WHATEVER HAPPENED
TO ECOLOGY?

WHATEVER HAPPENED TO ECOLOGY?

STEPHANIE MILLS

Sierra Club Books ♦ San Francisco

The Sierra Club, founded in 1892 by John Muir, has devoted itself to the study and protection of the earth's scenic and ecological resources—mountains, wetlands, woodlands, wild shores and rivers, deserts and plains. The publishing program of the Sierra Club offers books to the public as a nonprofit educational service in the hope that they may enlarge the public's understanding of the Club's basic concerns. The point of view expressed in each book, however, does not necessarily represent that of the Club. The Sierra Club has some sixty chapters coast to coast, in Canada, Hawaii, and Alaska. For information about how you may participate in its programs to preserve wilderness and the quality of life, please address inquiries to Sierra Club, 730 Polk Street, San Francisco, CA 94109.

The publisher and author gratefully acknowledge permission to reprint portions of "Revolution In The Revolution In The Revolution," by Gary Snyder, from Regarding Wave, copyright © 1970 by Gary Snyder, reprinted by permission of New Directions Publishing Corporation, and "Mother Earth: Her Whales," by Gary Snyder, from Turtle Island, copyright © 1972 by Gary Snyder, reprinted by permission of New Directions Publishing Corporation.

Library of Congress Cataloging-in-Publication Data
Mills, Stephanie.
  Whatever happened to ecology? / by Stephanie Mills.
    p. cm.
  Bibliography: p. 243
  ISBN 0-87156-658-3
  1. Mills, Stephanie. 2. Ecologists—Biography. 3. Human ecology—
Southwest, New. 4. Human ecology—Michigan. I. Title.
GF16.M55A3 1989
333.7′2′092—dc20
[B]   89-6294
                                                               CIP

Jacket design by Bonnie Smetts
Book design by Seventeenth Street Studios/Lorrie Fink
Production by Felicity Gorden
Printed in the United States of America

SIERRA CLUB NATURE AND NATURAL PHILOSOPHY LIBRARY
Barbara Dean, Series Editor

10 9 8 7 6 5 4 3 2 1

DEDICATION

To Bob and Edie for the gift of life;
To Phil, for a new threshold.

ACKNOWLEDGMENTS

◆

Thanks to: Hunter and Hildegarde Hannum for decades of exquisite friendship, and for generous support of this writing; to Barbara Dean for being a editor fine and compleat; to Phil Thiel and Phil Holliday for being major muses; to Danny Moses for a classic bookman's insight and courtesy, and to Barbara Youngblood for cleaning up my act.

Thanks to: Harriet Barlow and Kaye Burnett of the Blue Mountain Center for precious time, brilliant society, and progressive education; to Oswald V. Clark and Dennis K. Chernin, M.D.s for a leg to stand on, and to Pete Zoutendyk for a shoulder to lean on.

Thanks to: Anne Kent Rush for publishing counsel and lifelong trailblazing; to Earth Island Institute for grant administration; to Anne Ehrlich and the Stanford University Department of Biological Sciences, and to Dana Jackson, David Orr, and Harold Gilliam for quick and generous provision of background information.

Thanks to: Bob Russell, Brian Wanty, and Sally Van Vleck for having a look at the manuscript; thanks to Rob, Peggy, Darcy, Erin, and Annie for being most neighborly to me and my studio.

And thanks, finally, to all the friends not named here whose fellowship is my very oxygen.

DISCLAIMER

◆

What is recounted here happened long enough ago that the storyteller who occupies my memory has had her way with it. So this is just a version of a segment—not history, nor journalism, nor even autobiography, but memoir.

CONTENTS

◆

"We stand now where two roads diverge. But unlike the roads in Robert Frost's familiar poem, they are not equally fair. The road we have long been traveling is deceptively easy, a smooth superhighway on which we progress at great speed, but at its end lies disaster. The other fork of the road—the one 'less traveled by'—offers our last, our only chance to reach a destination that assures the preservation of our earth.

"The choice, after all, is ours to make . . . "

Rachel Carson
Silent Spring (1962)

THE FOX KNOWS MANY THINGS, THE HEDGEHOG, ONE BIG THING

◆

BEST TO BEGIN WHERE ONE IS. ONE IS JUST OUTSIDE OF TRAVERSE City, Michigan. This writing began in early 1986 in a ramshackle farmhouse known to its residents and their friends as "The Hovel."

Today may or may not be the last cold snap of winter. Outside, the brilliance of the sunlight rebounds from the snow. The icy wind buffets an aging apple tree, its branches still bedecked with a few wrinkled, rusty fruits. Sets of icicles have come and gone perhaps a dozen times this winter. Today they are plummeting from the eaves.

Phil Thiel, my husband, has gone to town to do some errands, relieving me of the powerful distraction and attraction of his company. Just before he left we were talking about bioregionalism—the avant-garde of the ecology movement, a biological politics so decentralized and wholistic that it all but defeats explanation. Phil and I are both involved in bioregionalism. That's how we met, coming as we did, in May of 1984, from considerable cultural and geographic distance to encounter each other, and a couple hundred more of our kind, at the first North American Bioregional Congress, held in Excelsior Springs, Missouri.

Bioregionalism is a clumsy term, but a good conversation starter. The word connotes a concern with the vitality of the entire fabric of life in realms not determined by man, but by nature. Bioregionalism is crafting a way of life that can be sustained within the boundaries and limits suggested by place.

Being bioregionalists means that we believe that civilization itself is destroying the biosphere and that neither resignation

1

nor reform is the correct response. We believe that the lethal ecological disturbances of our time, perpetrated by humans, have social causes and demand the creation, or re-creation, of social forms shaped by ecology. In short, we try to pose a sustainable alternative. We try to work in local and particular ways to create a culture reverent enough to seek harmony with nature, and we ourselves try to live on that basis.

Phil's rubric for right action is to ask, "What would happen if everybody did this?" which bespeaks the bioregional emphasis on lifestyle and responsibility to the entire biotic community. Day by day, it entails a willingness to fumble around, making sincere efforts at theorizing, organizing, consensus politics, and, above all, simple living. It means paying attention to the eco-logical context and attempting to live within it as harmlessly as possible. This is an evolutionary response to urgent, even catastrophic problems.

Even though by our parents' standards we live simply, to be well fed, well housed, well clothed, and well educated, and inhabiting a spacious pastoral landscape, is such an exceptional privilege that it makes me nervous. I figure the other wall of the postwar hurricane must be due through here any time now. Despite the secondhand nature of my knowledge of life in the Third World, I am willing to believe that my diet, housing, education, and ownership of transportation all go way beyond meeting basic needs. So, consequently, I marvel at happening to be a healthy, free citizen despite increasing hunger and desperation in the world. No special merit, just the luck of the draw. As the body counts attributable to malnutrition escalate (15 million infants and children per year), to be able to purchase just about any foodstuff I want from our clean little co-op seems extravagant.

The undeserved sleekness of my life, like the undeserved gauntness of the quarter of the human family living in abject poverty, is the product of an unsustainable global economic system, and of a civilization whose utilitarian bent is deadly to body and soul. Given that system's ultimate fragility, I look to my largely store-bought lunch to nourish me against a future in which I will either share in the general privation of human-kind or perhaps work with the rest of humankind to meet my basic needs simply and sustainably. However it shapes up, meals these days are nothing if not an occasion of grace.

Rapid human population growth is a cause and effect of the ecological, cultural, and spiritual simplification of the planet. Around 8000 B.C., the human population was 5 million. By A.D. 1650 it was 500 million. It was 1 billion by 1850 and has grown to more than 5 billion today. Stemming from a multiplicity of causes, the runaway multiplication of human lives vastly multiplies civilization's destructive impact and makes the creation of a sustainable lifeway all the more urgent—and challenging.

In the short two decades that I have been involved with ecology, a billion new humans have come into being. During that time the Earth* has not generated significant new surface or ecosystems capable of accommodating such increase. On the contrary, ecologist Norman Myers says that if present trends continue, by the turn of the century we can expect an annual loss of fifty thousand species. Much can be done to redress the desperate need that seems to pit humans against the habitats—and lives—of other species. By reverting to local agricultural production to meet local needs, the hunger per-mitted by the world trade in agricultural commodities could be mitigated. Sustainable farming techniques and inexpensive, appropriate technologies for providing the necessities—food, energy, and shelter—are being pioneered widely. These pos-sibilities are cause for hope, yet it seems clear that without

---

*Earth is capitalized herein because it is the proper name of our Mother planet. Earth is a living entity, at least as worthy of respect as God, the ol' gaseous vertebrate. About a decade ago Anne Ehrlich encouraged *Not Man Apart* to adopt this practice. Capitalizing Earth also seems to have occurred to many other writers and editors. High time it became standard usage.

dramatic worldwide curtailment in human fertility, and a dramatic reduction in resource consumption by the upper and middle classes, the human species will soon exhaust Earth's carrying capacity.

To admit that human population growth has been bad for the planet is an affront to the collective ego. Suspecting that our species has exploded in numbers beyond right relation to the biosphere is to admit that there might be something to Earth larger and more important than spectacular *Homo sapiens.* Beyond that psychological obstacle, the competition within our species makes dealing with overpopulation a controversial cause. Because human lifeways have been undone by colonialism, and the species riven by sexism, racism, nationalism, and the economic inequities that are the function of these, human impacts on the natural world are unequal. The poor hurt it less. In any consideration of the overall relationship of humanity to other life-forms, these differences, especially the difference between traditional and civilized people (and the possible difference between civilized and "future primitive" people), must be reckoned in.

However diversified and stratified we are, though, we are also undeniably organisms, determined by our biology. Being organisms, we are prey, mostly to our fellow humans; and habitat, to millions of bacteria, fungi, and protozoa, some of which inevitably must be our undoing. As one grizzled old libertarian tax resister put it, "The only thing I *have* to do is die."

• • •

There's a boddhisattva story in which the enlightened one shows compassion for a hungry tigress and her cubs by offering himself up for lunch. In your average, less-realized being, however, the life force, shackled to individual consciousness, generates an overpowering desire to continue as a self. That striving for persistence inevitably leads to some exploitation of the planet. Pending highest perfect enlightenment, one can only continue to grapple with the paradox of being human; to become a creature among creatures, bringing to heel our inordinate power to manipulate the environment.

The alarm has been sounded so many times that the clapper's broken. And disembodied programs and pronouncements have become wildly less convincing. Bioregionalism requires that I begin to practice the radical ecology I have preached for so long. It's a clear morality, and it can shape every facet of your life, from how you shit to how you pray. It is to be wed to place. Now that it's time to right and heal, it's what may come next. Peace on and with Earth, finally.

There is a whole literature of argument, anecdote, and science, all the impersonal information that rational actors could possibly require to be convinced that the ecological cause is paramount. It's not my calling to pile that mountain any higher. Rather I want to tell a personal story, to share my trials and errors in attempting to clarify my ideals, and to repent of my mistakes (by the making of which, and no other way, except by falling in love, do we learn). A lot of do-gooders, if my own conduct is typical, tend to sacrifice the intimate particulars to the general good. The consequent damage has led to the remedial awareness that the personal is the political.

It has taken me some years and a lot of experiences to learn the scope of the requisite change, personally and politically, to begin to talk about it plainly, but above all to try to live it. The intuition that all was not right between us and the planet was always there, from day one. For the life of me, I don't know where it came from (unless the wellspring of this concern is the very Earth). I do know how it got educated, though. And that's my story. I offer here a specimen life, an illustration— preliminary sketches, anyway.

For any new practice of the good to root, branch, and flower, there must be a seedbed in the heart. Our culture runs on abstractions, and theories abound. But I have come to believe that the most loving way to prompt change is through sharing our experience, strength, and hope with one another, each striving, above all, for integrity. As it turns out, the learning I report has developed from as nonlinear a conversation as that which goes on among the plants, the soil, and the weather.

As I have been writing this book, I've been nursing a badly broken leg. But even my doctor concedes that my recovery is not, in essence, a human accomplishment ("God has been very good to us," was how he put it). In the first moments of awareness after the automobile collision that crushed my thigh bone and broke several other pieces of leg (and damn near killed my husband), I awakened to the surety that life was living me. My conscious mind was a trivial fuddled thing, but the organism that I am, this collectivity of cells evolved out of wilderness, was mobilizing for survival.

By whatever incident one is awakened, or reawakened, the knowledge dawns that Earth is an organism of organisms, an interrelated whole, thriving in balance, with no preference for one species over another; that the task of our species is to find our way back into the web. The home truth is that all life wants to live; that life wants to speciate, diversify, and intertwine is immanent in nature. The knowledge that my habitat and, therefore, my existence as an organism are threatened is more than idea; it is at once visceral and transpersonal.

I love the Earth and its beauty; I love the free order of nature. The possibility of being in the generation that witnesses the end of these is real and appalling. To avert such immensity will require great fortitude and great change—a spiritual transformation; a willingness to find a larger identity in atonement with the biosphere; entire participation in nature; suffering death, and decay's power to transform.

As I write this, the sap is running. The phenomenal assault that is a northern Michigan winter is almost done. The trees and small plants of the forest floor, the grasses and wildflowers of the meadows lying latent in roots and last summer's scattered seeds—all of that quiescent tissue is ready to burst into life again. The birds are returning, insects emerging, mammals beginning to stir. All of those beings have learned their lifeways through long consultation with Earth and the cosmos. Despite deforestation, erosion, extinction, contamination—all the man-made threats—life continues to live through the myriad creatures. Life on Earth is the source of great strength and wisdom. It is to invite my fellow humans to sustain it that I write. Could there be a more crucial task than preserving our planet's genius?

A LITTLE VOODOO

◆

MY FAVORITE PLACE ON THE WHOLE PLANET IS AN INDOOR PLACE, actually, my 8-foot-by-12-foot writing studio. The long axis runs east-west. The door opens to the east; the horizontal peephole window in the back wall looks north to The Hovel and all the other buildings on the property, including the tumbledown wooden barn. The picture window in front of the desk provides me a commanding view of a meadow that was once a cornfield. A small rectangular window frames the setting sun. It is a space so intimate and crammed with information, so thoroughly occupied by little objects, images, and effigies, all laden with memories and connotations, that it's like another cranium.

Next to the west window, which now admits the iridescent, subtle glories of a late winter sunset, hangs a little watercolor that I painted months before I met Phil, months before I ever thought of Michigan as a place where I might live (in spite of the fact that both my paternal grandparents were born and raised a few hundred miles north of here, on Michigan's upper peninsula). What's remarkable about the watercolor is that it's nearly an exact representation of the scene out the window, color for color and contour for contour. In the sky are the pearly striations of pink and azure and rose and lavender and ivory. There is the blinding gold-and-ruby whorl of the sun's orb. There is the rickrack of an evergreen stand shadowed in ultramarine blue, and the expanse of white in the middle distance, flecked with saplings and other remnant vegetation. And in the foreground, a band of pink, suggesting the glow that suffuses a snowfield at dusk.

How did I come to see it? I painted it at a time when I never engaged in visual expression; I had all but abandoned that mode of understanding. But on the evening in San Francisco when I painted the picture, I was at a point of despair. The desolation of the moment was crystallized by an improbable love affair. The frustration and confusion and finality of it had driven me first to my library, looking for consolation. That literature offered none is the measure of the crisis. It was beyond the power of words to heal me, and perhaps less a job of garnering someone else's wisdom than of creating my own. It may be that I'd bankrupted my accustomed strategies. So I took out the paintbox and watercolor block I'd inherited from my grandmother. What emerged was a vision of the place where I would embark upon the second half of my life. That vision is my rivet.

PART ONE

THEORY

. . . Integrity is
wholeness,
the great beauty is
Organic wholeness, the wholeness of life and
things, the divine
beauty of the universe. Love that, not man
Apart from that, or else you will share man's
pitiful
confusions, or drown in despair when his days
darken.

Robinson Jeffers
The Answer

BEGINNING

———————————◆———————————

BOTH MY PATERNAL GRANDPARENTS WERE MICHIGAN-BORN. After they met and married, they lived for a little while in the town of Loretto. By the time I was born, my grandfather was the manager of a lead and zinc mine incongruously named the Iron King, near Humboldt, Arizona. Granddad had a long and distinguished career as a mining engineer, embarking from Loretto in 1920, with my grandmother and newly christened Aunt Edith, to work out of Georgetown, Dutch Guiana, exploring mineral properties. Then on to manage a mine and add my father, Robert, in Leadville, Colorado; a coal mine and two more children, Barbara and John, in Gallup, New Mexico; and finally the Iron King. Over the years his explorations and surveys took him to places, especially in the West, that were wild and still relatively unspoiled. His job, sad to say, was to start spoiling them. That's what mining is all about—writing finis to finite resources.

Tunneling into the Earth, extracting its ores—these are a daunting technical endeavor. My granddad's diaries are filled with mentions of problems with hoist motors and generators, with accounts of lines surveyed, and, during the war years in Humboldt, of dealings with national defense agencies, brokering economic relationships, trying to make the mines pay, and pay well, for their owners.

Mining is the most dangerous livelihood. "At noon Duncan died of bad air in a small shaft E. of Union. Worked all PM to get him out. Very hot."—the entry in granddad's diary for June 11, 1940. Dealing with death and occupational mayhem, going out of his way to secure care for the men who were injured on his watch, were all part of the lifework.

Granddad had begun his career as a mining engineer in the teens of this century and was, like his contemporaries, a generalist. He knew and used geology, chemistry, metallurgy, hydraulics, mechanics, architecture, calculus, business management, a little bit of everything. (Once at lunch, when he was well into his eighties, he dazzled the family gathering by figuring, in his head, the circumference of the Earth in fathoms.) On into the late thirties, when the terrain he was exploring demanded it, he took to horseback, which he noted in his diary, made him "very weary."

An irony of mining people—especially geologists—is their hankering to get out of town, to poke around in godforsaken places. But if they are lucky, a transient version of civilization— the mining town—will mark their passage.

My granddad was a shopkeeper's son, hardworking and comfortably middle class from the cradle to the grave. The family name was apt: Mills means "something or someone pertaining to the mill." Granddad's sons—my father and uncle— wound up pertaining to the mill too.

I'm sorry that I never asked my granddad why he chose mining engineering as a vocation. Did he have a passion for it? In his day engineers were magi, subjugating nature to man's desire. There were fewer fissures in the American sense that commanding nature was heroic destiny. Engineers were not the type to pause before the romance of the primitive. The fuels and metals Granddad wrested to the surface became the lifeblood and bone of industry, of modernity, of civilization itself. Never mind that the mining economy is inevitably boom and bust. The mines inevitably play out, leaving scars: open pits, tailings piles, hills riddled with collapsing underground warrens, ghost towns. Because of what metal is to civilization, mining has for centuries been deemed essential, a good and necessary endeavor, one of those activities that distinguished us from the apes. Especially in a young frontier state like Arizona, mining was a way of life, pursued in out-of-the-way places, spawning company towns, enclaves whose economies often were all but entirely controlled by the mining companies. Bisbee, Morenci, Superior, Bagdad, Jerome, Miami—these were one-industry towns. The ore-smelting atmosphere left them looking blasted and barren, but it was assumed that these rugged arid places were worthless otherwise.

This was the subculture in which my father was reared. Daddy grew up to be a mechanical engineer. He trafficked in heavy equipment, steel mill liners and grinding balls—shot put–like steel orbs used by the ton to tumble ore to powder so that it can be slurried off and smelted. So he took his place in the ongoing train of friendships across Arizona and throughout the West that had begun before he was born. Dad's main clientele was the copper industry. He drove all over Arizona and the intermountain west, anywhere there was copper or other ore being processed. Occasionally he'd take me along on his trips to show me man-made wonders like the Lavender Pit, the furnaces as big as houses, and the deafening ore crushers. Visiting the smelters, I'd have to crane way back to catch the full soar of the stacks. Females, even schoolkids, were not quite welcome in those places. Nevertheless, I remember the mine managers and others he dealt with as being robust and blasphemously good humored. Dad's brother became a corporate lawyer whose foremost clients were mining companies. At family gatherings, or parties, on the road, these mining men exhibited a lot of knowledge about the material world, and were current on all the copper gossip—their conversation was a pliant amalgam of human events and technical and economic goings-on.

A great thrill on these trips was to be traveling at night and see a cascade of red-hot slag being poured, adding to the great black windrows that became a new topography. The molten dross flowing incandescent as lava was, to my mind, purely phenomenal, and none of us questioned its rightful presence in that landscape.

In three Mills generations, there has been a peaking and decline in the copper industry. Viewed from the aspect of

history, you could say it happens all the time—the West whistles
with the ghosts of mining towns, tipples and plants that have
crumbled to oblivion. Therefore, it should come as no surprise that such a foredoomed, ill-starred way of life should be
dying, albeit not without a struggle. Some copper companies
have fallen prey to merger; others poor-mouth and insist on
union busting, or deny that copper smelting contributes to acid
rain, or shift their emphasis to Mexican operations, where environmental regulation is lax. The boom is long past. All that
enterprise is crumbling. Intellectually, I understand that that's
the way of extractive industry. Ideologically, I'm bound to be
glad, because the mining industry, more than most, tears
fiercely at the planet. Personally, however, I am, like the rest
of the bourgeoisie, confounded by the experience of such a
massive economic shift. (Although, as of this writing, the price
for copper has risen again.) When I was a kid, copper was king
in Arizona. It was the essential element of our family's prosperity. It seems peculiar to me, though I know all the reasons
why, that so prepossessing an enterprise, which required such
herculean effort from my granddad and thousands of miners,
should be passing, a little ignominiously, from the Arizona
scene.

• • •

The other day Steve, a friend of ours, native to the Leelanau
peninsula, asked me what it had been like growing up in the
desert. He'd visited Arizona once and hadn't been able to form
an appreciation of the landscape, he said. (He was also, on
that August day, making the sacrilegious remark that he was
eager for the cold weather to arrive. Clearly his disaffinity for
hot, dry places is genuine.) I told him that because the Phoenix
suburb we lived in had been Anywhere, U.S.A., an ersatz environment, I hadn't really grown up in the desert, hadn't known
it much.

Even so, there was something about its openness to the sky
that had got into my bones. That Salt River Valley was broad

16

and flat, rimmed with raw garnet-colored mountain ranges, with a few wind-sculpted outcrops of rose red sandstone adorning the expanse. And, yes, saguaros, the cartoon-cliché cactuses, and paloverde trees and ocotillo, all in the deep background. Now that I'm paying attention to natural history, the home desert has come alive with surprises—like eagles—that were there all along. (Alas, their riparian habitat is now threatened by yet another dam on the Salt River.)

While I love this northern Michigan environment of second-growth hardwoods and pine plantations well enough, when I return to the desert, the spare emptiness of it somehow looks righter. That corner-of-the-eye sense of proper relationship between Earth and firmament was instilled at the beginning. Likewise, an abiding sense of the preciousness of water, which has ingrained behaviors that are irrelevant in a place as wet as Michigan—stuff like overwatering the houseplants so as not to waste teakettle and vegetable-steaming leftovers. Is it that our fundamental responses to place are conditioned early on, ensuring that if and when we move, we will never again feel quite at home with what the sky does and how the air feels against our skin?

In Phoenix the ethic was to dominate nature. Not unique in the world, but the desert is extreme country, far less forgiving and forgetting than was the great forest or the prairie. The desert fantasy of command, marching under the banner of reclamation, was to reroute the waters of the Salt and Gila rivers and, with the electricity their damming produced, to make artificial climates. Thus there was always a tension in the environment. The sun, the heat, the light, the dry—all were like a lion at the gates. Every house had to be a walled compound, buttoned up and weather-stripped to keep the air-conditioning in and the truth of the climate out. In order to live in our accustomed fashion (which ecologist Raymond Dasmann calls "biospheric," meaning what we require the resources not just of our immediate ecosystem, but of the entire planet), we had to seal ourselves up in synthetic and, in ecological terms, extremely costly indoor environments. Yet none of this seemed anything less than our "natural" prerogative.

In *Dune,* Frank Herbert wrote: "Kynes the Imperial Planetologist said: 'It is said in the desert that possession of water in great amount can inflict a man with fatal carelessness.' " *Dune,* a great novel of imagination, is set on Arrakis, a desert planet where water's scarcity is the limiting factor, where colonial overlords engage in profligate customs of water waste, flaunting their consumption of an excruciatingly precious necessity. Reading *Dune* a few years after I left my hometown, I was struck by the correspondence between the arrogant water slopping of *Dune's* potentates and the crazy water orgy that characterizes life in Phoenix and much of the rest of central and southern Arizona.

Because of the state's many dams, and hence reservoirs, Arizonans are heavily into power boats. The world's highest fountain spouts manically in a development outside of Phoenix. To ballyhoo a dream-homes development in Mohave County, a couple of hundred miles northeast of Phoenix, some creative ironist bought one of the London bridges and transported it stone by stone to span an artificial lagoon. Also providing amusement that belies the true nature of the desert environment (where the average annual rainfall is just over seven inches a year) is a massive wave-making machine to provide surf for landlocked beachboys. Fantastic!

A typical summer day in the Salt River Valley, also known as the Valley of the Sun, brings temperatures over 110 degrees and ruthless light. So it is understandable that swimming pools abound and that the sound of plashing water refreshes the spirit of the shopping multitudes in scores of air-conditioned malls. But the groundwater pumping and river impoundment and diversion it takes to slake such multifarious thirst constitute a kind of hubris; and nemesis, in detail, stalks right behind.

My Mississippian mother chanced to fall in love with my Arizonan father and found herself living out her life in a place inimical to horticulture. Phoenix frustrated and finally defeated my mother's attempts to grow the plants and flowers that had surrounded her childhood. In her mind's eye a real landscape is green and lavishly blossoming. Time after time she would smuggle southern plants like dogwood, redbud, and camellias back from our visits to her hometown of Poplarville, only to watch them parch to death; so she felt a constant dissatisfaction with, and antipathy to, the place where we lived. Some backyard consolation was found in the creation of a little lily pond, with its own chortling waterfall. A blessed wet place, thousands of miles from the banks of the Pearl River. It is no casual thing to quit the landscape of one's early youth.

Phoenix has long been peopled by the uprooted. It's an immigrant place, become a destination for throngs of midwesterners longing to burst winter's chains, yet another place to seek high-tech employment. Because Phoenix's arriviste culture had insisted that the land adapt to us, our immediate surroundings were falsified. As a result, I never made a connection with it in Earthly terms. I just knew I didn't like it and couldn't wait to get away. Some of this restlessness must have stemmed from living in a region exotic to the nation's iconography (we don't warble about the burning deserts in "America, the Beautiful"). It wasn't normal to live in the desert, thought this teen. Normal was seasonal, broadleaf, New Englandly quaint. Thus, generic images of America helped subvert any allegiance I might have felt towards the actual place where I lived. Deserts are an acquired taste. Years later, through an intellectual interest in ecology, I would circle back to appreciate the life that had surrounded my hometown.

The desert's bad reputation, the possible dying of thirst, was scary. Youngsters just didn't go out in the desert to play. So "outdoors" to me was the irrigated backyard, the irrigated city park, and the air-conditioned mall. As soon as I got my driver's license, outdoors was behind the wheel. In high school I ran with the eccentrics, and we went to extreme lengths to keep ourselves amused. Those lengths were measured on Daddy's odometer. We'd drive hundreds of miles, back and forth across the valley. We'd drive as far as the road would take us up on South Mountain and spend a little while looking at the grids of lights glittering at our feet. Or we'd go to the north side of town, up Camelback Mountain, and look at the same lights from a different angle, moving nervous and aimless as leopards in a cage.

It was a confused and contrary place I grew up in. Water "reclamation" dictated an aggressive insensitivity towards the given environment, a macho striving to change the desert's character. The propaganda of common wisdom portrayed desert life-forms as malevolent — Jumping Cactus! Poisonous Lizards! It took pride in what man wrought in Bermuda grass: English manor-house lawns where only creosote and kangaroo rats had flourished before. This antagonism towards the actual surroundings makes for an essential derangement in the local psyche and helps account for Phoenix's solipsistic quality. It's hard to figure why there's a big city there.

Years later, Earth First! founder Dave Foreman, whom I first met at an organizer's conference, summed up Phoenix for me as "the most unbioregional city in existence: it's like a space station." And Foreman, an Albuquerque native, knew whereof he spoke, being then a resident of Tucson (which, Tucsonans claim, is Athens to Phoenix's Sparta). Long, white centuries have argued that the desert is the quintessential wasteland. Anglo settlers have always seen the Salt River Valley as a blank slate that civilization could not but improve. It's almost as though the indigenous life of the desert were invisible.

Phoenix was growing phenomenally fast during my years there. And maybe the rapidity of that change, the obvious over-shoot quality of it, suggested that *this* world, if not The World, was coming to an end. If Phoenix and its environs were blatantly contrived, it is only a difference in degree, not in kind, from any other American place, including Leelanau County. We are certainly closer to nature here, but this land, too, has been transformed by human activity, most notably by being denuded of its primeval forest. In Phoenix one was not much in the environment save for feeling the heat during the dash from the air-conditioned car to the air-conditioned supermarket, or basting in the ultraviolets at poolside. Here one is very much in it, up to the knees in snow sometimes, half-deluded that the woodlots are wild, but subliminally aware that it's a lesser version.

Even if the postwar settling of a million or so sun-'n'-fun seekers in the midst of a desert valley (which had been hard pressed to sustain a prehistoric Indian population of merely thousands) seemed like a good idea at the time, in reality it was insane. Growing up in a setting of constant environmental change and degradation was telegraphing a message about the human-nature relationship, namely that it was out of joint.

To continue this Oedipal railing against my hometown is too tempting. Phoenix is no tackier than any other sunbelt city. Like so many of them, Phoenix abandoned its short-lived center, churning outwards, laying down a flimsy and pseudo built environment that is shaped by neither a serious plan nor effective zoning, and precious little taste. At this point the horse may be long out of the barn. You can't zone chaos. After all the expansion, the center was rediscovered, and skyscrapers rose downtown. In the streets below, out in the burbs, the city is plagued by crime of both the organized and amateur varieties. The traffic flows in every direction. The drivers are savage. Everyone's abject dependence on cars means a severe carbon monoxide problem and smog. The dazzling clarity of the desert air is long gone. There's never a moment's peace, with police choppers and traffic reporters cruising overhead at all hours and sirens throughout the night. It has become a behavioral sink.

Now could this all connect with the fact that economic growth has been the civic objective throughout the postwar era? Phoenix proudly claims to have the best business climate in the country, and Phoenix's urban policy has been tailored to the wants of developers. The consequences are showy. Although many Arizonans were mortified by the shameless venality of their Governor Mecham, he is not an anomaly, just an extreme representative of the local booster community.

That boosting got under way back in 1867 when a cavalry wagoner, appropriately named Swilling, saw the potential in clearing the prehistoric irrigation canals he found in the vicinity of Fort McDowell. Crops followed. Settlers followed. In all, more than a thousand miles of new canals and ditches followed. In the language of reclamation, the god-sent torrents that brought sustenance to sparse Piman communities in the region are denigrated as "excess spring runoff," regarded as "lost" water if not put to an obvious kind of work. Regarding water as mere resource was both cause and effect of a poverty mind and a limitless thirst. The term *reclamation* (which betrays the delusion that we own what we are reclaiming) propagandizes for itself and obscures the will of the element it seeks, futilely, to exploit and control. This attitude is in stark contrast to the faithful, wild, and patient native practice of supplicating the gods, in due season, to continue the water cycle.

South-central Arizona's native peoples wooed the torrential summer thunderstorms and also the gentler winter rains. Their agriculture was attuned to the desert's radical turns, raising indigenous crops that throve on the widely spaced pulses of moisture and nutriment. Yet the suddenness of the area's rainfalls was experienced by Anglo settlers as further evidence of environmental hostility, along with the desert's ferocious heat and aridity.

Because of the perpetually foolish human tendency to build on floodplains—because of Phoenix's urban sprawl, there are multiple crossings of the Salt River, which almost every winter can be depended on to wash out a few roads and inconvenience thousands of drivers on their helter-skelter commutes—the cause of flood control is also sacrosanct. True, a gullywasher is nothing to mess with. Despite the fact that the campaign to engineer the waters into submission is quixotic at best, fraught with hidden costs, unable to keep pace with Phoenix's outlandish growth, reclamation is the state religion.

Lately, however, Phoenicians have become willing to think about limiting some of their less essential forms of water expenditure, like swimming pools and lagoons. Most householders disapprove of the waste that can occur when the biweekly irrigation ration (a controlled lawn-watering flood) overflows into the street. Municipalities have begun to make requests that golf courses use recycled sewage effluent (not as gross as it sounds), and to whisper that residential water conservation would be a good idea. Agricultural water conservation is still a taboo subject. However, with this growing awareness, Arizona has adopted what is called the most comprehensive groundwater law in the United States, a mix of regulation, taxes, and conservation measures. It may be too little and too late. According to the Arizona Department of Commerce, Phoenix is the second fastest-growing city among the top fifty cities in the United States. It is the ninth largest city in the country. Nearly 1 million people live within the city limits and another million or so in its outlying towns and cities, with more arriving and being born every day.

They say that if you try to plunge a frog in boiling water, it will, of course, try to escape. However, if you start with the frog in room-temperature water and heat that water gradually, the frog will become stupefied and suffer itself to be boiled to death.

On 1949 pastureland surrounded the vanguard suburb on the east side of town where my parents bought a comfy brick home. During all the years we lived there, the family at the end of the block kept sheep. The birth of a black lamb was big neighborhood news. Within a couple of decades, the neighborhood was surrounded by shopping centers. And now, despite a glut of commercial space, the shopping centers are giving way to office towers.

Phoenix got its name by rising, Phoenix-like, on the ruins

of a long-vanished network of villages built by a sedentary people dubbed the Hohokam—"the people who went away"—by
the Piman people who succeeded them and lived there in historic time. The reasons for the Hohokam disappearance are
matters of speculation: climate change and drought perhaps,
exceeding the area's carrying capacity, or salting up their fields
by excessive irrigation.

Like Phoenix's early Anglo settlers, the Hohokam were
agrarian canal builders. They also hunted and gathered. The
empty desert provided them with a diet that included rabbits,
birds, bighorn sheep, deer, turtles, frogs, lizards, snakes, and
possibly dogs; agave, corn, squash, pigweed, goosefoot, mes-
quite, cattail roots, cholla (that's jumping cactus), saguaro,
prickly pear, and mallow. The Hohokam lifespan was brief
by our standards—thirty to fifty years. Their skeletons tell of
hard labors and social stratification. Their artifacts don't dis-
close much to the untrained eye: posts and stone tools, impressions of cloth in the clay, shells traded from the Gulf of
Mexico. The number of Hohokam people was relatively small,
and the speculation is that the living was primitive, although
their hydraulics were highly sophisticated. Being pre-engineering
humans, or, rather, humans whose engineering feats were con-
strained by their lack of metals, the Hohokam made exceedingly
ingenious use of the local renewable resources, especially the
Salt and Gila river waters, and flourished for thousands of
years. But by A.D. 1450 they were gone, and no one knows
quite why.

To accuse present-day Phoenix of being an adolescent city
would imply that it has a chance of someday growing into functional maturity, of putting its excesses behind it. The ghosts
of the ruined hydraulic culture under foot might counsel otherwise. Like so many nineteenth-century entrepreneurs, Phoenix's
founders thought that they could way outdo the primitives.
They dug wider, deeper canals along the Hohokam traces and
extended theirs beyond, thinking that the trick was to do a
bigger, better job of exploiting the scant waters of the valley.

Oblivious to the desert's own canny ways of flowering diversity and abundance, they sought to compel it to produce in a more muscular and obvious fashion. One of the many ideas was cotton farming. Cotton is fond of heat, but, like other crops that started the agricultural boom, it has a powerful thirst. Another way was grazing—cattle ranching, which wreaks its own brand of havoc with the grasses, soils, and springs of arid lands. Citrus growing was another big enterprise in central Arizona. Perfume from the blossoms of the grapefruit orchard north of our house was a sweetness of summer nights that we took for granted until the trees were removed to make way for more housing.

At one time the five C's—cotton, cattle, copper, citrus, and climate—were said to be the pillars of Arizona's economy. Only climate and copper were truly native—one a mixed blessing (113 summer degrees at high noon is hardly clement), the other finite, difficult, and costly to get at. So the foundations of the Anglo economy were not what you could call bedrock. Phoenix's massive population growth—doubling about every twenty years—and the postwar shift towards manufacturing and services have not lent greater substantiality or sustainability to this weird metropolis.

Near the Phoenix airport sits a ruin, a vestige of the Hohokam era. It's called Casa Grande, but its grandeur is hard to spot. It's a mound of stone and adobe walls, some depressions where pit houses stood, and a "ball court" whose true purpose remains unknown. The whole of it, at least the parts that left material traces, is half the size of a football field. It would take a more tutored eye than mine to recognize its prehistoricity and distinguish it from any other disintegrating pile of adobe. A similar lack of recognition led early Anglo settlers to build their houses on such mounds elsewhere around the Salt River Valley, obliterating their tales forever.

It's a desolate ruin, all right, dissolving and blowing back into the desert soils from which it was molded. Jets arriving at and departing from Sky Harbor thunder and fume constantly in the background. Arteries visible from this rise teem with traffic across the valley's flat expanse. As I surveyed the scene on a pearly, choking, overcast day, the possibility that all of this new sprawl might crumble into obscurity hardly seemed remote.

People who seek a landscape or climate just to their liking are by definition malcontents and very likely short-timers. Phoenix, indeed the whole sunbelt, is populated by these Goldilocks, wont to find places too hot, too cold, too expansive, too close, too wet, too dry, too buggy, and never just right. So we cut the foot to fit the shoe, mutilating the world for our convenience rather than studying to adapt our bodies and minds to what is.

The place where I live now is the antithesis of the desert, this swampy, so-called temperate zone of the old Northwest, falling under the heading wet and cold, also buggy. A couple of years ago, when the levels of the lakes great and small were rising, according to some extensive fluctuation that cycles through time out of the human mind, some Michiganders, particularly those with lakeside property, began to think that their state might have a little too much water. Arizona is beginning to confront its future of water shortage; inevitably, there are techno-optimists who think that a happy solution to both problems might be shipping water from the Great Lakes to the Southwest. Fortunately, nearly all of the Lakes States governors and the premiers of the Canadian lakeshore provinces are adamantly opposed to the idea, and have sealed their opposition with a basin-wide pact.

The contrasts between the places in which I began the first, and then the second halves of my life are stark—Michigan is the cloudiest state in the United States, Arizona among the sunniest. Is Arizona yang? Is Michigan yin? There are also some underlying similarities. A bioregionalist landscape architect friend of ours, now also a Leelanau County resident, likens Michigan's sudden summer efflorescence, its desperate and beautiful capture of the season's fleeting light and warmth, to the desert's opportunistic blossoming after the ephemeral rains. In both places, there is a real urgency about growth and propagation, and marvelous adaptations to circumstances result.

The desert couldn't cradle my relationship to nature. That relationship has been continuous for an infinitely long time, reaching back, so far back, that there must have been a thread before the Big Bang. Nearer to now, that kinship stems from those steamy tidal pools of lightning-zapped amino acids on the rocky, wet, and formerly barren Earth. There are family ties with those strange benthic worms that make their lives on the hot, mineralized jets of water in the fathomless depths of seafloor spreading zones. We incorporate some chemistry of these states of being. Yet to call this embeddedness "relationship" is somehow ungainly.

All that picturing of our molecular genealogy is both memory and intellectual construct, something I had to learn and then awaken to later on. Yet the abiding passion informing the words and ideas does not seem to be a function of my individual consciousness, but of the Earth and the cosmos, the same passion that grows the cactus out of nowhere, talking.

• • •

Growing up in Arizona, I was an easy mark for Goldwater-style Republicanism. His rhetoric seemed to offer a few plain truths that the A-bomb–McCarthy era had rendered my young mind susceptible to. There was and is great allure in the myth of Liberty. I managed somehow to mentally edit out the fierce militarism, perhaps not grasping what a contradiction there is between having a vast secretive military establishment shading into a national-security state, and liberty too.

When the 1964 presidential campaign overtook Arizona, I was just a teenager, and if washing windshields and slapping on Au H$_2$0 bumperstickers would win me a trip to the Republican National Convention, which was to be held in *San Francisco,* I was supporting Arizona's native son. It was something to do. I didn't make it to the convention, Goldwater didn't make it to the White House, and his defeat did not prevent the war in Vietnam from escalating.

The following year I went to college, electing to go to Mills, a venerable women's institution in Oakland, California. It was a fortuitous choice that proved to be excellent, a decision I haven't regretted since the end of my sophomore slump. I was lucky enough to get in on the end of an era—the last hurrah of a pure liberal arts education. Some of my fellow students may have been planning their careers, but as far as I was concerned, my job was to go to college. It wasn't till the last hours of my senior year that I began to worry about what might come next.

My alma mater was beautiful—160 walled and wooded acres, with gracious and often-inventive Mission-style architecture (plus a couple of Victorian lulus), peaceful walks, and a reflecting pool that was featured in every edition of the college catalog. (My friend Karen Masotty called it "Propaganda Pond.") Only 750 of us populated this idyllic grove of academe, and we were taught by a solid faculty in an atmosphere that hallowed learning generally and art particularly. For the first little while, before the strife of the time penetrated the sanctuary, it was very genteel, with sit-down dinners and a gaggle of girlish traditions. Mills women were something special. Many of us were overprivileged, but many of us went on to lead. The best of our professors provoked us to individuality and achievement, and shared warmly in our pride at an original accomplishment.

Mills was a shelter, a hothouse, a bit quaint relative to its neighboring Titans, the University of California at Berkeley and Stanford University. Berkeley was a capitol of student activism, while Mills was a timeless enclave, a haven for less-worldly concerns. It was a perfect place for me to try my wings, although I didn't love it as much then as I do now. What a mercy is nostalgia for dissolving youth's callow bitterness!

Because the threat of the draft gave young men a personal stake in war resistance, collegiate youths raised a chorus of loud and principled opposition to this war, to war in general, and to the capitalism and imperialism that made the war inevitable. These great tides of conscience and political activism were crashing all around me, but they didn't catch me up. At Mills, not to be sheltered required positive action. It was perhaps in my freshman year that I spectated at the Vietnam Day Committee March, a big and early one. I went there on a date with a frat rat, and we gawked in a naïve and decadent way. The frat lads were no friends of the radicals, felt not much sympathy, not enough to draw them into the protest, anyway. They were throwbacks to the Jazz Age, perennial Joe College types, now rumored to be resurgent on campuses across the land.

Those years were about war, but the war, however thoroughly reported, was far away. I would like to think that in attending that march, as if watching a Saint Patrick's Day parade, I understood myself to be in the wrong spot—outside looking in. I was afraid. My more courageous peers were being dragged off to jail for protesting, being subjected to a physical experience of the violence that charged the atmosphere in that era. My experience of it was the intimate emotional violence of the family dinner table. All through my college years, I argued bitterly with my father about the U.S. involvement in Vietnam. It was, to be sure, an issue worth arguing. But part of what was going on all across the land was an intergenerational rupture, a wholesale repudiation of parents' beliefs. I can see now how terrifying that must have been for them, and how that fear may have incited such madness as the killings at People's Park and Kent State.

Student Power was a real uprising, obviously not a mass movement, since it was a privilege afforded by sixties affluence and the curious leisure of higher education. The students of today must find themselves hard pressed to imagine what it was like to be a college student then. Some of our elders, chastened, perceived us as the awakening conscience of the entire nation and projected on us the whole duty of idealism. The experimentalism of our generation was not dismissed as the mere sowing of ideological wild oats or acting out. The national soul-searching that finally ensued on the protest era was dramatic, but not unprecedented or unbidden. Its antecedents, century-long struggles on many fronts—labor, feminism, civil rights—offered many lessons and heroisms that had languished in the obscurity of racism, sexism, and class bias—the deliberately shallow memory of the comfortable.

The youthful outrage was nourished by the self-righteousness of the formative human. There was a definition about the stance that might suit only folks in their twenties, people who hadn't yet had time to shake hands with the devil within and have their pure self-images broken on the wheel of complexity. So it was, in some respects, war on war and dependent on the existence or identification of an enemy, much as the war it was warring on needed to demonize its opposition.

The student leaders and radical spokespersons were also perennial types, although at that extraordinary point, their numbers seemed to have burst the minority confine. Their interaction with the mass media made for a historic moment in social change, one we may not see the like of again. It was the best and worst of times to forge a concept of social change, because those of us who were trying to grow up then came away with a kind of implausible romance. Words seemed to be deeds.

I try to recapture the sense of that era, to put myself back in 1967, sitting comfortably on one of the couches in the gracious Alta California living room in Ethel Moore Hall, getting my news of the world from the *San Francisco Chronicle*. There was a war on, and there was opposition to it; often the reasons for that opposition invoked Marx and called the war capitalist imperialism. That gave me the creeps. For all the antagonism of my quarrel with the fatherland, I never flirted with the notion that state communism would be an attractive alternative lifestyle here, although it didn't seem worth it to battle it elsewhere.

I was paying just enough attention during the Joe McCarthy era, and subsequently in Goldwater's heyday, to have breathed the miasma of anticommunism and to have developed the (sound) conviction that totalitarianism was a bad thing. Also, I believed that what obtained in the Free World and what obtained in the totalitarian states were diametrically opposite. So revolutionary communism was something that I was culturally incapable of considering rationally. I was also, I now understand, psychologically averse to the strategic absorption of the individual. I did believe that the war was heinously wrong and that opposing it was righteous. I didn't understand then that principled and heartfelt opposition to the war didn't absolutely require embracing a particular economic or political ideology. So in my confusion and unease with ideology (as well as in simple timidity), I omitted to participate in antiwar action.

But then came the shock of California state violence in the occupied zone around People's Park in Berkeley. I learned that the policemen is not always my friend, regardless of the flag he's wrapped in. On my frequent trips to Berkeley to visit my beau, I witnessed men-at-arms, working for what I had until then considered to be *my* government, turning on members of my class and my generation. It was an uncensored display of state terrorism, orchestrated by the finally disgraced Edwin Meese.

I don't know all the reasons why I began thinking like an anarchist then and am only a little clearer now, but my minor brush with the forces of civil repression in Berkeley did not inspire me to join the opposition, whether they were the protestors on the scene or the revolutionary parties in Southeast Asia and Latin America. Plus there was Ezra Pound's conundrum—what do you do with the gunmen after the revolution's over?

All over the globe millions are justly aggrieved by their lot, but the architects of revolution are always an elite, and there's a cybernetic time bomb ticking away in the kind of we-they thinking that implies. Meanwhile, other species can't organize in their own self-interest.

One of the shortcomings of the student protest movement, and the substantive reason for my nonparticipation, was that it wasn't comprehensive enough. The war was atrocious, and a canker in the American soul. Protest was absolutely necessary. But the Third World War, the war on the planet, to borrow Raymond Dasmann's phrase, was being waged and won. And was being ignored by activists who wished to limit the focus to the political-economic conflict in Southeast Asia. The human oppression of the very planet simply isn't explicable in entirely ideological terms.

Churlish as the rightist jingoism of another American century is, I find myself just as rankled by lefty jargon, troubled by "progressive" assumptions about how power coalesces and flows. The myth is that power is latent in the masses and that those masses may be galvanized, politicized, and organized by activists under the aegis of a historically accurate (i.e., Marxist) analysis. And then we'll have democratic socialism, and most things will be better. This is an earnest, reasoned response to the plight of human injustice and makes a certain sense — mass response to massive problems — a more unified revolutionary force pitted against the uniform evil of capitalism. The practical consideration that the state, or even the party, can be as great an evil as the capitalist structure, and not just an instrument that can be disempowered once it has redressed the balance, usually doesn't get acknowledged.

Some leftists make me nervous (and because we're all involved in a social critique, some of my best friends are of that persuasion) because in round one, at least, they have all the answers. At worst they become a counterorthodoxy, propounding an exclusive and biologically callous worldview. What remains of the democratic-socialist movement is reformist, because it's still aiming at power-over, and a lot of the union-derived organizing tactics and bases have coevolved with, and depend on, industrialism and the factory system. Altogether too-large-scale utilitarian to make a creative difference (that is, if you accept the concept that the scale and locale at which social problems are joined is as decisive of the outcomes as the political theory shaping the tactics).

The socialist project is human centered, but what defeats it is human individualism, from possessiveness to preference. It was Jung's opinion that the world hangs by a thread, and that thread is the psyche. Hence, the individual's endeavor to understand the psyche is pivotal. The mind is the agency that wields the power to blow us all to kingdom come. So, really, it is in the mind that the survival of the planet will be decided. Introspection and individuation have critical roles to play in human and planetary salvation. We can't dismiss the soul or the quest to fathom it as just bourgeois conceits or luxuries to be deferred till after the revolution. Individual insight, contemplation, visionary "raids on the random"—all are essential for humans to develop the selfhood they need to function in diverse, ecologically responsible, place-located communities. These wellsprings of vision are just too vulnerable to being trampled in the mass.

Slogans don't do nuance very well. It's taking me a lifetime to understand what goes into my believing. Teasing out the threads, I find myself in the fabric of the human species, discovering my humanity and species-nature, yearning to draw closer not just in solidarity but in diversity.

Neither capitalism nor communism is a system within which traditional, tribal peoples can thrive (or are very often permitted to persist), and this tells you something about those big systems. To function most effectively, they require a standardized human. The public, the masses, the voters, the workforce, call us what you will (*human resources* is a particularly revealing usage), all become raw material for an other-directed "productive" process. Call it Progress. Whether the plutocrats' or the party's hands are on the levers, the differences are significant but slight. It all adds up to dull authority, which chafes my very soul.

"The mood of the ugly is crowd," quipped Stewart Brand,

Whole Earth Catalog creator. Sloganeering is a precursor to the psychic plagues of paranoia and fanaticism that could rage through the human monocrop. And if what's animating the masses is a handy oversimplification, the danger comes from the difficulty of keeping the masses loyal to a given oversimplification, which is in itself a form of violence. Reality is so infinitely complex!

If the imprint I received from the sixties was that everything was going up for grabs and that it was the potential and responsibility of the young to save the world, the deeper imprint I bore from the fifties was a horror of the state, through the fetish of anticommunism. It wound up not mattering very much to me whether the iron hand was the right or the left.

Buffeted among these prejudices, fears, and intuitions, shunning the drudgery of Marxism, I was without a vessel in the turbulent waters of imminent change, feeling nevertheless that it was imperative to sail into the dynamic, to participate in the generation-wide effort to Fix It and Realize the Ideal.

LEARNING

◆

ALTHOUGH I WAS AMBIVALENT POLITICALLY DURING MY STUDENT years, I had formed attachments to some other big ideas a time or two. During my last couple of years in college, I was dosing up on Jung, attempting to grasp as much of it (which was but a glimmer, given my youth) as I could. *Memories, Dreams, Reflections,* that anecdotal introduction to Jungian psychology by Jung himself was potentiating a deeper receptivity in me. The Jung matter is strong medicine.

All of this was going on about the time of the People's Park siege. My boyfriend, Steve Anderson, was a Berkeley student, a fey and gentle, honorable soul who was having to pass through zones of tear gas on his way to our rendezvous. He and several other student types inhabited a motley big flat southwest of the university campus. I remember greeting him with a kiss and getting some of that brimstone residue burning on my cheek. Late one night in Steve's psychedelic purple room (a color choice inherited from a previous resident), I consciously identified with Gaia.

There was a copy of the Sierra Club's exhibit-format book *The Place No One Knew: Glen Canyon of the Colorado* on hand. Having nothing better to do while Steve slaved over a model for an architecture class, I got stoned and read it. I regret having to relate that this first armchair wilderness epiphany was drug mediated. It would be a more uplifting story if the message had got to me without the chemical boost, but being stoned was a part of it too.

At the risk of sounding like a nostalgic middle-aged fossil, I must say that marijuana use was a little different in 1967 than it is today; different as the world is different. There were people around, although I proved not to be one of them, who were able to make ritual, judicious use of drugs, approaching them with the respect due a spirit-guide. Rightly or wrongly, we believed that we were getting another kind of knowledge by using them. As better minds than mine have discovered, it's all too easy to cross the line from use to dependency, especially in this culture, which both glorifies escape and leaves us almost nothing to do but to seek it. I shudder to think what today's reality would be like perceived through the preternatural awareness marijuana seemed to induce in me. Fortunately, I don't have to find out.

Twenty years ago, however, pot rendered this one, twenty years old and hungry for a vision, vulnerable to the tragedy of Glen Canyon's pointless destruction. The canyon fell victim to a power dam and now lies entombed under a 200-mile-long reservoir. Eliot Porter's astonishing photographs were the only remaining sight to be had of a place of pristine and unimaginable beauty. A place that no air-breathing creature would ever again be able to inhabit or see. The sanctuary depicted by those photographs of water-streaked sandstone grottoes was a haunting contrast to the social violence and ugliness outside the walls of that south-campus apartment. It felt like clear invitation to make common cause with the planet, its wildness especially. Somehow it was more possible for me to connect with the wordless beings of Earth and to take personally the threats to its wild places than it was to join the ranks of the war protestors (a false dichotomy, I now see).

There are good grounds for identifying with the planet: it is, undeniably, the womb that births us. Indeed, what's baffling is how we, as a species, ever drifted into an "I-It" relationship with the Earth. But what I think I was yearning after was the uninventedness of that life and beauty—its perfection absent thinking, strife, or agency; its suchness and freedom from the need to improve. The image of such a place—life-forms and landforms together shaping the wondrous beauty of the whole, all unpremeditated—hinted at the serenity of being, such a contrast to the strife of becoming and doing that was the lot of my late adolescence. But what really sealed my attention was the drama of the threat. It galvanized a desire to preserve the wilderness, intact, not unchanging; to secure its future evolution and perhaps dissolution, but to give it time.

The impresario responsible for the existence of the book that was having such an impact on my soul was David Brower, then the executive director of the Sierra Club. Brower was exercising the editorial dimension of his prodigal genius in publishing a series of exhibit-format books. Their purpose was to ally ravishing photography and stirring prose to inspire wilderness defense. It was an exquisite, effective form of propaganda. Revisiting the book recently, I was struck by Porter's artistry, the way he saw and loved and discerned his own compositions in the total beauty of Glen Canyon, and framed them in a way that showed that such dazzling beauty might reside in any pristine place, rightly beheld. Porter's pictures made me see what he had seen, made me see what seeing could be, but the heart-rending part of *Glen Canyon* was its being just a paper memorial to vanished splendors.

Brower's own writing and the selected texts accompanying the photographs state a philosophy of relationship to nature that made perfect sense to me: nature, epitomized and embodied in wilderness, was unsurpassable by any human artifact. Reading those words, seeing those pictures, inspired me to the noble cause of saving the world, or, more precisely, the Earth. Thus I am among the many who were spurred to ecological concern by the efforts of David Brower, one of many young people in whose destiny Brower had a hand. He had, unwittingly, but not unwontedly, set in motion a process that would, among many other things, eventually bring me into an attenuated apprenticeship with him.

Wallace Stegner, in *Glen Canyon,* was quoted in an opinion that allowed me to stroll into the ecology movement in street shoes. He said that wilderness is important "simply because it is there—important, that is, simply as an idea."

Writing of people who might never get to the Colorado Plateau, to any place like the places depicted in *The Place No One Knew,* Stegner said, "They can simply contemplate the idea, take pleasure in the fact that such a timeless and uncontrolled part of the earth is still there." The myth of wilderness is essential to the psyche as the fact of wilderness is to survival.

My wilderness experience remains scant—a few backpacking trips in the Sierra Nevada instigated by various friendly Sierra Clubbers. Those visits, too, were consequences of the chain of events triggered by the book. It's an anguishing thing to visit a wilderness: (a) they're virtually all threatened, so you're sightseeing in doomed innocence; and, (b) you never know when you're going to round the bend and meet fifty other hikers on the trail. One wants to savor wilderness in privacy, and having to take a number to go on a hike is an extreme illusion shatterer.

"A world from which solitude has been extirpated is a very poor ideal. Nor is there much satisfaction in contemplating a world with nothing left to the spontaneous activity of nature." Those words of J. S. Mill flanked Porter's image of "Cobbles and pool, Aztec Creek": rocks with an azure overtone in the foreground, water glowing midnight blue flowing by, and a quiet stretch mirroring the sunlit white gold of the sandstone cliffs soaring out of the picture frame. *Glen Canyon* is one long symphony of such juxtapositions. Word and image awakened me to the reality that the Earth I was born on and the Earth I would die into were bound to be radically different places.

The knowledge that the unspoiled places, not even board-certified wilderness, that I once visited or wanted to, are being peopled and built on and irrevocably changed is as unsettling as an earthquake. If you've ever felt the ground jerk under your feet, you know what a terrible betrayal it can be. This insidious conversion of the wild to the civilized is taking far longer than the eternal seconds an earthquake lasts, but the effect is just as vertiginous. It's a slow-motion version of that upheaval of the very ground of our being. Evolutionary justice demands that wilderness have a right to exist for its own sake, and for what it is to everything that lives—origin, atmosphere, continuum.

"One of the penalties of an ecological education is that one lives alone in a world of wounds," wrote Aldo Leopold. *The Place No One Knew* stamped my passport to that world. With or without such education, we all must possess some unconscious understanding of the wounding going on all around us.

If *Glen Canyon* laid bare the wound, it also was a brilliant introduction to the literature that calls for its healing. It was my first encounter with the prophecies of Thoreau, Eiseley, Leopold, Brower, and Krutch. I've encountered a lot of other wisdoms, programs for the soul, conceptions of justice, plans for a better human condition, but all of these seem provisional, as befits mutable human nature. The proposition that wilderness must continue, however, has a ring of the absolute.

Wilderness, the idea and the experience of it, has the power to move humans to bold exploits in realms from art to activism. And as this century careens towards the millennium, desolations like the damming-up of Glen Canyon on the Colorado, which are pushing not just individual species but whole ensembles and ecosystems to extinction, are becoming the order of the day.

Inevitably, opposing, if not equal, forces are rising to confront such mayhem and its causes head-on. Another David has come into prominence now as a wilderness defender. This one is Dave Foreman, a founder of the Earth First! movement.

Foreman grew up in Albuquerque, New Mexico. His family was urban oriented, yet he remembers always having been drawn to the out-of-doors and to wilderness, reading about it and getting out into it as soon and as much as he could. He was an Eagle Scout, a student of history in college. He earned a living as a farrier and a packer. Drawn into wilderness defense, his involvement eventually led him to Washington, where he became The Wilderness Society's chief lobbyist. That was during the historic Roadless Area review process. The "reasonable men" of the environmental movement were anticipating and incorporating the opposition's demands into "environmentalist" proposals for categorizing and preserving what remained of America's de facto wilderness. A lawsuit brought against the U.S. Forest Service in California to force a more inclusive and extensive wilderness proposal for roadless federal lands in that state brought Foreman to his senses. He realized that the reasonable men had been compromising prematurely. So in 1979, sitting around a campfire with Howie Wolke, who was then Friends of the Earth's Montana representative, Mike Roselle, Ron Kezar, and Bart Koehler, Foreman and friends decided that extremism in the defense of wilderness was no vice. Together they founded the Earth First! movement. Their battle cry is "No compromise in defense of Mother Earth!" Earth First! announced its existence to the world by symbolically cracking Glen Canyon Dam. A cadre unfurled a 300-foot-long banner of black plastic that remarkably resembled a huge crack down the face of the hated dam. A brilliant publicity stunt and spell to unleash the waters of Lake Powell and liberate the beauties eulogized in Porter's book.

Earth First!'s militance was sealed by its advocacy of monkeywrenching. Monkeywrenching is direct action, the stealthy sabotage of attempts to "develop," or, as Earth First! would have it, *rape* the wilderness. Tactical violence against the engines of destruction but not against their operators. Monkeywrenching consists of billboard removal, de-surveying, tree spiking, and bulldozer incapacitating, along with scores of other clever tricks to heave caltrops in the path of progress. The inspiration came from *The Monkey Wrench Gang*, Edward Abbey's adventure romance set in the slickrock country. In the book Abbey called monkeywrenching self-defense. It is, he declares, the literal protection of one's home. Leading the charge with monkey wrench upraised, Foreman may turn out to be the Sitting Bull of the counterinsurgency against civilization's occupation of wild nature. He's an enthralling orator and compleat propagandist.

Foreman describes his earliest conduct in Earth First!, when he was traveling and making stump speeches and doing grass roots organizing, as "being the bad boy of the environmental movement." According to the leadership of many mainstream environmental organizations, that's putting it too mildly. "Terrorist" is more like it. In fact, he edited the book on it: *Ecodefense: A Field Guide to Monkeywrenching.* In his introductory essay, Foreman takes the longer view:

> Many of the projects that will destroy roadless areas are economically marginal. . . . The cost of repairs, the hassles, the delay, the down-time may be just too much for the bureaucrats and exploiters to accept if there is a widely dispersed, unorganized *strategic* movement across the land. . . . Nationwide monkeywrenching is what will hasten overall industrial retreat from wild areas.
>
> Monkeywrenchers keep a pure heart and mind about it. They remember that they are engaged in the most moral of all actions: protecting life, defending the Earth.

What drives an Eagle Scout to such extremes of political rhetoric and guerilla action, I asked him. "We are facing the greatest event in biological history since the extinction of the dinosaurs. It short-circuits everything in your whole being to recognize that," he said. Not only that, but it tends to make you a little down on the human race as a whole.

"The most hard-core wilderness fanatics are misanthropic," he admits. Reflecting on the fact that our type, *Homo erectus,* apparently wiped out the other hominids, Foreman says, "We've been causing trouble for a million years now, like the obnoxious drunks sitting next to your table at a nice restaurant."

For opinions like that, and for publishing views sympathetic to the AIDS virus and pathogens in general, opining that the population reduction and related technological breakdowns caused by epidemics might be a good thing for the planet, and for his direct saying that food aid to starving Ethiopians and permissive immigration policies were just postponing the time when biological backlash would reduce human overpopulation, Foreman provokes a lot of outrage.

In spite of all that, he's an innocent, innocent of investment in society. He's simply awaiting the ice age, working to assure that maximum biodiversity will remain after its scourings. Part of what Foreman values about wilderness, I imagine, is being in a surround where you depend on your senses more than your wit, and the quality of your attention must be absolute. Death's nearness and nature's unsentimentality are bracing to the wilderness aficionado. Foreman nearly died once, in a kayaking accident. "It really did cause a certain change in my consciousness—it's all dessert now," he says, claiming to like the idea that if he dies in the wild, nothing out there is going to care.

We conversed while walking in the Santa Catalina Mountains outside of Tucson, Foreman's home. Hardly wilderness so close to the city, but spectacular and wild, rocky heights dressed in saguaro cactuses and other Sonoran flora. Dave Foreman was graciously doing the beginner's walk with me rather than a more aggressive hike with some birdwatching friends: sharing the outdoors blessing. As we paused a moment to revere the view, he said, "You can even feel the vegetation shrinking back from us . . . we just instill terror in everything . . . we're really very unpopular." The time has come, says Foreman, for a few of us to "tell that grass there 'I'm on your side.'"

Wilderness is a gut issue, not an amenity or marginal good. It's the mother of poetry. Preservation of all existing wilderness should be the minimum demand of any ecological crusade. Misanthropes and poets love the wilderness. In it they can escape the clamor of humanity and stand in the naked presence of something far greater than the self—the mother of all. What remains of North American wilderness is mainly the rocks and ice that were too forbidding to exploit. But lovers of wilderness will brave it all for the truth, for beauty, for awe.

"The only path to true wisdom and understanding is going out in the wilderness . . . and being able to be quiet and sit there and listen," Foreman muses, "You realize that you're a part of what's around you, not diminished by it, but part of that energy. To realize that it doesn't care whether you live or die . . . that you have no special status as a twentieth-century human."

One of the reasons Dave Foreman is enveloped in a swirl of controversy is his misanthropic Malthusianism; he is unlikely to persuade very many twentieth-century humans that they have no special status. But Foreman writes large, almost caricatures the wilderness-lover's presumption that man is not worth the death of a place, and the idea that humanity is a subset of nature.

Challenging humans to reconsider their role in the biosphere is essential and needs to be done and done and done again. Yet one must hope that the choice need not be between having compassion for humanity and holding wilderness sacred.

One puzzle, and one that Dave Foreman is as mystified by as I am, is the question of how or why any civilized human being comes to identify with wild nature. The west has been subjected, for a few thousand years, to Aryan sky-god hortatory proclaiming humans, particularly males, to be the only creatures ensouled. That anyone arrives at a humble sense of origin in wild nature is remarkable.

I once heard Dave Foreman propose the metaphor that if in general our species is to Gaia as a lethal virus, the Earth First!ers and their ilk are like antibodies. Certainly the reemergence of passionate devotion to Mother Earth has something of the quality of random mutation about it. Still, if the biosphere, let alone wilderness, is to survive, this devotion must become universal again.

I asked Dave Foreman how he got to be an antibody. He had speculated a lot about it, he said. For some people, he thought, it was basically a vision on the road, of the sort that struck Paul en route to Damascus, "but for me, I can't think of anything like that. It was always just there."

It is a lot about seeking a big enough relationship. My personal guide Zoe counseled me, in my loneliness, to seek the nurture of the Mother. For misanthropic mountain men like Dave Foreman, she's the impartial and ultimately life-claiming Tooth Mother. For me, she's the comforting funk of the humus, the embraceable strength and rise of a beech tree, the kindly beauty of the countryside. I fear what may become of us if we choose finally to orphan ourselves.

• • •

It's a vexing time to be alive. The big questions are becoming ever more pressing, and we each have to seek our own answers firsthand. By no coincidence the New Age has come along to soften our ideas and thinking. Mine, I notice, are blurred. In the course of tracking a number of informing ideas back to their sources, I discovered that sayings I had been attributing for years to Bateson, Illich, or Brower were often vaguely unfaithful impressions revised according to my prejudices, simplified to the point of being less-good poetry, and changed, the way whispers are in the game of Gossip, wherein the fun lies in discovering how distorted a phrase becomes in being passed around.

Because of that fallibility, I am grateful that there are still books, that there's still writing, that it hasn't all been reduced to magnetic flux variations. It's a good thing that there are still hand-powered paper objects that I can heft and open to a certain page, and read what people actually said, not what I would have liked them to have said.

Much as I enjoy literacy, it seems only fair to ask whether literacy has been beneficial to the Earth, or even our species. It has fostered the abstract mentality. It has narrowed our channels of apprehension and comprehension (mine, at least—I can't remember names unless I see them written; I first read the titles on works of art, sometimes forgetting to regard the art itself); literacy has stratified us socially and has supplanted the faculty of memory. In spite of all that, frozen language is an attainment of our species that is likely to endure, even among future primitives.

Reading is a rich, if vicarious, way to live and learn. Writing is still a powerful means of attracting people to causes. For people who don't get to waft around sniffing the blossoms in whatever form of spring befalls their place, or to scramble on the scree in hopes of seeing a grizzly, the written *idea* of being awash in the annual warming of the hemisphere, the written *idea* of a high mountain fastness that is home to great omnivores, may alert the reader to the real consequences — and potentials — of being part of that greater life. Of course, the map is not the territory, and a picture book is not a place, but a map can give you an idea of what you're getting into, as great nature writing can give you the idea of how to get into it. Inspirational literature can lead people to mend their ways, adopt a cause. As long as we are literate, we will always need print we can scan for the home truth, a sunbeam of enlightenment to excite the mind's eye.

Until all the wood-pulp paper crumbles, or until the Ministries of Truth dispose of our culture by logging it on disks warpable by electronic whim, those of us with or near libraries will have an archive and corrective, a means of learning and discerning the motion of ideas, of news, of science, of poetry. And once in a while we may even have the joy of fondling a triumph of the bookmaker's art: good paper, elegant type, proud colophon, and all. Where would the ecological cause be without lavish books like *The Place No One Knew,* or chapbook versions of *A Sand County Almanac* and *Silent Spring*?

• • •

It is important to my story that I got to spend some years in and around San Francisco, everybody's favorite city, and certainly mine. These years began with my attending college across the bay from The City, as I immediately learned to call it. The summer of my sophomore year, thanks to the bold suggestion of Merrill Provence, a wry, iconoclastic philosophy professor, I got a summer job at the firm of Freeman, Mander, and Gossage, a now-legendary and then-celebrated ad agency.

Howard Gossage was a maverick, a guy who gave full measure to the term *creative*, which gets bandied so freely about the ad biz, a genius in the field. He was a well-known San Francisco character, an eminently quotable sidekick to Herb Caen, the *San Francisco Chronicle*'s sui generis elegist and gossip-monger. I didn't know all that, however. Unaware of Gossage's celebrity, I phoned his office and somehow miraculously penetrated the Maginot line of receptionists he interposed between himself and the idly curious. Blurting out my situation to the man himself, I asked for a job and allowed as how one more summer in Phoenix, Arizona, might drive me either to suicide or parricide.

A gravel-voiced, wise-guy stutterer, Gossage growled that he didn't think he had a position available, but that it certainly sounded as though I needed to talk to someone over thirty that I could trust, this being the sixties and all. He invited me to visit his office a few days later. I borrowed a gray flannel suit to wear for the occasion, in keeping with the wise-guy theme. I must have made the right impression. Gossage hired me, on impulse, as an assistant nose picker. That is to say, the honorary summer job slot had already been filled by a friend's daughter, so he created another one, dividing a paltry work load even further.

The offices of Freeman, Mander, and Gossage were located in a handsomely appointed old firehouse in what had been San Francisco's Barbary Coast and was now a high-tone decorator district. Marget Larsen, a great designer and thoroughly dashing figure, established the style of the place. It was inventive and spare, original and earthy, gracefully lit and variously textured: Alt-Bohemian. The recollection of it makes me realize just how bygone such surroundings are. Their comfort and flair, their understated affluence all made possible by a fleeting coincidence of personalities and a permissive economy.

It seems improbable now, but that was a microera in which an ad agency could be a salon, with the likes of Gossage presiding. His office was a high-ceilinged, brick-walled, brass-chandeliered *salle* accommodating a great round table. This was the setting for lunches and conferences, where Gossage would hold forth with astringent wit. (We'll never see the like again, I sigh, much, I imagine, as the aging Edwardians must have sighed over the passing of the gaslight era.)

From this atelier issued Gossage's own opus of clever, knowing, ad campaigns (Eagle shirt ads making reference to Jay Gatsby, for instance). Gossage also had the acumen to have young Jerry Mander for a partner. Mander, a principled PR wunderkind, was author of the immortal ad headlined "Should We Also Flood the Sistine Chapel so the Tourists Can Get Closer to the Ceiling?" (This crowned a Sierra Club ad prepared at Dave Brower's behest in the campaign to block construction of two dams in the Grand Canyon. It was a tart rejoinder to the Bureau of Reclamation's claim that tourists boating on the reservoir proposed for Grand Canyon National Monument would be able to get a closer look at the fascinating geological formations higher up the canyon walls.)

I was astounded by all these savvy people, Marget and Jerry and the others, but mostly by Howard. He was a man with the uncommon sense to be unfazed by convention and hedonistic enough to have a great time going his own way. Seeing a group of tony iconoclasts, people who were succeeding by not playing by the rules, made a lasting impression on this sophomore. Gossage was living proof that you didn't have to belong to the establishment to flourish.

Gossage had played talent scout to Marshall McLuhan and he had been an early fan of Leopold Kohr's. Kohr, author of *Breakdown of Nations, Overdeveloped Nations, and Development Without Aid,* was E. F. Schumacher's intellectual godfather. He is a prophet of appropriate scale still too much without honor in his own time.

Acknowledging Kohr's prescience, Ivan Illich wrote, " . . . the values of smallness, multicenteredness, effective decentralization, deprofessionalization, deceleration and autonomous structuring which our generation has been 'discovering' had been just as clearly and much more humorously formulated by Kohr, before we understood what he was teaching."

Doubtless Kohr's influence led Gossage and his friend and associate, G. M. Feigen, to help foment, that summer of 1967, the secession of the tiny West Indian colony of Anguilla from the self-governing state of Saint Kitts–Nevis–Anguilla, which had come into existence earlier that year. This short-lived revolution (Anguilla returned to British colonial rule four years later—clearly not a case where nothing succeeds like secession) was abetted by running discursive full-page ads in the *New York Times* (a Gossage/Mander specialty) and Marget Larsen's design of a flag and currency for the minuscule new nation. This enhanced the excitements of my tenure there, which lasted but a brief couple of months.

I sat at the reception desk, mystified by the proposition of taking advantage of this lucky break. My possible rise to the occasion ended in a debacle of appendicitis, as did my brief acquaintance with Howard Gossage. A couple of years later, he was felled by leukemia. His memorial service was complete with mariachis and bagpipers, befitting an honest-to-god San Francisco character.

So that's how I spent the Summer of Love—hanging around the Firehouse and tasting the freedoms of a city teeming with vibrant creative life. By virtue of its incomparably beautiful setting and its relative proximity to the Sierra Nevada, by being congenial to nature-loving poets, bohemians, and fighting liberals, San Francisco has long been a hotbed of the ecology movement. The headquarters of the Sierra Club is there, Friends of the Earth started there, as did bioregionalism's Planet Drum. In addition to those, there have always been slews of progressive environmentalist and social change organizations being born, thriving, and passing from the scene in the Bay Area. It's a place that's always sprouting bright ideas, if not always fostering their maturation.

Maybe the basic environmental awareness is a function of topography. San Francisco Bay is ringed by hills and mountains, so you can get a literal overview of developments. This spurred the Save-the-Bay campaign, a citizen's campaign launched by Catherine (Mrs. Clark) Kerr, wife of the president of the University of California, and a couple of other faculty wives. Mrs. Kerr and her colleagues could see the bay filling at the foot of the Berkeley hills where they dwelled and grasped the implications. It took about a decade of their persistence—the mobilization of conservation groups, lobbyists, legislators, and busloads of supporters for protective legislation—to rein in the developers along the bayshore, but they succeeded. The whole issue came to a vote during my senior year at Mills, and I followed it in the *Chronicle*. The issue heightened environmental awareness all around, and the success of the Save-the-Bay effort demonstrated that developing a place to death need not be inevitable.

A few years later citizens would begin working to establish the Golden Gate National Recreation Area, a vast quilt of coastal lands primarily to the north of San Francisco, including the rangy grandeur of the Point Reyes peninsula. Activist efforts in those decades won gifts for future generations, and on an ambitious scale. Those extraordinary accomplishments, which originated in individual concern, seem heroic, macrocosmic versions of the local environmental struggles that surround me now.

The required education is a crash course in township and county politics. If we are to secure for ourselves and our neighbors such necessities as safe drinking water and such amenities as scenic roadsides, we have to engage in local self-government. Dealing in the microcosm requires confronting my neighbors' understandable desire to get whatever livelihood they can from their lands, and their equally reasonable resistance to abstract proposals for change. For now I'm still enjoying an elevated vantage point—the ivory tower of the writing endeavor—but sustained dealings with local folks who are, no doubt about it, struggling against nature to get by is tempering the ecological romance and teaching me that preservationist views have to come up against reality tests. If life in San Francisco was sustained education in the big, beautiful ideas of ecotopia, life in northern Michigan is a lab course in the fine grain.

CRUSADING

$\blacklozenge$

IN THE SPRING OF 1969, IN THE AFTERMATH OF ORGANIZING A student symposium on environment, my götterdämmerung gloom at having to depart the palmy groves of academe was given objective dimension by a reprint of Paul Ehrlich's "The Population Explosion: Facts and Fiction," a sermon he delivered at San Francisco's Grace Cathedral in 1968. Ehrlich's blunt insistence that human numbers could not continue to double without wreaking ecological havoc crystallized my feeling of environmental crisis. Inspired by his polemic, I began to interest myself specifically in human overpopulation; this interest led me to write a barn-burning sermon of my own on overpopulation, which I delivered as the commencement address at Mills in June before my graduating class of seventy-five and our assembled families and faculty. I titled my remarks "The Future Is a Cruel Hoax." Cheerless grad.

I focused on overpopulation for two reasons: Ehrlich's dazzling persuasions and a hankering for a coherent, even simple explanation of what was happening to planet Earth. "The Population Explosion: Facts and Fiction" found accommodations in my innate pessimism. Mesmerized by the global problem of billions of humans, rich and poor, perched at the top of the food pyramid, pressing, from need or greed, against the lives and places of every other life-form, I gloomily predicted widespread famines and plagues. I said we were breeding ourselves out of existence, predicted our impending extinction, and announced that as a result of all this mess, I was "terribly saddened that the most humane thing for me to do is to have no children at all." (Twenty years later, I continue to honor that commitment.)

Being educated at a women's college had helped confirm my feeling that only I had the right—and responsibility—to determine what I did with my life and my body. Therefore, when I rhetorically volunteered to do my bit to alleviate the population crisis by giving motherhood a pass, I just assumed that such a decision should be my natural prerogative. It was an obvious, comfortable, and, to me, reasonable sacrifice to make for the cause. Indeed, it seemed only common sense. I was genuinely surprised by the uproar I provoked at the commencement exercises, in the media, and among the audiences I would encounter during the few years of population/ecology chautauqua that followed. The feminist subtext of my speech was the barb on the news hook.

It turned out that my remarks were so shocking that I became somewhat famous overnight, and to some, a made-to-order heroine and token woman. I was catapulted into the gathering environmental movement. Quite unexpectedly I was called upon to expound a subject with which I had only a casual acquaintance, owing to my literary indifference to the best efforts of the Mills College biology department. At the end of my first day in the spotlight, I called Paul Ehrlich to confess that I was stealing his material and to ask whether it would be okay to continue. He genially allowed that I'd made a lot of people at Stanford's Population Biology group very happy and to go right ahead and help myself.

They don't make ecology like they used to. Back then pessimism was almost enough. Ecocatastrophe was big news, and it lodged a feeling of hopelessness inside me. I believed what I was saying; it wasn't empty rhetoric. I felt hoaxed, cheated of a livable future.

Empires come and go. Environmental exploitation is nothing new, and since the arrival of the sky gods, war has been the rule, not the exception. If the seriousness of the consequences of these typical human activities has increased, so has the scope of our approach to change. I can accept that now, but in 1969, Paul Ehrlich's quip that "nature bats last" seemed about right, and I figured that we, the visiting team, were about to lose in disgrace. That was fine with me. In my jejune depression I preferred the apocalypse to working on through the insurmountable task of living in a less-than-perfect world.

There were plenty of obvious, objective reasons to decry overpopulation. But I think it was my being by nature an outsider that disposed me to understand human overpopulation as the ultimate threat. It was a threat to my solitude and to my individualism as well as to the planetary ecosystem.

Our lives are guided by, determined by, our psyches; there's a lot more directing us than conscious choice or conscious purpose. The causes we espouse and the work we choose will evidence our inner being; or, if we try to adopt a vocation against the grain, that contrariness will result in suffering. Tutelary suffering.

Acknowledging the power and final mystery of one's inner life, recognizing that everyone has an inner life, parallels the recognition of the vast and complicated, ultimately mysterious dynamics of the global ecosystem, and leads to at least one obvious conclusion, namely, that one can never do just one thing. Deeds are done in systems whose interactions guarantee unforeseen happenings, random excursions from simple, causal chains of events. Call it what you will—grace, fate, accident, or luck—there are more things in heaven and earth than are dreamt of in our philosophy. Thus my population rhetoric was only the tip of the iceberg. There were unconscious factors that led me initially to renounce, occasionally to disdain, and finally just to forgo, motherhood.

My family was conducive to Malthusianism. Comfortably Episcopalian, we were never subjected to any religious proscription against birth control. But on account of their populous household's chaos and economic precariousness, the handsome Catholic family next door, blossoming forth each year with a pretty new baby girl, was mildly pitied and censured. At our house, by contrast, children were regarded as a mixed blessing: rottenkid was a single word.

Early on I sensed that I was an unplanned, if not an unwanted, child. My mother suffered the dolors of hospital obstetrics; she can't relate to the joys of natural childbirth. So I am an only child. And I knew, as soon as I could poke around under my parents' bed and read their marriage manuals, that they were practicing contraception.

As the only child, I was the focus of much considered attention, effort, and expenditure. The loot under the Christmas tree was, for the fifties, remarkably nonsexist and generally educational: an array of dolls and a microscope, toy bake sets and chemistry outfits, and always books. My mother, a small-town girl from Poplarville, Mississippi, a doctor's daughter, took the road less traveled by, first excelling in college, then going to live with her sister in New Orleans, and, most daringly, joining the Women's Army Corps. She became, by all accounts, a good officer. Although her independent strength of mind was pent by the feminine mystique, she remains nothing if not vociferous in her opinions, and my father has always shown a definite respect for her intelligence; their give-and-take was as equals. It never really occurred to me that it could, or should, be otherwise between a man and a woman.

Mom made every effort to expose me to such high culture as Phoenix offered and encouraged my checkered cosmopolitanism. She insisted on going for broke to provide me with a first-rate liberal education, and Daddy worked steadily to pay the bills.

My parents were mainly whom I associated with, rather than other children. Being an only child has a lot to recommend it, but a sense of ease with one's peer group isn't one of the benefits. Ours was a literate, discursive household; the emotions were taboo, magma. The outcome of all these conditions was that I got good at exhibiting the family virtue: intelligence. Smart, scared, snooty, and shunned—during childhood I was richest in time alone. Thus childhood was not a particularly happy time. Perhaps if it had been, I'd regard it as more sacred.

Forcing people to think about the ecological details of human overpopulation was necessary but tough. Technological optimists were more numerous in those days before Three Mile Island, Love Canal, Chernobyl, and Challenger. The innocently humane response to the problem of rapid population growth was a denial of the limits of growth and consisted of grand-scale fantasies to sustain a much larger population by feeding the world on a boundless, free lunch of algae or yeast, or by off-loading Earth's excess population to space colonies. The more-sophisticated, humane response was to notice that improved living standards, social security, infant survival, and, above all, women's literacy and economic self-determination and good family planning and infant and child care services demonstrably had reduced fertility in some developing regions. Hollow-eyed, large-bellied children had only just begun to haunt our TV screens. For all we knew—and hoped—their privations could be dealt with handily.

In the sixties and early seventies, back before the Reagan revolution drove a stake through the heart of New Deal liberalism, your average citizen (and a couple of presidents) thought public spending to meet basic needs was only common decency. The inequity between the developed and developing nations was seen not just as a strategic threat but as a moral challenge. This led to do-gooding like the Peace Corps. Some ahistorical trickling down of the world's growing economic wealth was not expected to quite do the job. Although development aid on a nation-state–to–nation-state scale has proven to be clumsy at best and self-serving and destructive at worst, the informing ideal was justice.

Some other things contributed to that earlier sense of possibility in response to the problem of human numbers. The Pill, then thought to be the perfect contraceptive, accelerated the happy pendulum swing toward sexual freedom. Family planning was publicly subsidized. The movement to legalize abortion was gaining energy and ground. Feminism was resurgent, extending women's roles beyond wife and mother. There were actual reasons to hope that humans might begin to be able to control their numbers, make cultural progress, and achieve ecological survival. The times, alas, have tempered all those hopes.

Overpopulation is a biological fact that offends politicos at every point of the spectrum, from far right to far left. It demands that the planet's finite ability to sustain humans be acknowledged, no matter what the power arrangements among those humans may be. Socialists tend to see overpopulation as a diversionary issue (although the socialists in the People's Republic of China have managed to overcome their anti-Malthusian scruples and implement a vigorous population-control regime). Capitalists may either focus on overpopulation to the exclusion of the issue of the distribution of wealth, or, even more insanely, imagine that it will spur the effective demand that will make the further extraction of vanishing natural resources "economic" or spur the development of substitutes. Whatever their coloration, political types seem to posit a lot more leeway for human increase than ecologists do. What humanist wants to admit that human numbers may overshoot and crash like those of lemmings and field mice?

Up close, the population problem diffuses and becomes a factor in the scale and seriousness of a myriad of human problems, from hunger to economic injustice. Contending with overpopulation directly means challenging the freedom to procreate and bucking the evolutionary tide of successful reproductive strategies. The idea of population control violates the privacy of the relations between the sexes, and a considerable chunk of the elevated human self-image. None of the actions to limit family size are popular or easy things to do.

What I did about overpopulation, apart from not procreating, was give speeches about it. Eighty the first year after I graduated. Here's what it was like: I was twenty-one, employed by the Alameda/San Francisco affiliate of Planned Parenthood. Although I was besieged by mail and invitations to speak, I had no secretary to shield me and sort through the clamor. I also had very little sense of geography, so I just said yes to everyone, more than once agreeing to appear on the same day at places so distant that even a Lear jet at my disposal wouldn't have spanned the distances.

Usually when I spoke, I extemporized and occasionally had almost mediumistic experiences during which, to borrow Mose Allison's phrase, my mind was on vacation and my mouth on overtime. During my fourth speech one day in Sacramento, I nearly had an out-of-body experience. On that occasion, I was saying the habitual things, the good ol' ecology rap, but simply disengaged from what I was doing, kind of cruising the auditorium in detached fashion. Although it was involuntary, it later seemed frighteningly irresponsible, because words have power and had better be heartfelt and consciously uttered.

I often spoke at ecology conferences (which were many in those days) and to college audiences. I desperately wanted everyone's approval. I was usually nervous at the outset, but it didn't always show. I was often described as "poised." I was once described as a crapehanger, because I would say things like this when I spoke:

"The world that we human beings have known and loved for all our history is rapidly being destroyed. It was a nice world while it lasted, but evidently we don't want it nice, so we are eroding it assiduously. Beauty is vanishing right and left — there will be no return to paradise. This is a fact — no amount of money or goodwill can bring back Glen Canyon or the passenger pigeon. More and more of our natural environment is lost to us forever. It is no longer a comfort to see untouched places near the city, since it is virtually certain that someday those will be 'developed.' It is hard not to see natural places and feel an impending sense of loss. The world is becoming a mangled corpse, an entity afflicted with the cancer of man." Furbelows of crape.

I also usually deplored our pursuit of the war in Southeast Asia, the concentration of political and economic power in too few hands, and the potential for racism in population-control programs. I was effective, sometimes eloquent, occasionally inspired, and more than once brought an audience to its feet. Applause was, of course, gratifying, but recalling that gutted feeling that would come while I was driving or flying home alone churns my stomach even today. I was in way over my head, but I couldn't stop to breathe.

How fortunate a thing it is to be able to get an audience for your views when you're young and unequipped to deal wisely with the distortions of notoriety is an open question. I had awakened the day after my college graduation to see my face on the front page of the *Oakland Tribune*. Thus began that brief episode in my life that handed me an entree to, and a vocation in, ecology, on a silver platter yet. It also, in Joan McIntyre's memorable phrase, "turned my head to hamburger."

I was swept up in a moment of opportunity. Ecology was becoming a crusade. Congress and the White House were paying attention, and the Sierra Club had grown big and strong. Bustling around the club's headquarters at the Mills Tower in San Francisco was a crowd of dedicated, ambitious young men, and occasionally women. We'd cross paths at numerous ecology powwows, becoming part of a green scene.

A few blocks north from the dowager Sierra Club, David Brower, the club's recently deposed executive director, never one to be without an organization, was setting up Friends of the Earth. Brower's parting of the ways with the Sierra Club he had built so dramatically is its own saga. "There was a problem of discipline and management, but Brower also outgrew the Sierra Club," wrote Stewart Udall. "His vision was too broad, his stance too militant for the old guard." The fissioning was deeply traumatic, but ultimately fruitful, for it led to the creation of Friends of the Earth, a new environmental organization that would extend the frontier of environmentalism into the halls of Congress, around the world, and even into physics, through its campaigns against nuclear energy. Friends of the Earth tended toward a casual bohemianism, while the Sierra

Club wore a respectable suit. Accordingly Friends of the Earth's first quarters were in the Firehouse, whose upstairs was occupied by Freeman, Mander, and Gossage.

Friends of the Earth was launched under the auspices of the John Muir Institute with a provocative conference held in Aspen. I was invited, along with John Ehrlichmann, Garrett Hardin, Jerry Mander, and a dozen other participants of varying degrees of renown or notoriety. I assumed I was expected to talk about overpopulation. I chose to confront Garrett Hardin's typically harsh rationalism with a venture into the metaphysics of the solution:

"A feeling of reverence for and responsibility to other life-forms is not characteristic of our culture, and it must be if we are to earn the right to survive. Obviously the status quo has got to be disrupted somewhat if there is to continue to be life on this planet. Again, magic and passion can help. The success of any effort to avert the global crisis will depend in part on spiritual awareness."

Talking about magic in front of a rather surly John Erlichmann was more sixties than seventies, I guess. Likewise my impassioned threat, in the heat of a later discussion, that we might have to become willing to take up guns in the defense of the environment. Hardly a cool thing to say before a president's man from an administration that would soon be impounding thousands of war protestors, just the kind of remark that reinforced our mutual paranoia. However, despite or because of the extremity of my rhetoric, Dave Brower asked me to join the Friends of the Earth's advisory council, which forged me a titular link with the organization.

So during the ecology boom, I speechified everywhere from the Yale University School of Forestry, at Stewart Udall's invitation, to a high school in Hayward, California (where I was pitted in "debate" against a mother of thirteen, founder and president of an organization called United Parents Under God), to the pulpit at Grace Cathedral.

The things that befell me in my fame and glory days seem

a little incredible now. John D. Rockefeller III summoned me to New York for some consultation on getting youth interested in the overpopulation issue. That first trip to New York also led to a meeting with Norman Cousins, another to a meeting with the hale and randy Arthur Godfrey. Still another trip was occasioned by an invitation to appear on David Frost's show. I was the subject of countless newspaper stories and radio interviews, was featured in *Look* magazine, won a *Mademoiselle* magazine award, and twice enjoyed Nick Von Hoffman's arch, but not ungenerous, journalistic attention.

The clips proving that all these things really happened are yellowing now, disorganized, in a scrapbook on the shelf. While I can only hope that that flash was useful in some wise to the ecological cause, it hyped my ego and led me to use people close to me. Lacking experience or assistance in coping with public life, I flamed out fairly fast. Ovations are habit forming. Although my friends knew and loved more of me than audiences ever saw, I was inconsiderate of them; the ratios were all wrong. I became isolated and inwardly lonely, indulging in ill-considered love affairs, abusing alcohol and drugs, and once in a while just collapsing and heading for the emergency room when it all became too much.

If this melodrama sounds hackneyed, it's because sudden fame has a predictable trajectory. The irony of my story is that it wasn't a hit single that led to the inflation and its attendant moral perils, but a resounding call to ecological consciousness. The further irony is that the adverse side effects of all that early recognition took me on a long detour through a consciousness antithetical to that serene and humble participation in life that is the essence of the change I began talking about so long ago.

Lots of sixties youths horrified their parents with the idea of a baby strike on account of the world's being too wrecked and crazy to bring kids into. I seem to be one of the few that launched a career from that position, the ecofeminist version of burning a draft card. If the starkness of my pessimism was noteworthy, so was the fact that I was a pretty, middle-class, white girl, exactly the type who *ought* to be a mother.

I had upset people who didn't want to think about the limits to growth, people who didn't want their lifestyle to change or to have their children's lives taking unorthodox turns. I upset people who didn't want papal, capitalist, statist, or industrial dogma challenged. Leftist war protestors whose analysis didn't include ecology resented being upstaged and grumped that environmentalism was a counterrevolutionary ploy. Bureaucrats and fat cats were offended by the accusation that their agencies, their companies, bore responsibility for environmental problems.

Given the podium, I was not uncommon among population crusaders in aggregating all of humanity and advocating grand solutions: perfecting contraceptive technology, promoting voluntary sterilization, and instituting tax disincentives to childbearing. None of these were new ideas when I was bandying them about, and all of them are now being implemented here and there in the developing world, in Asia especially. The more-progressive recommendations—combining family planning and maternal and infant health service, providing Social Security against the uncertainties of old age, promoting women's literacy and economic self-determination—guarantee deep cultural change. Nothing less than the rationalization of reproduction and a tremendous rearrangement of traditional sex roles.

Just as the more-sophisticated responses to the problem of numbers try to take into account the social and cultural systems in which humans are embedded, so do the more-sophisticated explanations for the rampant increase in population. Earlier on, the basic explanation for the radical increase in human numbers in recent times was simply "death control." This offered a nice symmetry to the birth-control tactic. Well-intentioned advanced nations, the explanation ran, introduced public health measures in their colonies and former colonies, thereby eliminating a number of insect- and water-borne epidemic diseases as checks to the expanding base of human population.

Centuries before that, however, tribal peoples were vanquished, or became peasantry, urban dwellers, or anthropological remnants. Agriculture, and with it civilization's relentless advance, disrupted traditional means of keeping population in rough balance with territory. Not all of these means were benign—they included fatal feuds and infanticide, along with the use of herbs for contraception and abortion, the practices of prolonged lactation and sexual abstinence. But they were tempered by being integral aspects of diverse indigenous cultures, none of them practiced uniformly or at a mass scale.

When hunter-gatherers stop moving and start farming, when a surplus develops and commerce begins, the illusion, enhanced by the buying and seizing of goods, that carrying capacity includes the whole biosphere, takes hold. This loss of an intrinsic sense of limits has become the curse of our time. If death control is not the sole reason that human fertility has gone into overshoot mode, birth control is certainly a necessary, but hardly sufficient, means to curtail it.

At the time of year when the deer could still browse without fearing hunters, a close friend was hospitalized in premature labor with her second child; a normal delivery followed some deft medical intervention and the early-arriving Max was placed in the hospital's nursery, where he could receive expert attention during the time it took him to get used to life outside the womb. Half a world away, when China was most stringently enforcing a one-child family policy, young villagers eight months into second pregnancies, needing to produce a son, were coerced into having cesarean abortions. In rural areas female infanticide was reported to be on the increase (To end such excesses, China has lately modified its policies.) Instead of suffering population collapse by the traditional agents of hunger, disease, and war, China is deliberately engineering a population stabilization and decline. The purpose is to ensure that everyone may have at least three bowls of rice and a few vegetables every day, but the application of this population-control policy must seem harsh as hell to the individuals whose lives it shapes.

Individual decisions are the little drops of water, little grains of sand, that, taken together, make up the continents and oceans of global problems. At whatever level society chooses to address these problems, they begin and end in the intimate sphere. And there is no more intimate preserve within an individual's life than desire. It is a violation of its sanctity to set desire and its flowerings in a macrocosm, and yet that is what dealing with overpopulation demands and why, possibly, it remains such an anathema.

Years after sounding the knell of planet doom at the hands of burgeoning multitudes, I see that there's always just work to do. I have learned that doing unalloyed and sufficient good is an impossibility, unless that good is so specific that it may seem insignificant to the faithless and invisible to the demographers. As Mother Teresa once said, "I do not agree with the big way of doing things. To us what matters is an individual. To get to love the person we must come in close contact. . . . If we wait till we get the numbers we will be lost in the numbers."

Simply assuring access to quality birth control for those who want it is an uphill endeavor. During the early seventies when big government and big foundation bucks were more readily available than they are now for worthy social purposes, Planned Parenthood was able to redouble its efforts to make every child a wanted child.

In those flush times Planned Parenthood/World Population had an 80-member board and was, like many another liberal organization, harking to the insistence that the militant young be given an official voice. Therefore, I wound up doing token youth duty on the organization's board. This board appointment, quite an honor, really, challenged and enriched my life for six years. My colleagues on the board were an impressive group of women and men, possessing much civic-mindedness and a wide range of expertise. The goal was to provide effective family planning and, a little less vociferously, to educate the prospective parents of the world to plan smaller families. At that time I believed that birth control was an unalloyed good and population control a necessary evil. I never questioned the goodness of my intentions and worked hard at promoting my own brand of good and evil.

Working at the national, and sometimes the international, level, the board, of course, looked at the Big Picture: the population explosion, the revolution in sexual behavior. We hoped to serve the millions of women and men who needed contraception and to secure for women the right to safe, legal abortions. Because they seemed, at the time, to be the most effective and, from the clinician's standpoint, the most efficient means of birth control, we promoted the use of pills and IUDs in the United States and abroad. These methods appeared to be panaceas for the problem of unwanted pregnancies. But as Stewart Brand astutely put it: "Panaceas are always poison."

A 20-year-old skier, a pill user, breaks her leg, and it's set in a cast. A blood clot develops in her immobilized calf; she can't feel its warning pain, and it travels to her brain, causing a paralyzing stroke.

A 35-year-old lawyer, having worn an IUD for seven years with little apparent ill effect, begins to try to get pregnant, having established her career and decided to start a family. But she can't. She learns that her fallopian tubes have been scarred as a result of a long-simmering case of pelvic inflammatory disease, aggravated by the device.

Personal calamities like these really do happen. Not a lot, but once is enough if you're the statistic. The point is that when you get to messing around with social change, you have to be ready to acknowledge your victims as well as your victories. Talking abstractly about overpopulation and human reproduction is safe. The changes are manifest in the personal details of people's lives, however.

Hanging around family-planning clinics and consorting with family planners, I acquired the unseemly habit of discussing my own contraceptive practice openly. In an era driven to "safe sex," using birth control is not only nothing to be embarrassed about, but a basic health necessity. However, I have always regarded avoiding an unwanted pregnancy as being equally a health necessity.

It is not only good luck, but conscious effort that has spared me from ever having had to resort to abortion. I have never had an act of what the family-planning biz refers to as "un-protected intercourse." I first used contraception thanks to the caution and responsibility of my first love, a doctor who was either cheating on someone or just habituated to the philan-derer's stealth. At the first opportunity to go all the way, we didn't quite, but practiced withdrawal. The second time, he presented me with a packet of pills, and we used condoms until the pills took effect. I continued on the pill for a few years after he scuttled out of my life and, fortunately, experienced no severe complications. Such cyclic craziness as the pill induced blended in with all the rest, and the slight changes that came about in my bodily ecology were a small price to pay for the sexual freedom I enjoyed.

Since then, I have had a Dalkon Shield, used a fitted and unfitted diaphragm, with and without spermicidal jelly, used the sponge, and a Copper-Seven IUD. So far, so good. Hav-ing access to the practitioner's gossip has put me in the desirable position of being able to make knowledgeable, if imperfect, birth control choices. Thwarting the exquisitely insistent pro-cesses of reproduction will likely always involve risk and effort. Yet after all the pros and cons are weighed, and sorry experi-ences shared, the fact that anatomy need no longer be destiny remains a positive—and radical—development. It may, in fact, be *the* adaptation that will allow us to continue as a species on the planet.

In the aftermath of a conversation with a Vietnam veteran friend about his taking of human life, it occurred to me that abortion may be woman's version of killing in combat; this analogy makes sense to me at least. I value the right-to-life movement for calling attention to the spiritual consequence of abortion and for asserting the marvelousness of conception and the sacredness of every single germ of life. The metaphysical questions this movement has so crudely posed have helped us possibly to recognize that aborting a fetus is not a deed to be undertaken lightly, although women have conjured, privately, with the gravity of the act since time began.

Appreciating that gravity doesn't mean that I wouldn't go to great lengths to procure an abortion if I had to. It doesn't mean that I agree with the sectarianism the right-to-life movement seeks to impose on this country. I want to live in a culture where people do make grave choices, according to the dictates of their individual consciences. Dictating those choices, proscribing the exercise of conscience, causes atrophy. Mortal choices force us to confront a reality which is ever more complex and less than ideal.

The right-to-life style of idealism and my early enthusiasm for population control demand and demanded oversimplification and a denial of the commonplace, quotidian nature of most human decisions. Whatever one's opinion about the morality of abortion, it is virtually ubiquitous in human societies. Thus, prohibiting it is as futile—and gives rise to corruption, economic discrimination, and rampant hypocrisy—surely as a prohibition against drugs or alcohol. It kills grown-up women bent on self-determination, a group fundamentalists seem to value less than fetuses. If abortion is an evil, it is surely a lesser evil than what Garrett Hardin terms "mandatory motherhood."

Once, under the influence of an impressive array of chemicals—cabernet, cocaine, psilocybin, and romance—I did embark on a sexual encounter with no thought of preventing conception. I was kidnapped by a fantasy of sailing off to Greece to raise this man's curly-haired love child on twelve cents a day. At the critical moment, though, my superego sent a neon flash: It's *Your* Life, uncannily adamant, and prompted me to think better of it and take the usual precautions. Some deeper sense of self and honor was speaking. If I had acted out that one-sided whim, there would have been two lives on the line, not just one.

Calling romance an intoxicant is not to put it down. Romance has done some very necessary complicating of my opinions. Over thirty and still unmarried, I experienced a ferocious bout of the hot-egg syndrome, that autonomous desire to make a baby. It hit in the midst of a relationship poorly suited to the parenting enterprise. Convincing my ovaries of that took a surprisingly long time, however. That powerful desire was a good teacher. It taught me what it feels like to want to be a mother, and about the blind faith that accompanies the impulse to parenthood. It broke through my longstanding incomprehension of the need and want of procreation. It made me yearn for love to find a way.

Never to give birth was not and is not a casual decision, but it went with my grain. I have not changed my mind about having children, and although the reasons for my 1969 "decision" have reassorted themselves many times, none of my questioning of that 20-year-old self's intuition has persuaded me that I should have children after all.

What's more, as I come to know myself better, I become ever more convinced that life without the opportunity for solitude and reflection would not be worth much, and I've never heard a young mother complain of having too much time to think. I doubt that I will ever be 100 percent resolved, but I'm at least 97 percent certain that, at least in this incarnation, I'm forgoing parenthood.

There are times when that sits as uneasily in the redoubt of intellect as it does on the rebellious, yearning heart. Is a heart's desire being thwarted by intellectual pride? Or is the desire so ambivalent that it rightly should be quelled by doubt? Well, if you have to ask, you probably can't afford it.

If population and sexism weren't such great problems, it might make sense to fall on the kid-making side of the fence. But living consciously entails choice, and all manner of foregone possibility. Publicly opting out of motherhood, I played a curious antihero role and liberated a few other women to try it themselves. It takes courage and, more important, company, to live with unresolved questions. Although civilization affords little support, even less spiritual imagery, and no role models for women who choose not to be mothers, there does seem to be an ecological demand for them.

Whence comes this demand for children, anyway? Not from the planet surely. I don't think ol' Gaia can handle too many more North American babies, even if they do wind up being vegetarians who join NOW and the Sierra Club. Motherhood should be an inalienable, but not unquestioned, right.

Other than refraining from producing one's own children or from having more than one, there aren't many actions to take in the individual realm to deal with overpopulation. The ideal unit for consensually restraining population growth would be larger than the nuclear family, smaller than the nation-state, an entity with a firsthand sense of the limits and of the persons involved. Such units used to be called tribes.

Nation-scale population control can and has involved coercion at its worst, profound violations of the person. Although my commitment to forgo having children was self-interested, it was also the "self-managing decentralist" thing to do. That the conduct of one's household should model the new order one advocates isn't always easy. Yet unless I assume the power and responsibility to do things in my own life according to ecological values, I can hardly expect the world around me to change.

CHRONICLING

———————◆———————

MY LIFE HAS BEEN IN WORDS FROM THE BEGINNING. MY MOTHER and father are both articulate and literate. Better yet, they're humorous. Their voices are distinctive, their language studded with regionalisms—Mom's southern, Dad's western—and pure invention, language that's nonsense outside our family. Their embroideries in conversation, their idiosyncratic letters, set me a good example of speaking and writing in a personal style. I listen to their speech with pleasure, for the apposite colloquialism and, in Dad's case, the well-told joke, a salesman's stock-in-trade. This verbal attention getting and attention paying worked both ways. My parents were wowed by my early talking. One of the consequences of having the floor as a child was that I became a punster and learned to relish a groan. Language had an impact.

In the Garden of Eden the situation changes when Adam begins the naming of things. Naming reifies the I-It relationship. It's the dawn of the pattern of dominion and control. This myth plays inwardly in my life in the endless sorting through the vocabulary bin for the right word, the exact name for a feeling or sensation, for the most euphonious syllable or phrase. It's an attempt to assert dominion over the wild garden within, to snare ambiguous feelings and run thoughts to Earth. This reflexive seeking for the aptest phrase must date back to my playground days, when as a standoffish and not very physical odd duck, I nurtured a fantasy of being able to defend myself and win everyone's admiration by slinging some skull-cracking words at whichever Goliath happened to be taunting me at the time. Needless to say, testing this notion deepened my unpopularity. However, it didn't deter me from becoming a writer, orator, and polemicist. Never say die.

Excepting the first five years of my life, I have always read and always written. I coveted books and organized my own lending library when I was seven; I was writing sarcastic letters to cornball local entertainers when I was ten. In high school and college I had newspaper columns. I ranted about wrongs—like the fact that some temporarily able-bodied students at North Phoenix High were making fun of the differently-abled students from the special education classes. Sometimes I was merely insulting, as when I wrote a stupid column in the *Mills Stream* griping about the fogey presence of alumnae on campus. (In the immortal words of the Who, "Why don't they all just fade away?") Sometimes I earned a slap on the wrist from the powers that were. Whatever else it accomplishes, the self-righteous posture of the editorialist helps valve off long-simmering angers. I was overlong a sucker for the stentorian style (which is what it sounds like when the evils and failings are all without).

Having been briefly an object in the media, I much prefer to be an agent. I like to be the one controlling the words and images. And that I have been able to testifies to the ready accessibility of print. It's cheap, relative to the electronic media. And from the Summer of Love through the early eighties, alternative publishing was a jumping scene in San Francisco. Starting with *Ramparts, The Sunday Ramparts, Organ, Oracle, Scanlan's, Rolling Stone, Earth Read-Out, EarthTimes, Sundance, Clear Creek, Earth, City, Rags, Whole Earth Catalog* supplements, *CoEvolution Quarterly,* and on through *Raise the Stakes, Processed World,* and *Gnosis,* just to name the local magazines of which I was either a reader or a writer, there was a wealth of significant periodicals created in those decades, but only a few of them survive today. San Francisco was a primordial-oozy estuary for these ephemera, nurturing a richness and diversity of young life happy in the fluctuation between sea and stream. A lot of these papers were constellated by a big idea (*CoEvolution*), a millennial perspective (*Oracle*), or a new politic (*Raise the Stakes*). Also enlivening the Bay Area periodical business were the numerous publications by membership organizations headquartered there (of which more later). Small-magazine publishing can be unremunerative (it's a great way to liquidate a trust fund), brain-racking, hair-pulling, hectic, sleep-costing, and completely anxiety-provoking. Journalists in general are the shortest-lived white-collar workers, but working for a daily must be like civil service compared to the compleat effort required to sustain a new periodical. Magazine work is also about the most fun a wordmonger can have. Live fast, die young, and leave a beautiful publication.

Once your mag is under way, you are wading in a rushing river of information, bucket in hand, dipping out samples, mixing them up for your readers. You're constantly scanning and opening, learning, making choices, and brainstorming. You presume to interpret the world, to shape it and order that interpretation, to lay it out and caption it. You get high on headlines, deadlines, and urgency. Juxtapositions lead to insights. Contributors wander in off the street with sheaves of manuscript, recounting their psychotic break, detailing their new theory of physics, or blowing the lid off some scandal. Within your paper world culling the mail is an exercise of terrible power. People hanker to get into print, and editors stand at the gate. The decision making takes a lot of nerve (and irate contributors sometimes tell you just how much). To make editorial choices is a brazen thing, a game of trying to stay one jump ahead of the readers' needs and interests, which sometimes you're just guessing, inflicting your own prejudices. Often the choices are circumstantial, a roll of the dice. It's catnip to some, affording the kind of exhilaration that theater does to directors and actors. It isn't so instantaneous or ephemeral, though, because your group labors result in an artifact—a magazine or tabloid you can hold in your hand, even keep for a while, to wince in hindsight at its shortcomings or congratulate yourselves on its sparkle. Having your work read and responded to is cake and frosting. All of these excitements were mine, at different times and in different editorships, over a period of years, beginning with a bright flash-in-the-pan called *Earth Times,* and ending at *California Tomorrow,* a solid civic bastion.

In 1970, under the nervous aegis of Jann Wenner, boy genius of the *Rolling Stone*/Straight Arrow publishing empire, *Earth-Times* was born. The idea was hatched by Wenner and Baron Wolman, who was a world-class photographer whose lens alighted tellingly on subjects as different as groupies and the California coast seen from the air. Wolman had been part of *Rolling Stone* from its humble beginnings in free office space upstairs at the Garrett Press. Feeling expansive with *Rolling Stone*'s meteoric success, Wolman proposed that they also publish an ecology magazine. It, too, might catch a wave of zeitgeist. At the very least, it would be worthwhile. More, I presume, with an eye to the value of my celebrity than of my nascent editorial abilities, Wolman suggested that I might be the person to edit this magazine. We had met and struck up a friendship when I was just graduated and being notorious and frequently photographed.

Wenner, at our first interview, sized me up, hired me, told me to find a staff (of one), and concluded by saying, "Ecology will never be as important as rock-'n'-roll." Starting out with Penn Jensen, then Lloyd Linford and Amie Hill, with art direction first by Bob Kingsbury and then the estimable Jon Goodchild, we began to create the magazine. Over the quick course of *Earth Times*'s four issues, we were guided by a procession of waggish, talented newspapermen, editors from *Rolling Stone*: Jon Burks, Jon Carroll, and Charlie Perry, all of whom were sojourning briefly in Wenner's halls before fleeing, or succumbing to the occupational hazard of the boss's mood swings.

Thanks to Wenner's great publishing acumen and unbeatable style, we were akin to *Rolling Stone* in our readability, although treating a less-commercial topic (and that lack of commercial appeal would be our downfall).

Our premier issue was timed to hit the stands just before the first Earth Day that spring. We covered a lot of bases, with just enough of a sensationalist touch: herbicides ("If They Try to Spray, We'll Shoot Them Down"); Southern Pacific's real-estate-development activities ("Sewage in the Surf at Waikiki"); chemical warfare; condors; an oil spill in Florida ("80 Million Gallons of Nuclear Waste"); "Why Dow Always Wins"; life on a New Mexico commune; the fate of the National Forest Practices Act; and so on. (If these headlines sound generic today, it's partly because we were shaping the genre, but, most important, because environmental problems are still the same, just worse now. Years later, at *Not Man Apart,* one of our basic headline formulas was: [fill in the blank]: Threat or Menace?

In subsequent issues of *Earth Times,* Penn Jensen interviewed César Chávez; we did stories on Buckminster Fuller, Frank Herbert, and Earth People's Park. One writer filed a report on "Clean Living in a Yoga Ashram." We gave extensive coverage to the American Indian occupation of Alcatraz Island in San Francisco Bay, in an issue that also included a map of North American tribal lands in 1493 (which is to say, the whole continent) overlaid with a scattered handful of halftone blotches indicating their remains as of 1970.

Our last, and best, issue came out about the time Nixon ordered the invasion of Cambodia. It featured a lengthy, passionate, and detailed report by John Lewallen, "Ecocide in Indo-China: How to Make a War Last Forever," and a tough editorial by me on clandestine U.S. defoliation flights over Cambodia. That happened to be our last issue, not because it was controversial, or pioneering—although by confronting environmentalists with the war in southeast Asia, it was both—but because the magazine's bottom line looked pitiful. *Earth-Times* was losing pots of money, and Wenner wasn't in business for his (or the planet's) health.

Skimming the thousands of inches of copy that got published during that short episode, I can relate to the cynics who suggest that there should be just one newspaper, a single edition once would be enough, because there's so little to report that is actually different. Lots is always happening, but it's generally more of the same distracting melodrama. *Earth Times* could be recycled today simply by updating the names of the corporate perpetrators of dastardly deeds, not because the villains are different, but because they've merged so many times that their computer-generated names have changed.

In 1970 we couldn't have seen that we were knocking ourselves out in a possibly futile effort. All that sound and fury, and the planet is worse. Then we were blind folks, reformists, groping the civilizational elephant. Economic and political analysis hadn't much penetrated the mainstream ecology movement. But there were exceptions.

Barry Commoner granted me a long interview in which he asserted, "There are certain actions which are beyond the competence of an individual or small group to do. It has to be done on a huge social level." ("It" being the restructuring of our system of production, which, according to Commoner, is the cause of the severe environmental degradation that characterizes the postwar era.)

"We're going to have to make our economic and political system responsive to the need for reorganizing things," he continued. Challenging my article of faith that population growth was hyping the degradation, he said, "Now this business of saying, well, we should control our population as an example to the world—that's nonsense. Why don't we control our avarice as an example to the world?"

Commoner went on to fulminate against the colonial legacies of injustice around the world, portending the split between "deep" and "social" ecology (of which more later), in speaking of "the deep responsibility we have to deal with the problem on the human level rather than the biological level."

Barry Commoner wasn't, and isn't, alone in imagining that if the good guys could get their hands on the big levers a bright new era of sustainability and social justice would be ushered in. He continues to advocate change at that scale, with unwarranted confidence in this nation-state's pliability.

Another significant encounter during my editorship of *Earth-Times* was meeting Peter Berg. Peter and his partner, Judy Goldhaft, are among the leading lights of bioregionalism. They are the founders of Planet Drum, an organization that has for years now challenged, expressed, and woven the bioregional movement. At the time of our first meeting, though, Peter was a leader of the Diggers, and bioregionalism was but a glint in his eye. The Diggers were a San Francisco band of anarchists serving the half-transient community in the Haight-Ashbury with free food, free clothing, and street theater, a mind-blowing acting out of a political philosophy calculated to outrage America's orderly, mercantile soul. (The name Digger paid homage to a small band of seventeenth-century English communalists who attempted to cultivate, or dig, the wastelands. In Surrey they planted a commons. Their short-lived community was destroyed by mob violence, fed by the antagonism of adjacent landowners.)

Prior to his Digging, Peter had written for and performed with San Francisco's celebrated guerilla theater, the Mime Troupe. Berg's genius for language and theater has a legendary proportion. Trickster legend. He's a charismatic pagan. And in he walked to my cubicle, with goatee and a samurai knot of long hair neat at the back of his neck, garbed in black. He hunkered intensely in the corner and made something between a request and a demand that *Earth Times,* in its next issue, publish and distribute free a four-page insert to be edited by the Diggers. I was too much of a sweet young thing to risk it, or be anything but intimidated and uncomprehending. I passed the buck to the publisher, and nothing came of these dealings with Peter Berg. It was years before I saw him again.

If *Earth Times* proved not to be as potent a tool for change as we had hoped, it is not to say that our efforts, and those of the legions of ecoscriveners to which we belonged, were too weak. Rather, it tells you that the system in whose toils we struggle is very, very strong and that naming its further boundaries is a good way to be diagnosed as paranoid, despite the clues provided by Watergate and Irangate.

During the 20-year wait for the system to start unraveling, I've pretty much lost my appetite for environmental news. Dragging myself through the news sections of the fine journals published by Earth Island Institute and Earth First!, I learn that things are still getting worse; I can absorb only so much gory detail before discouragement becomes catatonia.

The incessant flow of accounts seems to lack an essential rhythm and the ability to evoke a poetry worthy of the tale. News is meant to be disposable—it's a torrent, jostling the gravel of the streambed, taking ages to determine the shape of things and the direction of change. It's what ideas are watered with, but it takes a veritable deluge to raise a new possibility.

Most environmental news is a grand guignol. It becomes meaningful at the local level, in reporting on situations within effective grasp. The local stories are usually some variation on the theme of friends and neighbors waking up to discover that some outsize, out-of-town, or out-of-state corporation is clearcutting their watershed, developing their open space, or burying toxic wastes in the landfill. What's useful to learn about is when some third- or first-world community, resourceful and ingenious, wins for a change, or at least impedes a little carnage. What never ceases to amaze, and often inspire, is the fecundity of citizen action. Like unquenchable hope, groups and individuals all over the world keep springing up to sally forth against the forces of environmental destruction. I like hearing stories of How. Never mind my personal case of the vapors; a steady chronicling of the threats to the ecosphere and the valor with which they are met, nourishes the movement, establishes a detailed record, and stimulates a steady flow of mail and protest.

• • •

One of the penalties of an ecological education is that one lives alone in a world of wounds. Much of the damage inflicted on land is quite invisible to laymen. An ecologist must either harden his shell and make believe that the consequences of science are none of his business, or he must be the doctor who sees the marks of death in a community that believes itself well and does not want to be told otherwise.

Aldo Leopold
A Sand County Almanac

If San Francisco, as a city, was particularly congenial to visionary environmentalism and its expressions in every medium, then California, whose history, to the ecologically perceptive, is a tale of head-spinningly quick ecological transformation and degradation, was the mother of the vision. And the irony was, of course, that to the naked eye California, especially northern California, is gorgeous.

It may be that growing up in Arizona, a state where the pace of environmental change was equally breathtaking, and coming to reside in California, with its rampant grandeur and turbulence, hypersensitized me to the violence done by human occupation. Just as most of us, if we chance to see a badly mangled human, are shocked and sickened because the image of dismemberment doesn't jibe with the archetype of bodily integrity, inhabiting a landscape that is being simplified—and uglified—sickens that part of the human self that spent so many thousands of years developing in landscapes that remained whole. It was in keeping with my time and the fate of my dwelling places that I would be unsettled in relation to the Earth.

Raymond Dasmann's *Destruction of California* elaborated the reasons for that fundamental uneasiness in the California terrain. From the book I learned that most of those summer-drought, blondie-blonde grasses on voluptuous California hillsides are aliens, evidence of an ecosystem revolutionized a century before. The spreading stands of gorse and pampas grass and the pungent eucalyptus windbreaks are invaders. I learned that America's salad bowl—the Central Valley—had once been a vast tule marsh, a waterfowl habitat so rich that when its millions of birds took flight their sheer numbers blackened the skies. Dasmann's catalog of depredations (circa 1965) was as extensive and diverse as California itself, and it left me painfully aware that even when there are no gross scars on the landscape, the coarsening of the mix of vegetation and the loss of wilder species great and small debase its texture to something less than the rich suppleness of a climax ecosystem. What remains may be beauty, but of a superficial kind.

That is also the case with this new home place, northwestern Lower Michigan. My summer evening drives past cherry orchards, cornfields, hayfields, cedar swamps, and woodlots fill my heart with pleasure. The prettiness is thanks in no small measure to the man-made features of the landscape, the farmsteads and clearings and cheering pots of flowers that appear in front of every home in the warm weather. But what I'm enjoying, lively, rich, and abundant though it may appear, was bought for the price of a climax hardwood forest stirring with game. And the pastoral landscape can be maintained only with a struggle. Just as in California, it's strange that little more than a century could have changed a land so much, strange that it is surviving as well as it is, strange to think about the endless battling it takes. Biota is tough, but not infinitely so.

The most mind-boggling thing about Michigan's summer-flowering beauty, be it muttlike and non native, is what a loving response it is from a terrain that has had the shit kicked out of it for the last century and more. Likewise, California's glamour. That the Earth can't help but reply to a just-tolerable level of abuse with motley new flourishing foliates a fool's paradise. The beauties of a rural landscape are soothing and yet conducive to the delusion that we can continue to have our way with nature. In these times the soul-need is more often to let nature have her way with us.

My soul took enough of a hammering during my first couple of years in the natural cause that I needed a retreat. After *Earth Times* folded, I worked briefly for a slick monthly "photo-documentary" magazine called *Earth*. I didn't really know what I was doing, so it was not a happy situation. I dropped out. After a healing respite, I would go on to free-lance for a few years, editing a couple of books; writing a column for a Marin County weekly, the *Pacific Sun*; doing book reviews for Stewart Brand's brand-new *CoEvolution Quarterly*; and writing a family-planning handbook, *The Joy of Birth Control.*

Before I was restored to functioning, however, I had to recover from early celebrity and excess opportunities. Thanks to the generosity of Libby Gatov, a remarkable woman and gracious friend, I was able to repair to her weekend house in Bolinas, a coastal village in Marin County on the Point Reyes peninsula. The peninsula is a creation of the San Andreas fault. It is a little chunk off the Tehachapi Mountains, which are hundreds of miles to the south, an orphan landmass that has been inching northwards for millions of years. The lagoon that gives Bolinas its name is a depression indicating the fault. Bolinas Lagoon shelters one of the last heron and egret rookeries on the west coast and is a precious refuge for estuarine life. During my time on that shore, I let the beauties be a balm. I wandered around, consorting with the local populace of artists and poets, transported, often with chemical wings. I played in the Pacific surf, sunbathed, and marveled at the green opulence of vegetation in the creeks around town. During mescaline walks on the beach, I discovered mystic resonance between the ripples in the sand left by receding waves, and the striations in the clouds caused by the currents of the upper atmosphere—fluid dynamics, runic communications. It was good to have a place and time to try to understand those messages, and the freedom to pause and let those colors and fragrances and sounds, the lavishness of the vegetation, the skitterings of bird life, just wash me clean. I remember quite clearly an afternoon walk up towards the mesa north of town. I was passing by an ivied (truly) dell and noticed, amazed, that there was nothing in this haven to do violence to the eye or aesthetic spirit.

Then along came an oil spill. Early in the morning, one winter Monday, two oil tankers, the *Oregon Standard* and the *Arizona Standard,* collided just inside the Golden Gate. A dense tule fog had drastically reduced visibility, and the ships hadn't been in radio contact. A Coast Guard radar operator had helplessly watched the collision on his screen, unable to prevent it.

The *Arizona Standard* was breached. More than 800,000 gallons of bunker oil were spilled into San Francisco Bay. Within a couple of days, tides and currents carried the slick twenty miles northwards up the coast, blackening miles of beaches and shoreline, miring thousands of birds and other marine beings out in the open water.

Tuesday night a local underground radio station put out a call for cleanup volunteers. The radio also announced that straw, rakes, and pitchforks were needed for beach cleanups, and mineral oil and cornmeal for bird cleaning. Carrying primitive implements and home remedies, a long, straggling convoy of volunteers began to make the winding procession along Highway 1 towards Bolinas Lagoon and points north. (As it developed, there would be more volunteers in scenic Marin County than jobs for them to perform, while birds would die untended in the East Bay mudflats, where the oil had washed ashore earlier, before exiting the gate and moving into the open sea.)

An oil spill is so appalling that it beggars meaningful response. It makes for a desperate feeling. You want to battle it and not stand idly by as the ugly, reeking muck fouls the beaches, the meeting ground of earth and sea. And the miserable, defenseless birds, shrouded in stinging crude oil, innocent victims, become the totems of the entropy battle. With or without care, almost none of them survive.

In the earliest cleanup activities at a beach south of San Francisco, where the oil also had spread, overzealous bird rescuers donned wetsuits and waded into formidable surf to fetch out oil-clogged birds. Although well meant, these ministrations were so frightening to some of the wild victims that they fled back out to sea and sank, dying from the shock of human contact. Despite its general futility, bird cleaning after an oil spill is the ecology movement's version of the freedom ride—a way of getting your body on the line in the good fight.

By Wednesday Bolinas's main street was blocked off with a sign that read: No More Volunteers, Please. The community, in which ecological mystics were already well represented, had been swamped by all the concerned young longhairs so eager to help. I was just one of the dozens of willing, kerchiefed girls milling around, superfluous, looking for a way to pitch in. Doers outnumbered possible good deeds by about two to one.

The volunteer elite, all sporting brand-new rubber boots courtesy of Standard Oil, was constructing, from timbers the size of telephone poles, a boom to block the mouth of the lagoon and prevent the oil from entering, which, thanks to miracles of tides and water, it hadn't yet. Down at the beach under spotlights powered by rackety generators (also courtesy of Standard Oil), the people's carpentry brigade labored round the clock. They took just pride in their heroic endeavor and honest exhaustion.

On the beach at the mouth of the lagoon, esconced by bales of hay, was a hippie USO for beach reclaimers and lagoon defenders. Amiably freaky women were running a soup kitchen, and the spacey but generous town doctor had opened a medical station on the strand. Several foremen strode around shouting commands.

A marine biology station in Bolinas had been pressed into service as a bird hospital and rang with the indignant shrieks of the oil-soaked cormorants, grebes, scoters, coots, murres, and sea ducks that had been fished out of the murky surf. The lab also buzzed with activity around the clock (disasters don't sleep and neither can heroes). There dozens of hastily trained volunteers first bathed the birds in mineral oil (to remove the crude) and blotted them off with cornmeal. The station's resident biologist had been up for days supervising a flock of workers who would, after cleaning the birds, have to nurse them through the pneumonias that usually followed (a result of the birds' plumage having been contaminated and having lost its insulating property).

Since Bolinas was full up, I pushed northwards to the Point Reyes beaches, still looking for something useful to do. It happened to be a beautiful day, with magnificent surf and nary a bird or glob of oil to be seen. I had to satisfy myself by doing a quick trash pickup, during which I came across an odd artifact of the ongoing crisis, a cotton swab with a large clot of oil glistening on its tip, which must have been used to clean the nostrils of some victim bird down the coast.

Adrenalized by the climate of emergency, still wanting a piece of the action, I returned to Drake's Beach, hoping they wouldn't have given away all the birds by the time I got there. Arriving at the ranger station, I encountered the usual dozens of volunteers, half of them idle. Once again there were the harried young men shooing well-meaning people away from the beach—the birds had suffered enough shock without the additional trauma of being struggled over by a surplus of do-gooders. Things were getting a little competitive in the bird-rescuing biz. About the only help to offer was to taxi birds to the main infirmary in Bolinas. Offered a grebe to ferry, I was off like a shot.

About half of the birds caught in the spill were western grebes. They're long-necked, elegant creatures, with red eyes, a black streak atop the head, white throat and belly, dark gray wings, and a yellow stiletto beak. They're deep divers—fishing birds. At mating time they run across the surface of the water, necks akimbo like temple dancers.

My grebe passenger, stinking of oil, eyes shrouded with a rag, bobbed its head up and down and stabbed angrily at the sides of its cardboard box. It rustled around in its queer nest of shredded paper, frightened and disoriented, crying and keening, pretty well doomed.

The next day I decided to set up an angry letter-writing concession across from the bird infirmary in Bolinas. Posters showing addresses of various culprits and officials, suggested messages, pens, paper, and envelopes—all were available. A friend and I took up a collection to pay for postage. I sat beckoning to the throngs of passersby. Just a handful stopped to write. The rest were "out of politics," "going to write my letters at home," or "busy with the cleanup." Most of them were skeptical about the value of a letter to a congressional representative, and so, in fact, was I.

Although the redress of grievances is supposed to be available through our duly elected legislative bodies, petitioning a congressperson is a weirdly cerebral response to the life-and-death physicality of an ecological disaster. More appropriate, somehow, would be to grapple with these life threats mano a mano.

The great San Francisco Bay oil-spill excitement eventually died down, and life in Bolinas returned to paranormal. And that's the incredible thing, really: that oil spills are so unpersuasive. The oil platform blowout in the Santa Barbara channel catalyzed the ecology movement but didn't inhibit offshore oil drilling. Indeed, it's on the rise again. Meanwhile there have been oil-tanker crack-ups that made the San Francisco spill look like a grease spot on a tie. All of which, along with having lived in the time of Seveso, Bhopal, and the poisoning of the Rhine, has convinced me that environmental calamity is not an adequate educational process. Things change remarkably little in the aftermath.

TRAVELING

———————◆———————

HOW TO BRING ABOUT WORTHWHILE AND NECESSARY CHANGE IS, of course, the $64,000 question. Laying out a not-so-simple kit of information and devices before a generation whose rhetoric and sometimes even behavior were all about change was Stewart Brand's good deed for the decades. He called it the *Whole Earth Catalog*. Wishbook, dreambook, information overload, recipe for a sustainable culture—"access to tools" was how Stewart distilled his idea twenty years ago, just as the seventies hove into view. He figured it would be useful and interesting (and most respectful of their intelligence) to point his cohort in the direction of whatever goods or skills they might need in order to live out the *Catalog*'s injunction: "We are as gods: we might as well get good at it."

The *Whole Earth Catalog* began in 1968 as a sprawling (11-by-14), ragtag, newsprint affair, a virtually ad-free (and hence incorruptible) review of books, many of the how-to variety, and other tools to inform the simple life. Although these days, Stewart disclaims having envisioned it as a bible for the back-to-the-land movement, I think he demurs too much. His original aim was simply to be useful to his brave contemporaries, many of whom were starting from scratch out in the sticks.

Throughout many editions the *Catalog* arrayed a captivating wealth of information, in crudely graphic black and white. It attested not just *an* alternative, but dozens of them: individuals, families, and intentional communities could depart from Babylon and simplify, simplify. By meeting their own basic needs and by abandoning the systems that looked to be ravaging the planet—and the human soul—any outfit could pioneer, given the will. Especially in its earliest versions, the *Catalog* did have a certain survivalist flavor.

"Further," another of Stewart's maxims, only seldom implied a Promethean defiance of bounds. The reviews categorized under "Whole Systems"—somewhat of a philosophy department—limned the circuits of Gaia, her constituent systems, and the universe in which she travels, from a census of galaxies right down to the submicroscopic realms. The *Catalog* went about suggesting what interesting things might be accomplished by individuals and communities working within those flows, Taoist fashion.

Stewart is unsentimental, but not lacking in heart. "It's always a shock to learn that god is not interested in your pain," he wrote. "The best you can hope for is the help of other people." If he seemed slightly unconcerned with big schemes to help the victim classes, it was perhaps because classes are fictions that dwarf individual action. Stewart's great gift—and service—was to equip individual responsibility and local self-reliance. The *Whole Earth Catalog* was an exaltation of the value of tools, and of durable goods. Between the lines was the unmistakably libertarian hint that if you didn't like the way things were going, you could always change it, beginning with your own household, homestead, or commune. What transpired on the material plane was of real consequence, although heavily conditioned by our ways of knowing. Stewart was less interested in propagandizing than in tweaking the converted and piquing the curious. "Power to the person" was one of his dicta, and he shunned the right-left dialogue and dialectic as essentially unproductive.

One basic inference that could be drawn from the *Whole Earth Catalog*'s quick success was that among its devotees were a great many people who felt lifestyle to be a pivotal ecological-moral issue, an explicit summation of values and beliefs. This Early American insight did and still does go deeper than the well-meaning but superficial policy shuffling of mainstream environmentalism. In the immortal words of Anne Herbert (a brilliant writer who was Stewart's first assistant editor at *CoEvolution Quarterly*), "Behavior counts."

Because of that, and because of Stewart's pervasive biological literacy, the *Whole Earth Catalog* has been associated in the public mind with the ecology movement from the beginning. Just as he enjoys exasperating the liberals, Stewart also has delighted in giving fits to the oats-'n'-groats crowd on certain issues of doctrinal purity, as when, in the early days of *CoEvolution Quarterly*, he enthusiastically opened a discussion on space colonies. (A lot of us right-thinking, liberal oatie-groaties thought that abandoning the Mother would just be too easy.)

Members of the ecology movement felt, rightly or wrongly, that the *Catalog* and *Quarterly* should be toeing some standard environmentalist line. After all, Stewart had blazoned on his covers (and was, I believe, the guy who had originally procured for public view) *the* great icon of the movement—NASA's image of the whole Earth as viewed from space. So over the years when ecology types promoted a definition of political correctness, Stewart responded with annoyance, period.

Stewart's technological enthusiasms have expanded over the years, and he sees no conflict between them and a loyalty to Gaia. This perhaps admirable open-mindedness is a tacit reproach to the more purist and pessimistic ecofreaks (like me) because it's somehow so sanely accepting of certain promising aspects of what *is*. Terence's saying—"I am man: nothing human is alien to me"—befits the Brand catholicity of intelligence.

However the *Catalog* has evolved through the eighties, the early editions were strange and wonderful congeries catering to what in these decadent times looks to have been a slightly crazed, willful ignorance, or visionary innocence, that sustained the back- and heart-breaking (to say nothing of mind-bending) efforts of dropout communitarians.

As an aspiring, fortyish owner-builder, I can only marvel at the straight-aheadness of those early hippies who just bought— or squatted on—pieces of land, lived in rustic code-defying hovels, and flung convention to the winds in matters of sanitation, animal husbandry, childbirth, diet, and economics. The funk and daring of it all seem mighty valiant.

A mixed bag of technics to arm that valor is all there in the old *Catalogs,* this sampling of items from the fall 1969 issue: geodesic domes, simplified carpentry, plumbing and wiring, tipis, cabins, adobe homes, Aladdin lamps, seed catalogs, bee books, gardening manuals, pruning handbooks, woodstoves and windmills, foraging, solar-energy use, hardware, knot-tying lore, woodcraft, pottery, weaver's and jeweler's supplies, buckskin, how to build your own furniture and how to make cowboy horse gear and how to construct a classic guitar, always a little math, self-publishing, filmmaking, theater production, mail-order food and flour mills, *A Manual of Simple Burial,* emergency medical guides, *A Handbook for Conscientious Objectors,* camping and mountaineering equipment, tents, auto repair manuals, aviation, and always maps, massage, education, child's play, and of course the *I Ching.*

Books accessed in the *Catalog* came recommended by enthusiastic readers and judged by *Catalog* reviewers (whose claims to expertise were uneven) to be the best they had seen on the subject. So in one sense the *Catalogs* were a kind of hip, alternative *Consumer Reports.* Reviewers' tastes piped a tasty fount of resources for the autodidact, books of a sort that you seldom see in the mall bookstore. The net effect was that Stewart Brand, with self-assurance that grated a tad, removed all the excuses for not creating a better alternative by saying *Look It Up.*

The point was to point, point at good things and get out of the way, not to bore the reader with your theories and opinions. The Brand intelligence is voracious and focused, receptive to the new, and loyal to whatever will hold up as the true. Which is why the entrepreneurial, electronic-eighties incarnation Stewart Brand still concludes the latest version of the *Whole Earth Catalog* ("the *Essential* ") with a review of and consultation with the *I Ching:*

Gregory Bateson remarked once to his secretary, Judy Van Slooten, "I am going to build a church some day. It will have a holy of holies and a holy of holies of holies, and in that ultimate box will be a random number table." . . . All originality, he says, whether in evolution or in human learning, comes from "raids on the random."

The ancient Chinese Taoists who made this oracle may have had a similar idea, or they may have stumbled on it or coevolved into it, but obviously it served them. And it serves us. It profoundly served the generation that emitted the original *Whole Earth Catalog.* Ending with this review is a piece of homage to that time and those people, both passing rapidly, both remembered too easily for superficial and dismissable things rather than for the real risks taken with real clarity in the face of overwhelming opposition.

Clink clink go the tossed pennies. How about a statement for the end of the *Essential Whole Earth Catalog,* ancient random number table . . . Hm, 51, The Arousing.

What to tell you about the man tossing those coins? He was, at the time of our relationship during the early seventies, a striking figure. For special occasions—happenings and press conferences—he sported his Merry Prankster regalia: a magnificent handmade, fringed buckskin shirt and smashed top hat with a feather in the band. Stewart is tall and lean, with big unblinking blue eyes and vanishing close-cropped blond hair. He has a good beak and a sound chin, possesses a grin to wreathe more face than his in smiles, and also a withering stare. His face is rendered all the more engrossing by a thorough tracery of wrinkles begun in his twenties.

Most famous for writing and publishing, Stewart also wielded a pretty mean camera and relished designing large happenings—like the Trips Festival, the *Whole Earth Catalog* Demise Party, and the New Games Tournament. This art form was part party-giving and part cool experimentation. Stewart is bluntly unwilling to have his interests bounded by sentiment or dogma, even that of his friends. Given a raft of congenital advantages—brains, wealth, and strength—and the self-will to pursue his singular intellectual and sensory appetites, Stewart Brand is a formidable person.

During our while, we traveled together, socialized with the Bay Area's learned and hip, and conversed relentlessly. Stewart had a choice collection of toys—he was the first on the block to own a hang glider, a lapstrake Whitehall, or a Windsurfer—and at the time I knew him was asserting his freedom to play. Things between us were intense but somehow not close. His affection was peculiar and has left an indelible memory. He was, undeniably, a great date.

Our affair began shortly after Stewart, in an unprecedented act of success renunciation (and publishing derring-do), issued the *Last Whole Earth Catalog* and meant it. I had concluded my sojourn in Bolinas and was domiciled in a pleasant flat in Berkeley, with no phone. Stewart, whom I had met but briefly before, came a-courtin' on his motorcycle one day. After a few quizzical conversations, he invited me to join him on a camping trip. So began our spell of companionship. Among the treasures Stewart shared with me was his love for the desert. Although I grew up in one, it wasn't until my journeys with Stewart that I began to appreciate the look and feel of dry places. And, to mitigate the harshness, the Brand approach to outdoorsmanship always included hot-springs bathing, which took just enough of the rough out of roughing it for this sybarite.

Our first foray into arid lands was a truck trip around northwestern Nevada, basin and range country with hot streams and potholes here and there, ghost towns, gypsum mines, herds of sheep grazing in lava-outcrop uplands, and geyser-warmed cattle tanks fringed with cattails, hospitable to waterfowl (this, the most spectacular swimming hole on Earth, surely). Our ways were perfumed by sage and heralded by flashing antelope, anointed by the waltz overhead of eagle and hawk. We rejoiced in the total barrenness of the Black Rock Desert, a cracked white alkali flat stretching not quite endlessly off towards a horizon of harsh little indigo mountains. An uncomfortable beauty, not exactly the context for critters whose bodies are mainly water, ambulatory seas.

Even so, the desert is more about light than dry. It's as though the sparseness of the biomass—photosynthesizers are few and far between—means there's sunlight bouncing around, unconsumed, unabsorbed, and illuminating more. The desert makes you squint, and all its realities are stark. Much about nature comes clearer there. It throws its even pitiless light on self and soul both.

The next desert Stewart invited me to was Baja California, with a stop beforehand at Aravaipa Canyon in southeastern Arizona. The canyon was at that time a Nature Conservancy holding. What made it unique was its perennial stream, and its remarkably undisturbed ecology. Because the previous owners hadn't ranched it too hard, the uplands still hosted native grasses. And the untrammeled creek still was habitat for a number of Arizona's increasingly rare species of native fish. The year-round presence of water fostered exceptional growth of the indigenous flora, making it a lush, by desert standards, refuge for an abundance of wildlife, including cougars.

Clearly, a visit to such a place was not to be missed, but I was hesitant. I figured that roughing it in the desert was so inherently dangerous that even if the desert place we were visiting would have a stream babbling warily within yards of our trail, it would still require an almost superhuman outdoorsperson to be equal to the challenge. I figured that we might be confronting mortal consequences in Aravaipa Canyon, so I went looking for advice.

Superior advice was handy by. I was seeing a renaissance psychiatrist at the time, Sterling Bunnell. In addition to his medical and psychiatric training, Bunnell was also a practiced field biologist and teacher who understood both intuitively and in scientific detail the definite ground of ecological concern. A Jungian desert rat, tidepool aficionado, zen student, and possible deep source of wisdom.

So during my next 50-minute hour, sitting in the Eames chair, I asked him if there were any threats to be especially wary of out in that wilderness, any tactics he'd recommend, figuring that he'd remind me to shake the scorpions out of my boots every morning. Yes. As soon as we embarked from the car, we should put as much distance between it and ourselves as possible. That way we'd minimize our chances of encountering other humans. (This began to clarify my thinking as to which was the most fearful beast in the wilderness.)

While a desert encounter with another person can be a chancy sort of thing, there's another potential meeting in the desert that can be positively heart-stopping, that being the encounter with god. Not some doe-eyed, merciful, greeting-card Jesus, but an uncompromising, wily sort of godhead, built along the lines of a coyote, who kicks in your face the dust of obvious truths: attend the lifeways of your fellow creatures; be abstemious and tough; get smart or die; observe, above all, the spareness and grandeur of the expanse; face the blaze with due awe. Real gods abide in places where humans can't take it easy around nature. Desert canyons, playas, and plateaus are places like that.

While neither of us was surprised by god in Aravaipa Canyon, we were awakened by a startling midnight clatter in the remote stillness—a coatimundi (the Sonoran bioregion's counterpart to the raccoon) rummaging through our provisions. In addition to murdering sleep, the canyon's January chill was colder than we felt like being, so we cut short our stay and motored on down to Mazatlan, Mexico, to catch a ferry across the Gulf of California.

En route to the ferry, we camped out, and, tenderfoot that I remained, I began to feel grubbier by the minute, and ill-rested because sleep got in a bag didn't count. Thus, I was pathetically eager to claim that second-class berth on the ferry and make a beeline for the showers. The shower room, however, proved to be such a shockingly filthy mire that I emerged far worse contaminated, by the excretions and secretions of my fellow passengers, than I had been by simple road grime.

Nevertheless, by the time we docked at La Paz, I was ready to go to any lengths for a washup, and by cleverly busting a shock absorber manipulated the situation so that we'd be forced to spend our first Baja night in a hotel. But the joke was on me. There was no hot water, period; that's just life in the developing world. Frustrated into surrender mode, I had thus been readied to perceive the desert's utter cleanliness.

Tourist access to Baja wasn't total at that time (although discovering encampments of giant motor homes at faraway beaches thwarted our desires for splendid isolation). Our quest to get away from them all led to some fatigue-crazed, midnight forays through forests of cardon cactuses, trying to locate the seashore by smell.

We were at large in an extremely dry place, a stranded peninsula peopled by boojums. (These are weird cactuses that look like 40-foot parsnips doing headstands; they have as foils and compatriots little elephant trees that look like scaled-down baobabs.) It's a Krazy Kat realm, Baja, alive with freakish products of isolation and adaptation. This offbeat cast of vegetable characters emerges through the interstices of the desert pavement, an artless mosaic laid down by time, immaculate white gravel grouted with rose-ebony sand. It forms a delicate, even crust, permeable to the vanishing rains, to the millions of hopeful seedlings of intrepid desert plants. It takes almost forever for those bits of stone and sand to achieve that perfect repose, to structure the relationships that protect the desert earth from the cutting forces of thunderstorms, the lashing momentary deluges that sustain the thirsty, patient, desert flora.

I got very well acquainted with this pavement because, once we were out of town and dwelling under the cloudless tents of heaven, I was squatting to pee, which brought me close to those pebbles in their offhand patterns of beauty. I was able to study the miniscule forms of vegetation as well as the grander oddities. It dawned on me in that position that squalor is a human production.

Years later, recounting this pee epiphany to Dave Foreman, I learned that he and I both had seized on a line from *Lawrence of Arabia* that sums up the desert. About halfway through the movie, a sweaty Chicago journalist approaches Lawrence, definitively portrayed by Peter O'Toole. Lawrence sits on the rug-draped running board of a car, resplendent in white bedouin regalia, penning a dispatch. The newshawk wipes his neck and asks Lawrence why is he is so personally attracted to the desert. Lawrence replies, simply, "It's clean."

• • •

Another adventure with Stewart Brand, of quite a different character, took me to Stockholm in June 1972 to work in the vicinity of the United Nations Conference on the Human Environment (UNCHE).

Because it had been generated by a nonprofit corporation, the million and a half dollars in *Last Catalog* sales wasn't just loot that Stewart could frivol off (not that he was the sort who'd want to). It required philanthropic stewardship. Thus, the origin of POINT Foundation. With a board consisting of several of Stewart's brightest and most effective cronies, POINT Foundation began its first big project: Life Forum.

UNCHE was the stimulus. It was to be the first global environmental conference, and one of the largest international conferences ever held. (That it stressed concern for the *human* environment betrayed the essentially social orientation of the meeting.) In light of the fact that a presidential candidate in the 1988 election promised to convene an international environmental conference as a meaningful step towards dealing with global environmental problems, which are hugely worse than in 1972, it is worth asking how useful it was, or might be again. The Stockholm conference proved to be significant, but not particularly effective, for reasons anticipated by Mary Jean Haley in *Open Options,* her excellent handbook (a Life Forum project) to the alternative conferences in Stockholm:

The alternative groups say that since the UN conference delegates are representatives of their governments, they will be bound to represent the vested interests of those governments whether or not they coincide with the interests of improving the human environment. The alternative groups declare that the present environmental crisis is the result of a pattern of resource exploitation for profit for the few to the detriment of many, and that this pattern is an integral part of the social, economic, and political structures of the powerful UN member nations. Therefore, the critics say, the UN delegates will be unable to entertain the idea of changing economic and political patterns to solve environmental problems. In short, those who have organized alternative conferences feel that the UN Conference is so bound by existing governmental structures which have created world problems that it cannot play an effective role in solving them.

Another criticism of the UN conference is that the topics which it is able to consider are limited to those which are not sensitive to member nations. There will be, for example, no discussion of chemical and biological warfare, no discussion of overpopulation and population control, no discussion of the exploitation of the resources of underdeveloped nations by developed nations, no discussion of ecocidal American activities in Indochina.

Despite all those real shortcomings, the UN Conference on the Human Environment was a global event that signaled an awakening to the fact that we had, in economist Barbara Ward's memorable phrase, only one Earth and that it was suffering serious damage. In the San Francisco Bay Area ecology scene, hopes were that the Stockholm conference might be a great moment of global consciousness-raising. So with the logistic and financial aid of Life Forum, a handful of California's most noteworthy ecofreaks began making plans not merely to attend, but to launch an armada of counterculturalists, an eclectic assortment of ecologists, Native American elders, poets, and communards (the saintly Hog Farmers), who would constitute a de facto Fourth World legation.

My friends in Life Forum suggested that funding might be found for me to do my population shtick in one of the alternative forums. I demurred, being loath to expose my white, American, middle class self to developing-world assaults on Malthusianism. Having been rather wrung out by the previous few years, all I was feeling confident about at that point was my ability to give dinner parties. When I confessed that, funding was available almost within minutes for me to join the Life Forum gang and throw dinner parties. That is how I was ferried to Stockholm to establish what came to be called a salon. Funding me, a grasshopper-pauper-writer type, to throw real dinner parties opened that kind of entertaining to a crowd other than the wealthy.

Also in the Life Forum entourage were poets (Michael McClure and Gary Snyder); a traveling commune, the Hog Farmers, complete with their two buses; the aforementioned Mary Jean Haley; and Native American and Anglo members of the Black Mesa Defense Fund. The core group set up its ménage in the gallery and apartments at Pilgatan 11.

The Californios of Life Forum believed it their task to enrich and ameliorate a world gathering that they imagined might flower into a "Woodstockholm." The notion was that young people from all over Europe might converge on the meeting, so it would be kind to have the Hog Farmers there to do the sort of caring-for that they had at the Woodstock music festival, where they had provided emergency food, shelter, and first aid—real security, without armed force. The city of Stockholm gave characteristically straitlaced facilitation to the Hog Farmers by offering the use of an abandoned airfield some distance from town for the youth encampment. Because it is very expensive to visit Sweden, however, the Eurohippies for the most part gave it a pass, and so Skarpnack, the airfield, proved to be a desolate scene.

What a weird Tower of Babel Stockholm was, with all its political crosscurrents! The movers and shakers around the official UN meeting—advisors to it, preparers of white papers—

seemed to be mainly upper-middle-class, dominant-paradigm males: Club of Rome fellows, members of ruling elites. Lots of top executives from U.S. environmental organizations went over to lobby in the global arena, wearing their best suits. In such a milieu, Life Forum's hippies were vexingly outlandish. They were pricks of conscience, as when Calico the Hog Farmer ("a topkick with a heart of gold," Stewart called her) showed up at the conclusion of a lavish city of Stockholm reception to beg. All she wanted was some leftover hors d'oeuvres to take out to Skarpnack, where the teeming microtudes of youth were quarantined.

By bringing a caravan of vagabond do-gooders, Indians, bards, and bohos to the perimeter of that entirely too-safe gathering, Life Forum, thanks to Stewart Brand, was giving the world a look at an ecologically sustainable variety of American. More sharin' and carin' and less refining of the position papers was what the Hog Farmers implicitly advocated in Stockholm that summer.

Because of Sweden's nearness to the midnight sun, summer nights there are long and derange the biological clocks of folks from more southerly latitudes. Crazed by jetshock and collision with the Baltic style, by the concatenation of viewpoints, and the suffocation of bureaucracy, many terriers of ecobohemianism burned themselves out nipping at establishment heels.

Despite Mary Jean Haley's salient introduction, we hadn't reckoned with the combined abilities of the UN and our Swedish hosts to refine even the earthiest concerns into a noncommital diplomatic sludge. The "reasonable man" around the conference regarded the cause of Third World economic growth as impeccable. Brazil announced itself willing to endure a little pollution, if that was the price of growth (groan goes up from U.S. environmentalists). Macroeconomics was the soul of the meeting—the assumption that commerce (aka development) could provide the wretched of the Earth with greater equity. Once that was done, the thinking went, then environmental problems could be tended to.

This excerpt from a poem Gary Snyder composed in Stockholm is apposite:

Mother Earth: Her Whales

North America, Turtle Island, taken by invaders
    who wage war on the world.
May ants, may abalone, otters, wolves and elk
Rise!   and pull away their giving
    from the robot nations.

Solidarity. The People
Standing Tree People!
Flying Bird People!
Swimming Sea People!
Four legged, two-legged, people!

How can the head-heavy power-hungry politic scientist
Government   two world   Capitalist-Imperialist
Third-World   Communist   paper-shuffling male
    non-farmer   jet-set   bureaucrats
Speak for the green of the leaf? Speak for the soil?

(Ah Margaret Mead . . . do you sometimes dream of Samoa?)

The robots argue how to parcel out our Mother Earth
To last a little longer
              like vultures flapping
belching, gurgling,
           near a dying Doe.

(Snyder distributed the poem on the occasion of Project Jonah's whale march, of which more shortly.)

While the Earth obviously wasn't saved at Stockholm (had we even heard of acid rain then? of ozone depletion?), careers were made and broken, and a whole new international bureaucracy, the United Nations Environment Programme, was launched. Off in a side eddy, I was cooking and pouring, listening to friends and possible friends expanding their ideas under the rose of the primacy of ecological concern. This was the beginning of my salon. Such entertaining was my project in Stockholm, and my principal activity the following year at my home in Berkeley. The homeliness of housekeeping, marketing, and food preparation, and the intellectual electricity of the dinner conversation made a satisfying totality.

Assembling an interesting mix of guests, making introductions that would both set them at ease and pique their interest in one another's doings, minding the talk so that it elicited everybody's thoughts and wasn't dominated by just one guest— all these subtle efforts were a living form of editorship. The contributors appear live and in person, and the creation exists just in the moment. Attendance at these affairs was a special thing. It was understood that some thinking together was expected. Salons are spaces, psychic spaces, created to elicit the best talk from a gathering of minds—the custom dates from the Renaissance. I resisted suggestions to record or document those gatherings. That might have made people self-conscious: it would have been utilitarian and grandiose. The salons were art for art's, not artifact's, sake. They offered some special forms of nourishment for some exceptionally conscious people. One way and another, all my guests were working to save the world. It was an honor to serve them and to provide them with opportunities for new acquaintances and high-level play.

The Stockholm salon kept me on the streets with my shopping bag and out of political and media mischief. Every other day I'd compose a guest list and make the calls to organize a dinner to take place a few nights hence. Then I'd make a menu for the upcoming party and proceed to shop. I marketed my way round Stockholm with my transit map and phrase book, amusing fishmongers, grocers, and apothecaries (from whom, when in Sweden, you may buy your spices) with my spotty Berlitz Swedish clichés. I'd cook in the afternoon, serve in the evening, and clean up the next day, conducting most of these operations in a kitchen not much larger than a phone booth.

We had Native American dinners, steady-state economics dinners, population dinners, women's dinners (one of which was attended by Margaret Mead herself, archaically regal, sporting an embroidered red cape and gnarled walking stick), and a celebrated (by me) whale dinner. Maybe what I was practicing, unawares, was the "chop wood and carry water" truth. No matter what's transpiring in the great wide world, the doers eventually will want a meal or to slake their thirst or to come in from the cold and make friends. So hospitality—caring even for people whose basic needs are amply met—is a useful and simple thing to do. It was, to belie my chronic pessimism, an affirmation that life goes on, and that as long as they don't drop the bomb, some basic human covenants—such as breaking bread together—can be extended creatively.

More than most of the Life Forum envoys, I was blessed in having something tangible to do. The salon gave me a focus and a criterion of success far more attainable than just hoping that my ideas would prevail (and even in that unlikely event, there would still be dinner to get on the table). If any idea prevailed, it was the importance of setting the context: "a dinner party with a purpose." My guests' enjoyment was my reward.

Many of the Stockholm salon guests were warrior folks, trying to carry a vision within the formalized precincts of the United Nations or NonGovernmental Organization (NGO) conferences. At the salons they were able to unbuckle, to sit down and relax with other Earth-compatriots, to compare notes and refresh their big-picture vision. They also got a free meal, which in pricy Stockholm was no small thing.

One of the best parties we had was the whale salon. Joan McIntyre, the head of Project Jonah, an international whale-saving organization (and another beneficiary of the POINT Foundation), was the premiere guest.

Joan was ageless, compact, and rich as a hickory nut, woolly, brilliant, and alive in her sex, true to her femaleness. She radiated an intensity and integrity and was at once attractive and intimidating. Joan was part of San Francisco's tangy Bohemia — beat literati, North Beach habitués who were not merely rebellious, but learnedly so, polymaths of an ilk increasingly rare. Intellectual range and poetic diction were standard equipment. With her 16-year head start in this life, Joan McIntyre was a heroine to me, and a role model. She paid the price of her individuation in the coin of sensitivity. It seemed that everything she turned her hand to was rooted in insight and executed with style.

Other participants in the whale salon were: an Aleutian Inuit whose lifeway revolved around whale hunting, a White House advisor on wildlife conservation, a British cetologist, a Canadian marine biologist who implored us not to overlook the plight of the salmon in our enthusiasm for the whales, and Michael and Joanna McClure. Sundry members of Life Forum and POINT Foundation rounded out the party.

The highlight of the evening was McClure's reading of one of his *Gargoyle Cartoons,* a goofy one-sided conversation between a Swedish and a Japanese garter snake concerning the relative merits of being a seal, a mackerel, or a whale on a nice day out in the waves. McClure's deadpan rendition of his work, with vaudevillian accents, had us all rolling in the aisles. All in all, during what was a terribly mental occasion, the salon provided me with sensuous riches. Other people may have vibrant memories of agreements hammered out or agencies begun, rumors squelched or orations delivered, but I can still taste the salt tears I cried over a cutting board deep in chopped onions.

• • •

Conservation, environmentalism, and the ecology movement were and are, like most movements, directed by male honchos. Needless to say, there were always women behind those thrones: crucial and dutiful wives; patient, admiring mistresses; supercompetent, self-effacing executive assistants — auxiliary engines to the masculine world-saving heroics. Sexism was the element we swam in, the prevailing current in which women had to navigate. We dealt with it usually in silence, repressing or forgiving, accepting or resenting, and, sometimes, finally protesting all the vague and explicit patterns of domination and exclusion.

In this preserve of executive timber and great white fathers, then, a woman like Joan McIntyre was doubly exceptional. In the minutes of a POINT Foundation meeting at which she'd been invited to serve as the Elijah (a one-time, critical observer), we read of Joan weeping openly in frustration at the insular patriarchy of the foundation board, accusing the members of being typical representatives of "the male-aggressive world that will not listen to other voices." Denying her perceptions, the board protested that, of course, she had been heard. Nothing in the process or the content, however, seemed to change. Civilization's constant denial of the female perception of male hegemony ("Woman is the nigger of the world," said Yoko Ono) is reflexive and, ultimately, crazy-making for all concerned. It takes a very concentrated soul to sustain the confrontation and to carry on a life's work as well. Joan McIntyre, as I knew her, had that strength.

When we first met, she was working for Friends of the Earth on a campaign to make the wearing of fur coats by humans unfashionable and thereby protect the original owners of the skins—spotted cats, seals, foxes, coyotes, wolves, and others. Boldly, she'd rounded up a pack of San Francisco glitterati who took, with great fanfare, a public vow of abstinence from pelt consumption. The press conference was a smash. At the same time that Joan was bringing off this stunning PR coup, she was writing an "Animal of the Month" column for us at *Earth-Times*, portraying a few of the creatures it was her passion to defend:

> A wolf goes about his business of being a wolf with surety
> and joy. He or she, with rare exceptions, has a place in a society

of creatures that share pleasures and pain and each other's company with a kind of conviction and authenticity that would serve as a model for the realized self. Wolves know what it is to be wolves, and they enjoy it. Orphans are cared for and adopted into other families. Strangers, if the territory and range permits, are afforded a place in the pack. Hunts are arranged, dens are dug and watched, pups are bred and born and cared for with affection and love. They are fantastically gregarious and interested in each other and in all of the rest of creation. Anything that moves or doesn't is an event.

Watching Joan McIntyre move in Stockholm was fantastically interesting. While the delegates, mostly male, to the conference passed the time nitpicking declarations and debating how much pollution they were willing to accept as a price for national development, Joan busied herself with organizing a whale march, a circumambulation of the parliament building where the UN conference was held, just a little demonstration to remind the delegates that some fleshly, life-and-death issues were being obscured.

The Hog Farmers obligingly dressed one of their buses as a whale by contriving a skin, fins, and flukes of black plastic (and writing "Maybe Dick" in masking tape on the side). They rigged up an elaborate sound system to play recordings of whale songs during the procession. And while the parade assembled, Joan was buying up all the cut flowers in Stockholm to array the marchers. As we got under way, the elaborate sound system failed. Joan asked us to sing the whale songs ourselves. Gamely clutching our lilies of the valley, we followed the whale bus downtown, bellowing, bleating, whining, squeaking, and generally rupturing Stockholm's circumspection with our display of fancy. Just a few days later the conference moved to recommend a 10-year moratorium on commercial whaling, as the U.S. Congress had done the year before. Joan McIntyre had undeniably succeeded in making whales the symbol of the Stockholm conference and a totem of global environmental concern thenceforth.

After Stockholm, she continued her efforts, making saving the whales a children's crusade with Project Jonah, encouraging schoolkids worldwide to badger the leaders of Russia and Japan to stop whaling. In a phenomenal spurt of energy, Joan McIntyre and her advisors and colleagues—Jerry Mander, Diana Shugart, Eugenia McNaughton, Maxine McCloskey, Gail Madonia, Joe Bacon, and Barbara Belding, in concert with the British and French Friends of the Earth—made saving the whales a global movement, which, despite having secured some protection for some species, is still battling the intransigence of the whaling nations. Even if Joan didn't succeed in her ultimate goal, her work continued to be influential long after she transformed herself from activist-author to compleat nature mystic and dropout.

Joan McIntyre is not unique among ecological women in her ingenious ability to do things on the cheap, and to identify and address the fundamental needs rather than the impulse to self-perpetuation. It's a kind of maternal directness about getting the other cared for, a virtue necessitated by women's second-class citizenship and economic standing. Like a lot of women organizers, she had a sensible simplicity of approach. The degree of her radicalism mothered this necessity, positively ensuring no sudden deluge of funds. She chose to operate on a simple, nomadic basis, traveling and conferring widely with other whale savers. The Project Jonah office, with its loose staff, was housed in Joan's Bolinas home. There was less physical weight to lend the whole thing inertia.

If she were of the opposite sex, I imagine that she'd have been slightly more available for institutionalizing her approach and gathering an edifice around her. Once whale saving became a popular cause, she was content to leave the field to others and move on to the next thing, seeking to extend her consciousness.

Joan McIntyre's imaginative empathy with other life-forms, exemplified in *Mind in the Waters,* her anthology of writings on cetacean intelligence, and *The Delicate Art of Whale Watch-*

ing, her journal of her life in Hawaii, is extraordinary. As an anthropologist, she is well aware that an equal regard for other living creatures had been characteristic of human relations with nature among tribal peoples for millennia.

In an *Earth Times* column, Joan wrote:

> The yearning for totems is a primal desire for sacredness. In all the years of our memory, along forest paths and across deserts, we have carried with us, in intimate company, animal figures that make reality sing and space vibrate with particular meanings. Totems. Figures carved out of mind, in fear, loneliness, and joy, to walk with us through time and shed light in the dark spaces of our animal soul. These figures are distant now. They have been reduced to Disneyland; paper dry, one-dimensioned pets—poodles and parakeets. The animals that peopled the world of our ancestors and brought hope, light, and terror to the forest clearing; that were consulted in reverence, invoked in danger, and appeased in hunger, are now safely under our control. And we are smaller now—and much less wise.

Feeling awe before the mystery and identity of other life-forms is not a pathetic fallacy but an essential moral step beyond objectifying and mining the lives of those members of other nations. In the last decade, animal rights have become more thinkable in our culture, but it is taking a long time for environmentalists to begin to accord *Thou* rather than *It* status to other living creatures. At least a decade and a half ago, Joan McIntyre made honoring the selves of the cetaceans the ethical cornerstone of the Save the Whales campaign. In a statement to the United Nations, she announced, "We consider the whales themselves a nation." At about the same moment, legal scholar Christopher Stone was exploring the question *Should Trees Have Standing?* And a few years later, Peter Singer would make an academic philosopher's case for *Animal Liberation.* Joan McIntyre, however, by weaving together intellect and intuition in a basic PR lady's understanding of the common mind, was introducing these revolutionary ideas to public consciousness before the hairsplitting could begin. She was a biocentrist before the term was even coined.

In 1975 a slick women's magazine solicited some articles from me. The editors contracted for, but didn't use, a story on Joan and Project Jonah. In the course of writing the article, I interviewed Joan at length. In our few hours of talk, she issued a whole body of wisdom. I'm sorry it has taken this long for it to see print.

Joan McIntyre was among the few ecological activists in the seventies who stated unequivocally that ecological crises were a function of our civilization and its debasement of our souls. She had the anthropologist's acute observation of social forms and was poignantly attuned to the moral content of our species' interaction with others.

"Dolphins when they get into trouble go to each other," she said. "Sperm whales go to each other when they're harpooned, so then you can harpoon one after the other. So there's this pattern which worked perfectly well for 35 million years, which is 'take care of each other,' which is how they got taken care of in the sea, because they didn't have anything that they could count on outside of themselves, because they weren't manipulators, so they couldn't build something to take care of themselves. They had to take care of themselves by their social order, by their common understanding."

Joan's sense of the magic of a common understanding—what might be termed "species consciousness"—pervaded our talk: the entrainment in flight of starling flocks, and in rest and play of schools of dolphins; the coherence produced by the ceremonial cycles of traditional peoples. She spoke of the psychic value of a multigenerational community, or authentic ways of raising human energies through dances and festivities that include people of all ages, and of the collective transmission of culture and personal empowerment. These essentials have long since vanished from most of our lives.

"Everything's been taken from us," she said. "We can't sing, we can't dance, we can't make music, we can't heal our own bodies, we can't run, we can't smell anything, and most of us, because we've been defined as having bad vision, can't see anything except through glasses. So we have this incredibly affluent society where everything that could be owned by us is stripped away from us, and everything is replaced, none of which can we fix, make, in any way produce, take care of, or even know what to do with when we're through with."

Ideas like this haunt me when I push my cart through the aisles of the local hypermarket, an emporium that sells clothes, food, sporting goods, electronics, building supplies, pets, baked goods, deli food, toys, tools, hardware, geegaws, jim-jams, and knick-knacks—a little of everything, catering to the wants and needs of debased human protoplasm. So many of my fellow shoppers look gray, overweight, poorly nourished; even the kids seem broken down and disaffected. The gaggles of fat, dull, covetous children in places like that are enough to break your heart. What kind of society reduces the holy vibrance of childhood to pettish, mean consumerism?

Joan McIntyre's stridency echoes forward: "We're having this thing done to our minds . . . it's like a D & C . . . it's an abortion of anything that we might have known in the past which could help us now. Scrape it clean. So read a *National Geographic* and look at the natives as quaint and answer all questions with 'We can't go back.'"

At times this alienation Joan describes so vividly has me devoured by what the *Book of Common Prayer* calls "faithless fears and worldly anxieties." The possibility of global disaster, internalized as definite personal mischance, gnaws at me. The house could be struck by lightning and burn down with us in it; a wheel could come off the car and send me crashing into a ditch; inadequately refrigerated mayonnaise could poison us with salmonella; my sphere has constricted down to the dot on the exclamation point. What the hell is going on?

Joan McIntyre anticipated such compounding morbid paranoia years ago. "Particularly as things get more chaotic for a while, your ability to deal with fear is going to be very important in terms of how you feel the life to be," she said. "Right now we could all be totally crazy, no matter what our condition was, because we would always have something to be afraid of."

Courage is making meaningful choices despite fear. Fight, flight, and transcendence seem to be the basic options. And the latter can be attained only by making peace with the fact of death. In one of the most memorable passages of our discussion that day, Joan described an entranced meditation on the death of a wild thing:

"Sterling [Bunnell] brought me this hawk . . . and it was dying . . . and I tried to keep the hawk alive for a week, and the hawk got a little better, and then it got worse. . . . And then the hawk was clearly dying . . . and I sat on the floor with the hawk for a long time. I realized how slow dying was. . . . It was like a dimming, not a snuffing . . . and after the hawk was dead . . . I didn't want to bury it. . . . I didn't want to throw it in the garbage can. . . . I didn't want to leave it lying around because I didn't want it torn by dogs and cats. So I put it in this basket, and I hung it in front of the house.

"So I watched the hawk. And I thought, Okay. You stay with the spirit of it. I mean the hawk can do less now than he could do. And the maggots came and ate it. And I watched the hawk becoming, in flesh, something different, but still connected with it.

"Understand that death occurs. . . . I was talking to some people last night about what it is to think of your form changing . . . a maggot eating at the soft tissue in your nostrils . . . my nostril . . . and to either look at that with an incredible kind of repugnance or to look at that as this incredible biology which just continues . . . and we come out of that biology. Because we can only come of the flesh of things which have been eaten and have been eating." We must make peace with what we are.

Years before, imagining the mental state of the cetacean, Joan had written in *Earth Times:*

Being. Mind activity unrelated to words—to ideas as we know them. No concepts, just the essential shapes of reality, colors or forms, density, the quality of weight, emanations from stars, the presence of "other" in its feeling state. Light, temperature. With fewer things locked into place by learning, there is more chance for the random. This is where play is truly possible. There is no great need to do anything—so anything can be done.

Not long after our interview, I heard that Joan had gone to Maui to spend her time swimming with dolphins, exploring the surf, and playing in the waves. This past January, I received a note from Joan, now Joana McIntyre Varawa. She wrote: "I'm living the ecological reality now—married to a Fijian, living in a grass house—bathing from buckets and lighting our starlit nights with kerosene lamps. Eat mostly fish and cassava, which we catch and grow. . . . Love Fiji, its soft ways and natural highs. Live on an island—go everywhere by boat— even see porpoises once in a while—but am not concerned with their consciousness. . . . " Years earlier, explaining why she was withdrawing from the corridors of activism, she said, "I had to stop being a PR lady and start living some of it, if only to find out about my own self that way, to test my own assumptions."

In twelve-step programs they talk about the futility of the "geographical cure," meaning that you can't evade your life problems by moving away because they're your *life* problems: an ongoing function of personality. Similarly, with the advent of systemic environmental contamination like acid rain and ozone destruction and poisoned groundwater, all functions of industrial civilization, no place safe from those consequences remains. Moving anywhere just forces you to confront another facet of the problem.

"There's no way to hide," Joan McIntyre said to me fifteen years ago. "There's only a way to begin to make it better— there's no place to go now except to make it better."

LABORING

———————————◆———————————

IN THE UNITED STATES ONE OF THE MOST POPULAR APPROACHES
to the job of "making it better" is the cause-oriented membership organization. The woods of environmentalism are full of
them. With the conservation battles of the late sixties, conservation organizations began to diversify their concerns and
their membership. The vocal minority was growing in numbers
and included indoorsmen and women—the breather's lobby—
as well as mountaineers and bird-watchers. David Brower
played an important role in fostering this growth and change.
He had made his first communion with the wilderness as a
child, and his abiding love of wild places infused his language
with a special power.

Brower's eloquence in conversation, at the podium or
wielding a pen is purely captivating. Like any great bard's his
voice has range and wit. He called for the preservation of homely necessities like topsoil, and of conspicuous glories like the
Sierra and the slickrock country with equal conviction. The
old Archdruid (a derogation gone awry that found its way into the title of John McPhee's 1971 *New Yorker* portrait of
Brower), whatever his failings, is nonpareil at making you care
about the fate of the Earth.

At countless podia Brower would stand shyly, almost absent-
mindedly. Tall and broad-shouldered, with a mountaineer's
expansive chest, he speaks in a melodious alto. Over the years
he has embroidered variously on the back-of-the-envelope
calculations at the core of his basic speech, yet it is always inspiring. This version of it appears in his introduction to *Only
a Little Planet:*

If we squeeze time . . . and compress the earth's four billion years into the six days of creation, the earth began only last Sunday at midnight, life arrived Tuesday noon, to grow, spread, diversify, and become ever more beautiful. Neanderthal man came 11 seconds before Saturday midnight, agriculture only 1½ seconds before midnight. The Industrial Revolution began its attack on the earth 1/40th of a second ago.

It is midnight now, and high time to slow the attack. So far almost all nations have been asking for more speed, believing that some kind of technological magic will stretch the earth. There is no such magic. We ought soon to learn to ask, before starting a vast new project, What will we gain if we don't build it? What will it cost the earth?

One thing it will usually cost is wildness, the wildness that holds answers to the questions man has not yet learned how to ask. We are surely able to demand less for ourselves, to live within the earth's income instead of scattering the capital the earth took billions of years to bring together.

Unequivocal credos, great energy, and charisma, with a generous admixture of obstinacy, combine to make Brower a great leader of the environmental cause. Although he was capable of it, compromise was not his long suit, and Brower's convictions about the sanctity of nature led him out in front of the conservation movement. For all the criticism of his managerial errancy, Brower's tenure left the Sierra Club the legacy of being a major force for environmental action, with a membership diversified and numerous beyond the original Berkeley hills preservationist and hiking coterie. And, as history would repeat itself, with variations, Friends of the Earth, which Brower began in the wake of his ouster from the Sierra Club, also fissioned as the result of an internal power struggle. Consequently, Brower, well into his seventies, has launched the Earth Island Institute. Characteristically, there is an excellent new publication, the *Earth Island Journal,* for one of David Brower's greatest talents is editorship. His abiding faith in the power of the pen and the press is in itself a noble preservationist sentiment.

In establishing Friends of the Earth, Brower created an atelier where some of the ablest young environmental thinkers and campaigners in the world, creative dissenters for whom friction is elixir, could be given a desk and some letterhead. The result was a surprisingly functional amalgam of the quixotic and the purposive.

Even a partial catalog of the array of issues that Friends of the Earth/U.S. addressed over the years suggests that its relatively small staff and membership covered a lot of territory (perhaps what follows should be sung, à la Gilbert and Sullivan): Whaling, the conduct of the International Whaling Commission, the right of Inupiat people to subsistence whaling; imperiled wilderness (Rainbow Bridge, Mono Lake, Alaska, and countless other irreplaceables), roadless areas throughout the land; the failings of nuclear power's technology and economics; protesting the damming of wild rivers; forestry practices; pesticide and herbicide use; endangered species (condors, wolves, the snail darter, legions of others); UN conferences and agencies; recombinant DNA; a sea-level Panama Canal; acid rain; bottle bills; waste recycling; opposition to the development of the supersonic transport and the B-1 bomber; alternative energy technologies and development (Amory Lovins's famous "Soft Energy Path"); noting the link between nuclear power and nuclear weapons development; objecting to superhighway construction; coastal protection; protection for Antarctica; the Clean Air Act; exploring steady-state economics.

By 1975 the drift of friendship and events found me working at Friends of the Earth. It was a yeasty surround. The members of the sixties generation that Brower talent-scouted and employed, however, had grown up in a "peace"-time that had provided no convincing experience of hierarchy or honorable vassalage. Hence, the staff's rebellious attitude and atmosphere of ongoing volatility. Things might have worked better for David Brower if he had surrounded himself with yes-men on staff and boards, but that was not his inclination. He looked for the spark of genius and the capacity for self-starting, and assembled himself a headstrong outfit. Everybody was permitted to charge off in his or her, but mostly his, chosen direction. The worthwhile array of pet causes was finally limited by Brower's guidance and the vagaries of Friends of the Earth's perpetually uncertain finances. In its heyday, Friends of the Earth was maddeningly unbureaucratic and refreshingly non-professional. It really couldn't afford to be otherwise, and the result was some real camaraderie and social enjoyment throughout the organization.

Like most of the women at Friends of the Earth, at the outset I was employed not in a policy role but in the service industries. My first couple of years were devoted to a dubious outings program and a stint at direct mail, writing letters that read like editorials and produced, alas, very few new memberships.

As director of membership development, and all during my tenure at Friends of the Earth, I was involved in fundraising, with never enough success. At one point Brower and I tried calling personally on some Friends of the Earth supporters. Those forays occasioned my longest sustained contact with Brower, but didn't lead to the mentorship I hankered for. One trip was a bootless voyage to Martha's Vineyard. Our arrival at the wrong side of the island truncated our visit with a potential donor who chose to stay potential. We straggled away from that encounter like a threadbare missionary and his spinster daughter.

Another distinguished couple had other plans for their day and graciously packed us and some box lunches off to a beach to await their return from a sail. I made the acquaintance of the Atlantic that bright day, swimming and frisking in its warm mild surf while Brower roamed the shore, totally absorbed in beachcombing and contemplating the essence of the rocks that inevitably venture into his seeking hand. Each of us was contained in a different element. Later, when we sat on our hosts' deck, it was my place to listen respectfully while he and Brower discussed the state of conservation in America.

Being in Brower's ambit at Friends of the Earth, I was among the seraphim, within earshot of Gabriel's voice. But as an editor and editorialist, I longed to step out of the choir. Membership development clearly was not my destiny, but I needed the job and liked the company. Fecklessly I awaited another big break into editing.

My big break came, as they are wont to do, with slow-healing complications. Tom Turner, the longtime editor of Friends of the Earth's paper, *Not Man Apart* departed for a sabbatical year in New Zealand. David Gancher, a puckish wit and snazzy thinker, succeeded Turner as editor pro tem. Gancher was almost immediately thereafter offered the greener pasturage of the managing editorship at *Sierra,* the Sierra Club's monthly magazine. He jumped at it, and the *Not Man Apart* editorship stood vacant again. President Brower, hero and inspiration of my youth, then bestowed the job on me. This was not a popular choice. Most of the paper's staff were partisans of Mary Lou Van Deventer, the dedicated and highly competent managing editor, who was next in line for the editorship. In loyalty to her, they threatened to walk out on me. Brower's response was that if it came to that, we would put out the paper on a mimeograph machine. Fortunately, it didn't. Mary Lou resigned, but with remarkable grace and magnanimity, and stayed a month to orient me. Despite her kindness, it was a rocky shakedown cruise.

Eventually the staff came together, and we began to extend the territory of editorial concern. In so doing, we had the advantage of *Not Man Apart*'s near decade of publishing excellence, which was the cumulative accomplishment of years of effort and attention from Brower, senior editor Hugh Nash, Tom Turner, Trish Saar, Bruce Colman, and a generation of other staff members and contributors.

In contrast with the *Earth Times* experience, this time I was taking the helm of a substantial and well-established bimonthly news magazine, with a flock of regular departments. *Not Man Apart* provided regular coverage of regional issues throughout North America, thanks to reports submitted by Friends of the Earth associates and field offices. Being the organ of a not-for-profit organization gave us the enviable freedom not to pander.

Interesting and valuable as Friends of the Earth/U.S. was in its American context, the most significant thing about the Friends of the Earth idea was its internationalism. Friends of the Earth/U.S. was one of a sisterhood of Friends of the Earth organizations throughout the world. At the planetary level, anyway, Friends of the Earth was decentralist. There was no international headquarters. Hence, the idea flowered in a real diversity of approaches worldwide: Friends of the Earth organizations engaged in everything from electoral politics (France), to appropriate technology development (Mexico), to high-stakes civil disobedience in defense of the rain forest (Malaysia).

In 1978 Jamie Nelson, *Not Man Apart*'s managing editor, and I had the choice assignment of covering the seventh Friends of the Earth International meeting, held in Brussels. In the course of working and traveling together, Jamie and I became loving friends and live-in companions. Returning from Europe, as partners we wrote:

> Fifty people (representing sixteen sister organizations) gathered in a city that houses the headquarters of numerous supernational institutions. These fifty Friends constitute a living cell, the life of an organization, not an institution, whose center is everywhere and circumference is nowhere. Nice contrast to the impassive grey edifices housing courts, parliaments, and bureaus. Nice that Friends of the Earth is nowhere drawn and headquartered.
>
> The bravery of Friends of the Earth demonstrators and organizers, and that of their allies in other organizations, is considerable. Police reaction to the Creys-Malville demonstration claimed a life. In Germany, the government is putting the

jobs and reputations and possibly the lives of antinuclear activists in jeopardy.

. . . One of the best, if one of the most obvious, lessons of the international meeting was learning that the ideas that inform Friends of the Earth are easily translated. What we have is not an ideology—it is simpler and more elegant than that. We share the thought, as Tom Burke put it, that the earth needs friends.

In addition to the Brussels meeting, my itinerary included visits to other European Friends of the Earth sisters. My first destination was to be Frankfurt. When the train rolled across the French frontier, the douanier with the tricolor ribbon adorning the sleeve of his jacket left the train and German customs men, wearing jodhpurs and holstered revolvers, boarded. I was all alone with a valise full of international antinuclear propaganda, speaking not one syllable of German at a time when Germany was cracking down on antinuclear activists. Nation-state borders are delineated with visceral threats.

Thanks largely to the political sensitivity and multicultural awareness of Jamie Nelson, *Not Man Apart* editorials began to address larger social issues. We were going beyond what were, strictly speaking, environmental concerns. Devoting column inches to subjects besides bugs 'n' bears and nukes was a bit controversial, even in Friends of the Earth, the liberal wing of the environmental movement.

For instance, Jamie remarked that a World Wildlife Congress was to be held in Johannesburg, South Africa, and allowed that that circumstance probably shouldn't pass without comment. So we wrote:

We'd like to depart, in this writing, from environmentalism as narrowly conceived, and discuss a nontraditional approach to saving the earth. We wish to discuss human social ecologies.

Recently we received an information packet announcing the World Wilderness Congress being held this October. The meeting is expected to draw some 2,000 delegates to hear 30 speakers discuss global problems of national parks and game preserves. . . .

What's unconscionable about the Congress is that it's taking place in Johannesburg. . . .

No doubt South Africa will be beautiful. It is spring in the southern hemisphere and the almost subtropical climate won't be uncomfortable to the delegates.

But the political climate of South Africa will continue to be intolerable for South Africa's black majority. . . .

Respect for life and a love of diversity are articles of environmental faith; they are among the values we must cultivate if we are to survive. And if environmentalists choose to amputate a significant chunk of conscience by choosing not to apply these values to a human situation, then the movement suffers a fatal flaw.

Certain ideals follow other ideals. We are not suggesting that environmentalists shift all their efforts to the elimination of racism; we simply feel that we cannot, in any of our efforts, condone it. We are loath to pick internecine fights; there are few enough of us engaged in the effort to preserve the planet's wildlands; but *Not Man Apart* feels that there are some lines to be drawn and one of them is here. . . .

To which David Brower replied in personal correspondence to Jamie and me, propounding a bonafide dilemma:

Which brings me to the "Of Parks and Apartheid" editorial, which I liked very much on first reading, but which I now find worries me. . . . It ignores Pete Seeger's good advice: walk along as far as you can or there will be no conversation. If we refuse to meet to talk about saving wilderness because our hosts are, in your opinion and mine, beastly to people, I am not sure we will straighten them out in either their treatment of the wilderness or people by confronting them. . . .

. . . *Not Man Apart* speaks for an organization, one with international pretensions, one with a hope that whatever the form of government, it treat the earth better. It may often not be possible to get other people to see things our way with ink. If we must use ink, and if we want to hold on to diversity, seek equity, and make our own contribution toward defining justice and administering it, we have a lot of good work to do on the home front, setting examples here. Other lands may take it better from there — from our example, not our ink.

In addition to Brower's internal communiqué, we received a shocking little spate of letters from a handful of Friends of the Earth members who figured an end to apartheid would be the beginning of miscegenation and worse in South Africa. It was unpleasant to discover that there were, evidently, a few items on the progressive agenda that were regarded as irrelevant or flat wrong by the Friends of the Earth membership. We had innocently presumed them to be with us all the way. More happily, we received a lot of endorsement for "Swords into Windmill Blades," an editorial congratulating the Carter administration for canceling the B-1 bomber program and articulating a link between environmentalism and disarmament. Clearly, it was callow to assume that everyone who got to thinking about ecology would inexorably be led to a radical social, political, economic, and cultural critique. If we were to be serious about our work of rescuing the planet, it seemed to me, nothing could remain the same. Therefore, I was happy to be able to publish, in the fall of 1977, Peter Berg and Raymond Dasmann's "Reinhabiting California," the afterword to Planet Drum's *Reinhabiting a Separate Country*. In sedate but seditious prose Berg and Dasmann shot right on past reform to something else entirely:

> *Living-in-place* means following the necessities and pleasures of life as they are uniquely presented by a particular site, and evolving ways to ensure long-term occupancy of that site. . . . It is not, however, to be thought of as antagonistic to civilization, in the more humane sense of that word, but may be the only way in which a truly civilized existence can be maintained. . . .

Reinhabitation means learning to live-in-place in an area that has been disrupted and injured through past exploitation. It involves becoming native to a place through becoming aware of the particular ecological relationships that operate within and around it. It means undertaking activities and evolving social behavior that will enrich the life of that place, restore its life-supporting systems, and establish an ecologically and socially sustainable pattern of existence within it. . . . It involves applying for membership in a biotic community and ceasing to be its exploiter. . . .

Reinhabitation involves developing a bioregional identity, something most North Americans have lost, or have never possessed. . . . The term refers both to geographical terrain and a terrain of consciousness—to a place and the ideas that have developed about how to live in that place. . . .

. . . Shifting to a reinhabitory society, however, requires basic changes in present-day social directions, economics, and politics. . . .

The bioregion cannot be treated with regard for its own life-continuities while it is part of and administered by a larger state government. It should be a separate state. . . . Perhaps the greatest advantage of separate statehood would be the opportunity to declare a space of addressing each other as members of a species sharing the planet together and with all the other species.

Dasmann and Berg here raised a crucial question: Can you cure civilization of its ills using its own bureaucratic approaches? Or is the ecological crisis tied to the scale of the polity? Our nation-state, the U.S. of A., is, in terms of sheer economic influence and firepower, the biggest and baddest on the planet. And this was the entity with which the domestic environmental movement tried to coevolve during the seventies.

There were good reasons, it was thought, to try to influence the U.S. government, so Friends of the Earth was deliberately designed to be a capitol lobbying organization, which, at the time, was something of an innovation. In reformist terms, Friends of the Earth's presence in Washington may indeed have been valuable. The lobbyists celebrated some legislative victories, possibly bought time for the environment through their efforts (but by the same token insulated the corporate state by acting as if it could be successfully regulated). Friends of the Earth's Washington office and all the other environmental lobbies validated the principle of federal government. Being credible lobbyists foreclosed the vigorous advocacy of decentralist, or antistatist, strategies for building a sustainable society.

At this late date, we are still trying to discover how to save the Earth. Given the track record, it is a fair question whether national organizations are the appropriate tool. On the one hand, it seems like an inordinate amount of energy is expended for only minimal effect. On the other, given the inertia of the problems (and the hegemony of their perpetrators), it's amazing that environmental organizations have persisted as long, and enjoyed as much lip service, as they have. But some questions about the body language of reform are pertinent.

Is it well for environmental groups to function as specialists for hire, shops of professionals who, for a small fee tendered in the form of membership dues, will work politically to try to nudge society along the sustainable path? Does signing the check mentally absolve the individual from integrating these civic and biologic activities into everyday life?

And a question for the questioners: Is it ever really useful for would-be radicals to flail away at liberals? (Not everybody wants to spend their evenings disabling bulldozers. The majority of us still crave that popular chimera, security. As yet, those (mostly white middle class) who take an interest in conservation still believe that they have too much to lose to break with the system. In the United States (if you're the right color) the sanctions against advocating a decentralist, nonstatist form of social organization or a noncommercial economy are not yet as dire as being disappeared, jailed, or tortured. The penalties for holding minority viewpoints consist in being marginalized economically and politically.

Never having been a fan of the nation-state, I was becoming increasingly persuaded by bioregionalist arguments for the importance of rooting social forms in ecological reality. At the last Friends of the Earth staff convocation I attended, I suggested that Friends of the Earth's field offices might be reorganized along bioregional lines. Friends of the Earth's political adepts courteously, but indulgently, explained that that would be impractical. Bioregional offices would be as irrelevant to the existing political units as those straight surveyor's lines are to watersheds, migration routes, and biogeographic provinces. Besides which, chances of a voluntary devolution of power to communities and a peaceful dismantling of an economy predicated on growth seemed remote. That hinted at the further question: Would Friends of the Earth officially join in nonviolent resistance to environmental destruction when all obedient means of recourse had been exhausted? The obvious answer was that we couldn't expect both to advocate civil disobedience and then seek legislative and/or judicial remedies for environmental problems. It made sense, if not progress.

For an opportunity to rant about the futility of playing footsie with the Feds, I had to wait till *Not Man Apart*'s annual April Fool's Day issue (we thought they were the funniest things in print since Mencken's day; and they were amusing, albeit mainly to the magazine staff, a harmless yearly self-indulgence that was dependably censured by the funless Pecksniffs who begrudged any frivolous consumption of newsprint and, by extension, trees).

Cloaked in the nom de plume Anne R. Kist, but quite sincere, I wrote:

> More direct experience of nature would benefit everyone, especially the *soi-disant* capitol hill ecologists in their three-piece suits, shuffling around that whited sepulchre, that city reeking of death, presuming to save the environment with words and laws, not deeds.

The environment is above the law—in a less synthetic situation, the environment would be legislating *our* behavior.

There is no way for us to continue living an urban-suburban-industrial existence without continuing to destroy the planet. Reform is futile, revolution too scary, and evolution takes too long. Secession from the mess, refusal to collaborate with banality seem to be the healthiest, purest, actions. Otherwise we are fighting fire with fire and producing further holocaust.

The environment will continue to suffer as long as two institutions—the state and the profit motive—continue. . . .

Whatever happened to non-negotiable demands? Whatever happened to pig-headed opposition? Why bother to ameliorate the difference? Why not get furious at the vast stupidity of the conventional approach?

Let's stop trying to play ball with the badguys, to beat them at their own game, the game whose rules they wrote.

Face it, environmentalists, we're mostly poor and crazy anyway—in that situation about the only luxury you can afford is conscience.

That was Anne R. Kist's one and only print appearance. Not too long afterwards, she departed Friends of the Earth to become a free lance again.

These days when I go to environmental conferences, I feel like a ghost. I was doing this when half these people were in grade school. And few people seem quite aware of how protracted the struggle has already been, and that the plight has been deepening in spite of it. The fact that we continue the same set of issues suggests that we may be battling corporations and agencies on the wrong front; so far reformism hasn't accomplished nearly enough.

Originally I planned the account of my time at Friends of the Earth to serve as an indictment of the failings arising from Friends of the Earth's actual conventionality, to point out that its design came not from nature, but geopolitics. I intended to mention that its centrist approach produced no fundamental cultural change, not even in the homely particulars of its workers' lifestyles. Friends of the Earth, a national organization, focused its efforts at the macrolevel. "Think globally, act locally" is, for some of us, a recipe for discontent, and the discontent has to do with ego—wanting to be *the hero*—and an inability to function well in the new reality of collectivities for change—affinity groups, support groups, even large coalitions. Groups make more sense in our populous, information-saturated world than looking to a great man or a great woman to spearhead the necessary change.

I hope that we are moving into the time when we will abandon our dependence on great men. Leaders can't be hesitant, ambiguous, ambivalent. They've got to know who's on their side, and who are the partisans of their values. Part of the confusion and disarray that has been kicked up around David Brower in his organizations is a portent of this change. We will have to mature beyond followership: change from the grassroots is a less efficient, untried proposition. But things may never turn around unless we budget the bulk of our do-gooding time not at the level of the nation-state, but at the level of topsoil. We've got to become our own leaders now.

Some middle-of-the-road conservation exec is credited with having said, "Thank God for David Brower; he makes it possible for the rest of us to look reasonable." One person's radical is another's reformist, I guess. And that is faint praise for the function radicals perform.

To express a perfectly radical vision helps stick that vision's nose into the tent of possibilities. Thus, the innate power of ideas. Proclaiming a vision invites its fleshing out. If the idea that the Earth needs friends was powerful, the idea distilled in the phrase Earth First! is potential dynamite. The Earth First! movement—not corporation—is a self-affiliated group of people who will work towards the realization of a world in which mankind is not king, where existing tracts of wilderness are held inviolate while others are being restored. Earth First!ers' outrage is given creative expression in the pages of *Earth First!*

The Radical Environmental Journal, where, by dint of finding company, many formerly "insane" notions are edging their way across the border to common sense. You never know which weird little sect may gain ascendancy half a millennium hence, and "practicality" has nothing to do with it.

Earth's ultimate fate is equally the fate of the self. Thus ecodefense, the nonviolent direct action practiced by some members of the Earth First! movement, is simply an extensive form of self-defense, one that transformed the movement's founders from frustrated, politically adept Washington conservation lobbyists into ruddy, fierce logging-road blockaders. The lives of ecodefenders can be and are demonstrations of the vitalizing effects of courage, the sublimity of nonviolence, and the liberation of knowing that since none of us gets out of this thing alive (in his or her accustomed form, anyway), a futile clinging to comfort and security costs the very integrity that makes life worth living.

Talk is cheap; deeds are eloquent manifestos in body language. Earth First!'s direct actions, such as camping out seven stories up in an old-growth Douglas fir to impede logging or chaining oneself to a Forest Service tree-mangling juggernaut, speak revolutionary volumes. The lives of ecodefenders and other activists are like wild places, reservoirs of *élan vital* and evidence of diversity, relieving the sameness of an exhausted psychic landscape, even if the only good realized by this movement, finally, is the solemn transport of the Ghost Shirt Dance.

What I like about Earth First! is the sterling simplicity of its stance. Cooler heads may object that its rhetoric is polarizing, and that uncompromising positions and vilification of one's opponents are self-defeating in the long run. Certainly some Earth First! propagandos talk like graduates of the Symbionese Liberation Army Language School. But their craziness, if that's what it is, is small potatoes compared with what passes for sanity in the executive suites these days.

The Earth First! journal is rife with redneck lampoonery

of the bad guys (the U.S. Forest Service, timber companies, mining companies, ORV buffs, and numerous senators and representatives, among others). In addition to fulfilling primitive name-calling urges, Earth First! brickbats and canards serve the strategic purpose of eroding respect for the powers that be. After all, it is said that Madame de Staël's salon shortened Napoleon's reign by providing a setting where his lieutenants didn't have to take him seriously. At her parties the clay content of the Corsican's feet was an acceptable topic of discussion: skepticism, satire, sarcasm make a serious arsenal.

The Earth First! movement, like Friends of the Earth before it, deliberately extends the frontier of reasonableness. In comparison to the Earth First! demand for the designation of millions of acres of public lands as wilderness, and the restoration to wilderness quality of millions of other publicly owned acres, other previously extravagant environmental demands begin to seem like polite, even modest, requests. And that, too, is a strategic point.

George Sessions and Bill Devall are intellectual god-uncles to Earth First! by virtue of their authorship of *Deep Ecology*. Devall's stint as president of the Earth First! Foundation and his hard work for the preservation of biodiversity, especially old-growth forests near Arcata, California, his home, testify to his deep devotion.

Deep Ecology is an attempt at codifying a scattered body of ecological thought into a philosophy that places human beings on an absolutely equal footing with all the other creatures on the planet. Devall and Sessions call this relation "biocentric equality." The worldview they extrapolate from it is quite different from that which informs society today, including the society of earnest professional environmentalists. Devall and Sessions suggest that the ideal of biocentric equality, by its very existence, can revolutionize conventional, or "reform," environmentalism.

They, too, are about the much-despised but quite necessary

work of saying, *This isn't radical enough.* Ideological purists may be lousy on near-term results, but they keep the earth-works way out there. Yet their philosophy—that the ecological crisis is mortally serious and that human consciousness is the origin of the problem and must be changed—is gaining ground. Consciousness change is slippery stuff: talk isn't the same thing.

Because the ecological crisis is too urgent to allow for the luxury of disposing of any insufficiently radical technique that might buy time for the Earth through mitigation, *Deep Ecology* criticizes but does not condemn the conventional environmental tactics that keep man at the center of concern and that rein-force, through use, the forms of central government. The philosophy of deep ecology calls for the stabilization and then reduction of the human population. In unadorned terms deep ecology means tough shit for individual humans, but not for the species. A fundamental text in the Earth First! movement, *Deep Ecology* is a gauntlet thrown at the feet of environmental humanists.

More and more, as I dig around in my studio print middens, I am beginning to realize the benefits of never discarding printed matter. Thanks to my book hoarding, I could revisit *Wholly Round,* Rasa Gustaitis's thoughtful, clear-eyed account of the ecology movement during the late sixties and early seventies. In it she provides an affectionate and respectful biographical sketch of Ponderosa Pine, an activist-communicator who is the granddaddy of all the bare-knuckle critics of environmentalism. Pine was variously the publisher of *Earth Read Out* and founder of a press agency called Living Creatures Associates. His latest publication is the *Deep Bioregional Action-Examiner.* I first met Pine when he went by the handle Keith Lampe, and was helping to organize the gatherings at which the manifesto "Four Changes" was proposed and discussed, later drafted and polished by Gary Snyder. Pine articulated early on some of the basic ideas of bioregionalism and biocentrism. His antennae and intelligence swept way out, and so does his behavior. Irritatingly, he insists on acting on his conclusions. The ideals of harmlessness and nonconsumption led him to become a barefoot mendicant chanter and general thorn in the side to people of lesser mettle. Pine plays John Woolman to the ecology movement, a guy destined to make us all deeply uncomfortable in our insufficiency of action. He plays the heady role of outrider, stalking-horse for the extreme. A bit of a Torquemada, he can be quite merciless and sometimes petty in his assessment of deviance from the ideal. Which is why, I suppose, a lot of his germinal contributions are overlooked and why he has taken to an indirect clamoring for acknowledgment. His stridence poses a pure dilemma: he's correct in his radical asceticism, and can't be accused of ever having been a reform environmentalist; but even though he's living proof of the practicability of his beliefs, they still seem incapable of attainment by less fanatical souls (which isn't to say that fanaticism about ecological collapse is unwarranted, just that walking the talk is a rare trait). So Ponderosa Pine is a progenitor of ecological radicalism, one of those people whose contributions and influence will always exceed their reputations, a visionary who will never make an amenable dinner guest, or safe and reasonable company.

A lot of times in this sinner's life, I've been broke—not poor, because my basic needs are met. And, being more of the grasshopper clan than the ant, I'm not very frugal. So I'm just broke, as in having no pocket money, nothing to spend on anything that's not basic. This is what comes of trying to live on the munificent recompense of environmental action and literary endeavor, I guess. Being broke, I spend a lot of time distracted by cravings for things I can't have. The desire for those unobtainable sweets becomes a maggot in the brain, and not to be able to have them results in a sense of deprivation. So the taste for luxuries, extravagance, or nonessentials can be a severe psychic and economic liability. Of course, the definition of superfluity is subjective—the more stamina or saintliness you possess, the more burdensome objects and "conveniences" become. The renunciation of wants, however, goes against the grain. Our civilization is based on addictions—to physical comforts, mobility, variety, cultural diversity, and privacy. The more we are able to cater to those addictions, the more desperately we resist the personal and social structural change that would liberate us from our dependencies. The dealers are not about to relinquish their markets, much less support a thorough restructuring. So marginal support for token reforms is what we get.

Deep ecology contends that environmentalism is denatured by its anthropocentricity. Ponderosa Pine thinks that shoe wearing is liberalism, that you're a sissy if you haven't taken a bust (as Thoreau said through the bars to his "free" friend Emerson, "What are you doing out there, Waldo?"). Pine holds that environmentalists who haven't frugalized their lives or put their convictions on the line are just playing games, trying to have it both ways. Earth First!er Dave Foreman feels that the situation is so urgent that he doesn't have time to become a frugal homesteader; his idea of an appropriate technology is an 80-penny nail suitable for tree spiking.

Quibbling over whether a particular tactic or organizational style is drastic enough is a pitfall of a scarcity model of social change. The assumption is that there's a finite number of possible participants, and so the different factions of do-gooders vie with one another for followers and support. The rads foolishly try to lure the libs further out by chastising them for the inadequacy of their vision and commitment. This puritanical approach, massively unappealing, guarantees only a tiny following of visionaries and masochists, folks who function best when guilty.

So I read Ponderosa Pine's analysis of everything from shoe wearing and hair cutting to land ownership and civil disobedience, and I do believe him to be correct. I also know that I'm not about to go barefoot anytime but during the summer in northern Michigan, or risk getting beat up by irate loggers. I must also admit to not wishing to have to choose, finally, between the unshod paths of the Ponderosas, the moonless marauding of the monkeywrenchers, and the better-worn trails of the Browers. I can only pardon this weakness by quoting Wes Jackson, who says, "It is one thing to be caught in the system and quite another to defend it."

The heartbeat of the problem sounds like "either-or, either-or, either-or." The mantram of the paradox is two syllables: "yes, and; yes, and; yes, and." Dualities and choices look real to me, but excluding anyone from the earth-saving club, or forswearing any nonviolent tactic doesn't make gut sense. Doing violence to the belief systems of others causes pain, and it may be necessary, or it may be counterproductive. Some ideas will gag even the most earnest synthesizer. Drawing the line is serious and personal: there are slews of situations in the ecosphere that present no comfortable options. And consensus may be generations away, while time is in mighty short supply.

Just at the moment when panic and fierce reaction seem to be unavoidable, we confront the opportunity for patient, gentle work on the self, and through it, society. Relinquishing violence and anger, delegitimizing them in my heart, is a dandy spiritual exercise. Yet all around me in the lives of other creatures, I see a universe of unselfconscious competition for sustenance, territorial defense, and occasionally lethal reaction. None of which should be used to condone human violence, anger, or even our passion for conquest and intellectual dominance of those with whom we disagree.

Routing out those reactions, which are bred in the bone along with our biological capacities for tenderness, altruism, and cooperation (see Kropotkin, *Mutual Aid*), is an uphill process of unnatural selection. Sometimes it's right down to the basics of fight or flight.

Despite my intention to relinquish violence, I've been damaging my karma by murdering every wasp that dares to venture into my studio. I had never been stung, and I was phobic about it, so I didn't even flirt with the idea of sharing my space with them. Therefore it has been an ongoing slaughter of the

Valkyries. Whenever a wasp would enter the confines, terror adrenalized me: my armpits prickled. I'd roll up some high-toned periodical—the *New York Review of Books* has about the right heft—and smash the intruder, hoping that my aim would be true and that I wouldn't become prey to the insect's justified wrath. It was never much of a contest, and I beat dozens of those incredible diehards to flinders, not remorselessly, nor with impunity, but in grave good sadness. I did feel like I was getting away with something.

Then one day, as I reached into the mailbox, I felt a fierce sting to my palm and then my little finger. I yelped and wondered for a second what was going on and then realized that I'd been attacked by a wasp whose confined space I'd invaded. I flicked it away onto the road to die of its aggression. There was no need to kill it. It had counted coup fair and square, and the price it paid, unlike my pittance of suffering, was a mortal one.

Getting that tiny experience of pain over with trimmed my fear down to just proportion and steadied my exterminating blows. I still have no desire to attempt indoor coexistence with brave wasp warriors, knowing they are made with erratic tempers. Stinging is what they do—not a moral issue.

Wasps and cats will try even the fondest pathetic fallacy. When we got a new kitten (actual brother, a litter or two later, to our first cat, Simone), the new boy, Tyrone, was as adorable as a postage-stamp-size kitty could be, and into everything. I, of course, delighted in Tyrone's antics. Simone, however, growled, hissed, and spat at him. For weeks. When Tyrone got within closing distance, she'd take a swipe at his eyes.

"Be nice, Simone," I'd coo. But *nice* is irrelevant to a cat whose territory has been violated. What I was witnessing was a reflexive jostling for dominance. Given the artificial circumstances of pethood, Simone and Tyrone have by now achieved détente. Given their respective sexes, Tyrone has naturally displaced Simone from most of her favorite nap spots. This sorting out was unsentimental and had nothing to do with justice: cats enjoy the sometimes enviable but unobtainable (by us) "freedom" of predestination.

Another day I forsook my studio to lie on the Earth, belly down in the sunshine. There, while I nearsightedly inventory the six square inches of biota under my eyes, my peace was raped by the overflight of some air national guard fighter jets that had come all the way from Ohio. Lethal black and supersonic, they push a shock wave ahead of them: engines of war. A horrendously loud screeching, and, to my surprise, tears followed in their wake. Imagine what those planes could do to Leelanau County! The overflight/show of might is a commonplace, and that that is so is to weep over. Abominations like that—let alone the unleashing of their destructive force— are part of the life.

And another day I went for a walk around a quiet pond, listening to the peepers, watching a pair of mallards take flight, and guessing that the indistinct mammalian shape I just noticed at the margins of the cattails might have been a muskrat. As usual, I also looked for what I wasn't seeing—occupants of niches emptied by human progress—and listened for what I wasn't hearing: silence gone, contaminated by the noise of a mile-distant highway. Watching my mind work thus, I realized that I've never not thought that the Earth is in trouble. And I understood that everything I've learned since has tended to reinforce that perception, and that what I've preferred to learn has been to reinforce it. Is this a case of information fitting a true pattern, or are we talking close-mindedness here? I am willing to wonder whether there might not be a parallel sense in which things are improving (maybe that's it: *things* are improving, while creatures are vanishing), but that's about as far as my paradigm flexes.

In an atmosphere of either-or, with violence as the conflict-resolution method of choice, and the stakes in the land-use game rising, confrontations intensify. In the fall of 1987, ecofeminist-bioregionalist Judith Plant wrote, describing a town meeting in British Columbia:

Our small community, which lies 20 miles out of town, has been actively involved in a major environmental issue involving a watershed—the Stein River—50 miles to the east of us. Last night's meeting was called by the Western Canada Wilderness Committee from Vancouver—250 miles to the southwest—to give the various interest groups in Lilloet a chance to discuss their differences. WCWC gave a slide show, mostly of the pristine wilderness of the last remaining intact watershed in southwestern B.C., during which burly, half-drunken and enraged loggers cheered at the sight of clear-cuts and groaned lustfully at the sight of virgin stands of fir. As soon as the slides were over, the local logging king began, at the top of his lungs, to insult and badger the WCWC people, not letting them or any one else in the crowded gymnasium respond. I thought he might die from heart failure—the intensity of his behaviour was frightening, for his own health as much as ours. Soon he stomped out, with his following close behind.

He's operating from fear, and his behaviour is meant to intimidate as a defence. It does, too. We are so divided here that some people are concerned for their safety. This is what has happened in our community over the issue of preserving the last piece of major wilderness left—not just here in B.C., but if this is one of the last in B.C., it's for sure one of the last in Canada, and Canada is thought of as one of the last places on earth where there are still places untouched by the exploitative human. The sad thing is—and I think this is at the bottom of my emotions—that it is not just a matter of winning a debate with the loggers. The fact is we are all losing, and after last night I wondered how we would ever be able to work together. And this is what we have to do—figure out how we can live here in an ecologically and economically sustainable way. The Stein Valley is not just the last major wilderness. It's also just about all that's left of accessible timber for the logging industry. Then what? But we're so polarized we can't begin to have the question. Perhaps our enraged neighbor is afraid of this, though it hasn't quite come to his consciousness.

I wish I could trust the process of candid and hopeful sharing, the "open space" so wisely advocated by thinkers like

Robert Theobald and Anne Weiser, to produce a higher synthesis, a life-sustaining social form. No question that we need new processes of self-government, processes that don't structure the polarization in. Beginning with respect, striving towards trust, the ideal would be an utterly peaceable approach not even countenancing intellectual or ideological dominance, let alone conflict.

But I'm not sure that I'm entirely willing to hear my fellow humans who disagree with my perceptions about the peril to the life of the planet. Human atrocities against humanity and nature make me angry. It is hard to have compassion with people, like the loggers, who dandle precious life in the balance. The best I may be able to manage might be to learn to hate the sin and love the sinner, to regard earth-destroying behavior as but an ugly garment on an innately good being.

Environmentalists who are patiently, conventionally trying to turn public policy towards sustainability; social theorists and visionaries who dream of democratic, egalitarian, life-enhancing political forms, are working the decisive human angle of the ecological crisis. But in terms of triage, the most critical ecological work is species saving, ark building, habitat preservation. We've got to save the irreplaceable living beings (which ultimately means saving their surroundings); no time to await the dawn of that happy day when all of humanity sees the light. Salvaging these fragments of ecosystems, from which a partial version of what once was might, with intricate, patient effort, be reconstructed, is desperate work. It's like rushing into the burning house to save the babies.

An equally necessary proposition, one extending forward into the blank reaches of the future, is learning how to heal the arsonist within, to change the misperceptions that lead us to torch the domicile in order to warm our hands for a few minutes. It isn't reasonable to expect the firefighters to lead the group therapy. Nor is it wise to imagine that the efforts to preserve relict species and places can succeed within our present civilization. Until the context changes, humans will always be able to rationalize frying up the last snail darter.

Teaching the sacredness of the whole and healing the wound that parts humanity from other life require the temperament of the peacemaker. There are people who have come to terms with the conflicts within and who abjure physical or even rhetorical violence. They work away from our dualistic adversarial mode of thought and towards something more systems oriented and compassionate. Becoming a peacemaker means kicking the justified-anger habit, a deed that is at once both selfless and pragmatic. Peacemakers are angels, an essential part of the cosmos. Yet there is no change without the dialectic spurred by devils, revolutionary/radical critics (like Earth First!ers). We need the angels to be gliding serenely on high, sharing their grace, and the devils to be jabbing our lazy asses with their pitchforks and outrage. Either constellation of virtues in absence of the other would be inane.

LEAVING

$\blacklozenge$

MY STINT AT FRIENDS OF THE EARTH MAY NOT FULLY ENTITLE me to criticize organized environmentalism as a whole, but critics are born, not made. As an employee, I always tended towards disgruntlement. Much as I admire the peacemakers and aspire not to rain on worthwhile parades, the critic-daemon is by far my more vociferous part, and reasonableness is not my long suit.

I'm usually in the mood to find fault, and the bigger the windmill—like the state of Arizona, the nation-state, industrial civilization, hierarchy, anthropocentrism—the better the tilt.

Consequently, in 1979, about a year after I left Friends of the Earth, when Jerry Mander invited me to help plan a conference called "Technology: Over the Invisible Line?" I was delighted. It meant there would be large gathering of fault-finders, a group of people willing to join in a critique of a very large given: technology.

After Freeman, Mander, and Gossage had passed into history, Mander founded Public Media Center, America's first public-service advertising agency. He also wrote a tome titled *Four Arguments for the Elimination of Television*. Diana Dillaway, an ebullient fundraiser at the Foundation for National Progress, was so inspired by Mander's book that she proposed a conference to essay similar analyses of other mass technologies.

In the proposal for the conference, Mander dreamed that a possible movement against technology per se might be catalyzed by such a gathering. There already existed, he wrote, a significant number of activists in disparate movements who "all share this radical perception: some technologies cannot

134

be reformed and should be scrapped. What remains to be agreed upon is whether such analyses of specific technologies might also be applied to technological society as a whole." So the purpose of the gathering was to wrestle the broader imagination right out of the grip of technology.

With a premise like that, dominant paradigm types were in the minority. With some choice reading lists and address books being consulted by the conference committee, which also included Lee Swenson, Carol Levine, and Toby McLeod, we developed a guest list that produced just the right cacophony. There were radical lesbians and longshoremen encountering one another with bemused respect. There were left-wing East Coast academics attempting to interface with West Coast Jungian scholars. There was Murray Bookchin, grand old man of American anarchism, railing at Harriet Barlow, a longtime peace activist, also a founder of the Institute for Local Self-Reliance and of the short-lived Citizen's Party. We enjoyed Wes Jackson's Will Rogers demeanor as he detailed the destructive consequences of a petroleum-based agriculture. Peter Berg's Mephistophelean affect and vanguard bioregionalism gave another large context. We delighted in Leopold Kohr's foxy grandpa decentralism and lilliputianism and, overarching it all, Jerry Mander's plenipotentiary Luddism. Virtually all of the participants came with real curiosity to do some bold thinking. Defenders of high technology were scarce. Exponents of appropriate technology, like New Alchemy Institute and *Whole Earth*'s tool wizard J. Baldwin, were the conference's version of liberals. J.'s paper roamed hither and thither through the psychology of industrial design (including the lamentable tendency for market considerations, rather than durability or functional elegance, to determine products) to a description of the New Alchemy Institute's arks—self-sufficient dwellings that incorporated solar storage, greenhouse-ecosystem food production, and wastewater purification—homestead "bioshelters." J. concluded, "We think that clear demonstrations of soft technology will be able to fire the public imagination sufficiently to take a stand against the take-it-and-run people. We are the answer to Armageddon chic."

Not nearly so hopeful was Raymond Dasmann, who in his paper presented an early, mortuary census and elegy for the myriad creatures being driven to extinction by technological civilization: " . . . with an increase in human abundance there is a decline in biotic diversity," he wrote. "We are going to have to get by with tattered remnants of the old, wild world." And then he quit mincing words: "It is my belief that the people who are alive today may be the last generation that can significantly alter the future of the world. By this I mean the long-term future, such as forever."

The most eloquent and unblinking observations were made by the Native American statesmen who attended the conference—Oren Lyons, John Mohawk, and Michael Meyers of the Onandaga nation among them. "So now we need to begin a critical examination of all phases of the technology," wrote Michael Meyers. "Not just the mechanical ones, but the institutional ones as well. . . . And the bottom line of this examination is: will what we choose to keep be of benefit to the seventh generation on?"

John Mohawk, editor of the indefatigable *Akwesasne Notes,* commented:

> The hunting-and-gathering culture had lasted through several ice ages and seemed to have survived the test of time. By that time, man had evolved so far from his origins that for all practical purposes there was no place left on earth where he could survive without his devised method of evolution—culture.
>
> Western cultures and Western technologies have been defined, by the objective, inherent in the culture, of supporting overly large concentrations of population.
>
> Civilization-supportive technologies have always been ecologically destructive.
>
> The conventional wisdom has it that technologies benefit mankind. The historical fact is that technologies were invented to benefit civilizations. There is a difference.

These were the dicta that cut to the root, put by unvanquished survivors of civilization's technological onslaught. Cautionary words came from Chief Oren Lyons in the course of his spellbinding explanation of the Iroquois lifeway: "Don't look for mercy where there is none."

That Indian voices were the steadiest and most assured at the conference surely had to do with the holism of their philosophy, which Michael Meyers described as "a belief system that honored all the life-forms in a given environment, and taught an understanding about the complex relationships of living things to one another."

It is our proud indifference to that vital complexity that has led us to a historic moment when we must question all the givens, and weigh against them the well-being of not only the seventh generation, but of the children who are here now, because the "side effects" of today's comforts may prove to be next year's teratogens.

There once was a time when ecology wasn't a subject or concern, an element of public awareness, or a popular cause. The spreading incidence of groundwater contamination resulting from the burial of all manner of waste—from municipal to radioactive—has been a sharp consciousness-raiser, though.

As I sit with my neighbors plotting our latest siege of opposition to blind progress—an effort to prevent the doubling in size of the landfill a mile to the south which is rapidly becoming a regional dump—the main thing on their minds is the possibility that groundwater contamination will cause cancer in their children or grandchildren. In rural areas like this, we are all dependent on our wells. Well drilling is a significant fraction of the cost of a dwelling and if your well goes poisonous, you're shit outta luck. So with the dawning awareness of the extent of the chemical contamination of groundwater caused by toxic-waste dumps and just plain old dumps, we confront, as a people, a sinister form of pollution that has the same pervasive DNA-mangling potential as the A-bomb, but without the sirens sounding warning.

Late twentieth-century people had already been worried about the seemingly random scything that is cancer, despite the fact that we're all becoming more experienced with the disease. But the idea that your grandbaby might be stricken by an environmentally induced illness makes toxics and groundwater contamination an environmental issue of wide interest and of greater immediacy than, say, wilderness or endangered species. Toxics is a subject that is thrusting a lot of people into learning mode. And now that community activists are beginning to look beyond disposal problems to the whole process of toxics production—starting with product development and marketing—the education is sweeping. The toxics threat drives home the point that we live in a time when there's no refuge from environmental problems, not even in rustic Maple City, Michigan.

Sometimes it seems that in this thoroughly technologized, helplessly dependent society, every human action except to think, sing, and pray can damage the future. At one point Phil and I lived in a household that included a roommate's two lively daughters. They happened to enjoy drinking through plastic straws. Those straws, along with the countless plastic film bags in which we tote home the tofu and the semireusable yogurt containers and the cartons of soy milk and the jugs of cider, help compose our modest quid of trash, all of it destined for the neighboring landfill. Like every landfill in existence, it is contaminating the groundwater. Rain percolates through its contents, distilling a bitch's brew, a little plume of contaminants flowing underground to the east and north, which is to say, in the general direction of our wells. So the girls may someday be imbibing a fine blend of deteriorated drinking straws and tofu bags. In other neighborhoods in America, mothers are no longer wondering where the deformed babies came from, or the cancers, or why so many miscarriages.

But how do you explain these connections and consequences to a child, a child whose life almost inevitably must include television, with its dazzle of advertising and only the cheapest and stupidest renditions of what it is to be alive and human? It's a long chain of events.

• • •

Directly after the technology conference concluded, I went to work as assistant editor at *CoEvolution Quarterly,* reporting to my old buddy Stewart Brand. *CoEvolution* was the periodical blossom of the *Whole Earth Catalog* vine. Stewart called what we published "conceptual news," and whatever that was, we got a lot of it, often from our readers. They were the type to take pen in hand to extol their favorite tools and authors, their pronounced reactions to the magazine's contents, in fact, to the world itself, and in salient detail. This and *CoEvolution Quarterly*'s own subscription to dozens and dozens of other quirky magazines made the mailbag, whose contents it was my duty and pleasure to winnow into manageable piles for Stewart's attention, a fabulous source of intelligences.

While I was at *CoEvolution,* an augmented staff, headed by the crashworthy Art Kleiner, produced *The Next Whole Earth Catalog,* with a heroic effort that in some ways resembled the construction of the bridge on the river Kwai. It was a doozy—a 608-page behemoth containing (in the second edition) 3,907 separate items. Serious value for your book-buying dollar! My involvement with the *Next Catalog* was limited to some proofreading. (I was never so aware of all the possible skills in the world as when scrutinizing reviews of how-to literature on everything from knife making to glassblowing to zymurgy to ecological restoration. It was an invitation to dream big dreams of usefulness.)

Stewart Brand, like Jann Wenner and David Brower, is an editorial genius. He created a form. He espoused good principles. I learned a great deal from his criticism, and from watching him in action, irritable though I was throughout. We did have some substantive conflicts. I was particularly infuriated when Stewart hewed a lovely collection of reviews of books on feminism that Anne Kent Rush and I had assembled down from a spread to measly page headed "Women's Politics." (The gentlemanly art of fly-fishing, however, rated an entire spread.) Most of my problem with Stewart, though, was ego clash, and in one of those, as any fool should know, the boss always wins. It has been possible for me fully to appreciate having worked with a great man only after the fact. In the midst of the association (in order to survive psychologically), I was in inward rebellion against not just the authority but also, alas, against masculine truths. A cat can hiss at a king.

Fortunately, the antagonism wasn't reciprocal, so in late 1981 Stewart trusted me to guest-edit, with Peter Berg (whose inspiration it was), an issue of *CoEvolution* on bioregions. It was a happy chance to be able to work with Peter and to publish a collection of pieces that is still a useful introduction to bioregionalism. The issue included the now-famous Where you At? quiz (see page 150); essays by Jim Dodge, Peter Berg, Murray Bookchin, Wes Jackson, and S. Mills; articles on small nations reemerging in northern Europe, on the political importance of keeping native tongues, like Welsh, alive, on the Navajo-Hopi struggle against forced relocation at Big Mountain; bibliographies on the North Woods and North American prairies; among other features.

After working on a few more issues of *CoEvolution Quarterly,* I was offered, and eagerly accepted, the editorship of *California Tomorrow,* yclept *Cry California.* This prestigious publication was the journal of California Tomorrow, a respected mainstream organization advocating planning as an instrument for achieving environmental quality. (Well you may ask what an erstwhile anarchist was doing in a central planning establishment. Satisfying my craving to be an editor-in-chief again, that's what.) However, California Tomorrow was faltering, and the powers behind the scene had taken a flier on Isabel Wade (also a Mills grad, class of 1969), a spitfire organizer who became the organization's executive director. Wade, in turn, took a flier on me, a firebrand editorialist.

For my debut, on the occasion of George Deukmejian's election to the governorship of California, I wrote:

It's time to admit that economic policy is a statement of values, to identify the values that have led to the nation's and hence the state's economic distress, and to embark on the collective adventure of reconsidering these values, rejecting some, keeping some, and forging some anew. Our state's big problem may be most evident in the financial and governmental arenas, but it won't be solved there. Our best hope is that resolving it will occasion a widespread change of heart; a discovery of enlightened self-interest, a humanly generous response to scarcity and inequity. . . .

Is it merely prejudice to assume that a pro-business administration in California might fail to serve the wider public interest? It all depends on your definition of that interest. There are few instances in our history where giving enterprise a free hand has led to environmental preservation, fair return for honest labor, decentralization of economic power, or the equitable distribution of wealth. Those things would not, in the short term be economical—or profitable. Advancing those causes is old-timey radicalism, granted. It has yet to succeed. Why? Is it that the majority of us don't want such things? Or that the value system that would make them work is denied, precluded, or overwhelmed? . . .

. . . the institutions whose leaders we choose at election time have become irrelevant to our real problems. Our governmental system of checks and balances has a genius for reconciling various points of view, and an inertia that's built in. It seems misfitted to the urgency of the socioeconomic crisis we face. Public policy is incapable of addressing the sheer scale and complexity of things, and hamstrung by the official dogma of free enterprise. . . .

How can we begin to go beyond our own self-interest and act on behalf of others, even in behalf of other life forms, as well as generations of Californians to come? Finding answers to this question will mean turning to historians, anthropologists, hucksters, holy men and women, storytellers, mothers and fathers, neighborhood heroes and heroines. It will call for information from a myriad of sources: academics, entrepreneurs, solons, religions, traditional cultures, children, and poets. The attempt itself supplies an answer. Any wide-ranging, free-thinking, participatory inquiry into a timeless human question *is* an organizing process.

These fine sentiments did not sit too well with a few glossy Angeleno lawyers on our board of directors. They tried to pass a resolution prohibiting me from writing anything for the magazine I edited, but they did not succeed. Still, despite, or perhaps because, of our best efforts, California Tomorrow closed its doors within a year of the Wade-Mills advent. One friend of mine close to the situation claimed that this was in part to save the board the blatancy of having to can me for my populist/decentralist editorials. Whatever the reasons, Iz and I were out on our ears, and about a year later the organization was resurrected under progressive Republican (not always a contradiction in terms) auspices and now serves California as a socially conscious good-government think tank.

This dismissal brings our heroine close up to 1984, feeling, like Howard the Duck, trapped in a world she never made. The real-estate boom was making being a renter in San Francisco an increasingly treadmillish proposition. Nobody had a magazine for me to edit, and the straight environmental organizations around town were fully staffed, while the fringier outfits couldn't pay a salary that would let me live in the manner to which I'd become addicted. After California Tomorrow gave me the silver handshake, I was, fortunately, able to find work as director of development at World College West in Marin County. It is proving to be an exceptionally relevant, rigorous, and useful experiment in higher education. Dick Gray, a very remarkable man, who was at that time president of the college, bent over backwards to give me a working schedule that allowed me blocks of time to pursue my writing.

However noble the cause, though, fundraising was still a disagreeable occupation. It is, more than most, an enterprise that demands new clothes (something Thoreau advised us to beware of), and proposal writing is a real style killer. Too often I was having to dude up in a downtown look, wear ankle-busting high heels, and swallow my convictions. I was a car-driving commuter, living in what was to me an expensive but wonderfully pleasing Telegraph Hill apartment. I wasn't recycling, wasn't growing anything. I was being a mere, if unenthusiastic, consumer. My friends and I were turning into blasé, harried yuppies. The moral vacuum of the computer world sucked in most of my old environmentalist colleagues, and advertising took care of the rest. From where I sat, it looked like the counterculture had degenerated into a quest for interesting dining experiences.

California, even northern California, was starting to seem like a done deal. Everyone had discovered it, and everyone's values seemed corrupt. People had taken to working just for money and to celebrating entrepreneurship. Full-tilt consumerism was no longer morally dubious, provided you were tastefully chic about it. We were all becoming hard, in our careerist ways, and soft in our inability to function without a lot of money. It did not seem to me like a way of life with much predictive, or survival, value. I wanted time and space. I wanted out of the urban "ecosystem" of humans, houseplants, shitting dogs, and cement. The thought began to take hold in my mind that the hip thing to do would be to leave California before the rush.

That San Francisco was changing is nothing new—it has always been a boomtown. North Beach old-timers opined that the neighborhood had been gentrified well before I was a gleam in my father's eye, but even the traces of character that I so enjoyed were being erased to accommodate the lifestyles of the rich and banal. For me, the end drew nigh when the little shingled cottage at the end of the lane, a digs that had housed a succession of flamboyant bohemians, Richard and Mimi Fariña among them, was razed to make way for a 4-story, vulgarian condo.

The sixties were long gone, but I still missed them. It began to feel as though the values vaguely at their heart—pacifism; decentralization; personal liberation; living poor with style, as Chick Callenbach put it; community; ecology; and a return to the land—were just quaint now, dated, absurd, and irrelevant. San Francisco seemed less congenial to idealistic ways, and in my mind was one of the handbaskets the world was going to hell in. I was increasingly bothered by its gloss and preciousness. Striking out for a new life, however, a life more self-reliant and physical, less dependent on cash—and developing the ability to meet my own needs—was an entirely confounding proposition. I was all dressed down with no place to go.

Which is about the crisis of conscience I experienced in May 1984 on the eve of the first North American Bioregional Congress. The timing was true synchronicity: the central issues of bioregionalism are where and how you live. Having been an aficionado of bioregionalism—and bioregionalists—for years, I needed no persuading that the North American Bioregional Congress would be the most interesting and relevant political/spiritual/cultural gathering of that fateful year, Republican and Democratic national conventions notwithstanding. So I found a way to get myself to Excelsior Springs, Missouri, where the congress was held.

A bioregional congress, whether local or continental, is an assembly of peers. Each member is vested with equal authority and responsibility. All the participants may join in setting the agenda, and decision making is by consensus. Ad hoc and standing committees focus on such specific issues as agriculture, economics, education, health, ecofeminism, Native American rights, forestry, media, and appropriate technology, proposing policies and strategies for meeting human needs and remedying ecosocial problems at the bioregional level. Bioregional congresses are, in effect, shadow governments, starting from a more meaningful set of premises than conventional governments, and designing for peaceful sustainability rather than short-term ascendance.

Using what congress organizer David Haenke called the "ecological discriminator," the first North American Bioregional Congress drew an eclectic two hundred participants, people actually walking the talk of ecological awareness. Participants were thoughtful, independent, hard-working sixties relics, a high school reunion of back-to-the-landers, vegetarians, anthroposophists, appropriate technologists, geographers, community organizers, economic cooperators, journalists, land trustees, small-farm preservationists, theosophists, musicians, mask makers, map makers, wholistic health practitioners, and comrades in the struggle to maintain the land base of the Native American peoples. (Some polymath bioregionalists manage to play several of these roles at once.) Being with all these kindred souls for the five days of the congress put a cutting edge on the inherent contradiction of my lifestyle. I had living proof of possible alternatives. My practical hypocrisy was gnawing at me. In San Francisco, belief in the need to live more simply and conscientiously was little affirmed in my life or anybody else's. I was as crazy as Thoreau, lacking only similar endowments of guts. At the North American Bioregional Congress, confronted with practicing believers, I knew I was going to have to change my ways, or die of quiet desperation. But I couldn't see how or where to begin.

Well, you can always make a new start by falling in love. The epicenter of the North American Bioregional Congress's impact on my life was Phil Thiel, a northern Michigan boy. Gorgeous and witty, he was certainly the most inspiring individual I met at the gathering. At that time he was making his living as a hippie carpenter. In his spare time he was organizing the Great Lakes Bioregional Congress, serving on the board of directors of the Michigan Federation of Food Cooperatives, and volunteering for the Northern Michigan Environmental Action Council. A classic do-gooder.

When I first noticed him, he was chatting with Carolyn Estes, the conference facilitator, after the bioregional movement committee meeting. Phil's slangy, astute analysis of what was going on caught my ear, and I wanted to hear more. It's only fair to mention that in addition to being very smart, having an accurate worldview, and being dedicated to all the right causes, this guy was also big and funny and handsome in a sort of godlike way. Once we got to talking, it took us about fifteen minutes to fall madly in love, and an interbioregional romance was well and truly under way.

Less than four months after we met, I'd quit my job at the college, sublet my apartment, stored my books, and raced off to Leelanau County in northwest Lower Michigan. I eagerly anticipated my new existence as a voluntary simpleton, living-in-place, marrying poor. I'd been blessed with a life partner, a partner who, to his credit, wouldn't confront me with the poser "What is bioregionalism?"

PART TWO

---◆---

PRACTICE

He who would do good to another must do it
    in minute particulars;
General good is the plea of the scoundrel,
    hypocrite, and flatterer:
For art and science cannot exist
    but in minutely organized particulars.

William Blake
Jerusalem

MOVING

◆────────────────────────────────◆

THE BIOREGIONAL MOVEMENT'S CREDO, DRAFTED AND ADOPTED at the first North American Bioregional Congress, was titled "Welcome Home." Finding a home, knowing home, making a home, feeling at home, and staying home are essential psychological processes of reinhabitation. It takes time. Sometimes it's a matter of discovery and wonder, sometimes of resistance and confusion. Ultimately, reinhabitation is a cultural more than a technological endeavor, which is why individual character and local style are main ingredients.

Where we have become rootlessly mobile, bioregionalism encourages an adamant loyalty to place and an intimate knowledge of the plant and animal life and seasonal changes that define the home place and determine livelihood. How to begin knowing home? Read on. The Where You At quiz, which kicked off the special bioregions issue of *CoEvolution Quarterly,* is one of the most reprinted items *CQ* ever published. Compiled by Leonard Charles, Jim Dodge, Lynn Milliman, and Victoria Stockley, the quiz is "a self-scoring test on basic environmental perception of place." The authors admitted that "the quiz is culture bound, favoring those people who live in the country over city dwellers." (But for city dwellers to develop the X-ray vision it takes to answer these questions revolutionizes perception.) The scoring is tough: 8 to 12 correct indicates "a fairly firm grasp of the obvious"; 13 to 16 that "you're paying attention"; 17 to 19 means "you know where you're at," and if you score 20, "you not only know where you're at, you know where it's at."

My Leelanau County score ("just paying attention") is far better than my San Francisco score, which I'm too embarrassed to recall. But where *you* at?

1. Trace the water you drink from precipitation to tap.
2. How many days till the moon is full? (Slack of two days allowed.)
3. What soil series are you standing on?
4. What was the total rainfall in your area last year (July–June)? (Slack: 1" for every 20".)
5. When was the last time a fire burned your area?
6. What were the primary subsistence techniques of the culture that lived in your area before you?
7. Name five native edible plants in your region and their season(s) of availability.
8. From what direction do the winter storms generally come in your region?
9. Where does your garbage go?
10. How long is the growing season where you live?
11. On what day of the year are the shadows the shortest where you live?
12. When do the deer rut in your region, and when are the young born?
13. Name five grasses in your area. Are any of them native?
14. Name five resident and five migratory birds in your area.
15. What is the land-use history of where you live?
16. What primary geological event/process influenced the landform where you live? (Bonus special: what's the evidence?)
17. What species have become extinct in your area?
18. What are the major plant associations in your region?
19. From where you're reading this, point north.
20. What spring wildflower is consistently among the first to bloom where you live?

Obviously, to know your home, you've got to watch and listen and sniff the air, to hear and see and taste the rain, or to let a snowflake melt on your tongue. That was a lot of what I did on my arrival in northern Michigan a few Septembers ago. Uprooting myself and starting a new life with a new person in a new place was a darn bold move. Settling in was harder than I had imagined it would be. So when things became too much with me, I would hike out back of the house, to get sur-rounded by the woods, or just sit facing south, gazing at the meadow for hours, witnessing a first fall.

What we have here is a pastoral landscape, much altered and not a little confused by the hand of man. On this penin-sula a hundred and fifty years ago, I suppose I'd have been blinking in the dim green hush of a maple-beech forest. Those original monarchs were cleared or logged off to build a little of everything, including the fortunes of timber barons. What forests weren't razed to make way for settlers, or converted to cash, were reduced to ash in deliberate and accidental holo-causts. Openings of fragile, yet demanding, farmland followed. Picture fields and woodlots and hedgerows and usually im-maculate small farmsteads, often with For Sale signs in front. Scale makes these northern Michigan farms picturesque; they're not whole counties of monocrops; you can see them entire.

Our back eighty, like most of Lower Michigan, is a ripple of sand hills, ground out by glaciers and sculpted by wind. Dead ahead, shock troops of the sugar bush, a rabble of young maples, this day just past an orgy of gaudiness, advance. Their blinding hues of ruby and vermilion are toned down now to bronze, copper, and gold. Most of the grasses are dun, but there's an undertone of green still cast on the hillside.

The autumn sun is setting in a sky that is all but clear, the monumental white and indigo clouds of some hours ago hav-ing scattered a few drops of rain and mysteriously disappeared. Shadows of the maples in the woodlot to the west are creep-ing across our sunken "meadow" (an exhausted cornfield, in truth), lavender now with the blossoms of millions of knap-weeds, cousin to the cornflower, exotic to North America, blooming in ominous profusion.

This landscape possesses nothing of the stark drama of the arid West where I spent my childhood. It's a thoroughly sub-jugated terrain, valiant in its self-regeneration and yearning towards diversity and fertility, nonthreatening topographically. Awe and drama are in the province of the sky: thunderstorms,

tornadoes that swathe their way through Christmas tree farms
and trailer settlements, the massive snowfalls and frigid gales
of winter. The gods of weather and the sweetwater seas deal
out fate in these parts.

To the south among the encroaching saplings, the deer
browse discreetly, being just a subtle presence in a state where
it doesn't pay to advertise that you're game. I am transfixed
by that glimpse of their amber flanks and balletic footfalls. So
much beauty and peace pervade this scene that I might almost
rest content were it not for the problem of trying to reconcile
my idyll with the Big Strange Picture. And becoming reconcil-
ed has always been a bit of a problem for this one.

This story was originally conceived in the happy vacuum
of an urban, urbane existence in San Francisco. I imagined that
the past, at least a little more readily than the present, would
hold still long enough for me to learn its lessons conclusively,
that I could develop a meaningful, maybe even predictive critique out of my years around the ecology scene. What's more,
I understood that I had only been talking a good game of
cultural transformation. I wanted to be wed to a place and
a person that would offer the chance to practice some ecological
integrity. And I've got that. So I embarked on the road to
Michigan and the trip to the altar with a grab bag full of hopes.
In my unsinkable naïveté, I thought that by being bopped with
a couple of magic wands—marriage to a bioregionalist and
a move to the country—a reinhabitory life and an easier conscience would be mine.

I regret that I ever heard of Saul who became Paul, because
I've been wandering the road to Damascus ever since, looking
for the right spot for a conversion experience, waiting for the
blinding flash that will make me what I'm not, yet: strong,
or driven, enough to be pure. The ultimate question, the one
I can't answer, is: How do you come up with a soul that's willing to go all the way?

Absent the blinding flash, there have been shocks and awak-
enings. First, that a happy and contented partnership with my

husband was going to take some work. Marriage is a lot like that these days. So that was one realization that tempered the dream.

Quite a terrible shock came when, about a year after I arrived here, and just a few months after we were married, Phil and I were headed downstate for the third Great Lakes Bioregional Congress. He was driving my car. He pulled out from behind a slow-moving truck to pass on an uphill stretch and encountered another car, coming downhill in the same passing lane. They call them suicide lanes, and we now know why. In the split second before the head-on collision, we were both pretty sure that our numbers were up. Imagine our surprise when we came to in the wreckage, immobilized but conscious.

We were rushed to the hospital in a screaming ambulance and routed to separate bays in the emergency room. There it was learned that my right leg had suffered a "maximum sustainable injury"—smashed thighbone, kneecap, and bones of the lower leg—and that Phil's head, especially his jaw, had been knocked around, and that he'd suffered a cracked rib and collapsed lung as well.

I was put in traction and wheeled up to the orthopedics ward to stabilize and await surgery. Phil was placed under observation in the "intermediate" intensive-care unit. Two days later, as the result of air embolisms entering his brain through an injured artery in his neck, he had a couple of strokes, becoming incoherent in midsentence during a friend's visit. He was CAT-scanned, put on the critical list, and, after much quick consultation, operated on. After his surgery, he was placed right across from the nurse's desk in the intensely intensive-care unit. We later learned that they didn't hold out much hope for him just then. In fact, he was hovering around death's gateway for days, close enough that a few days later he had to have further surgery. That helped turn the tide.

Meanwhile, I had had the first of what was to be a protracted series of six operations and was receiving a steady stream of visitors—on Phil's behalf as well as my own—and many bouquets, cards, and phone calls from more-distant friends. It was an overwhelming, and entirely life-sustaining, flow of love and concern. Our community's earnest tugging on the lifeline made the vital difference and carried us through an indescribably horrible occurrence.

While he was still hospitalized, there were fears that Phil had been brain damaged, that he wouldn't be able to speak, and there was no answer to those fears until they got the various tubes out of his gullet. That was excruciating suspense. Miraculously, about ten days after the ordeal began, Phil made it out of the woods and off the resuscitator. He was walking and talking again. Four days after that he was out of the hospital and embarked on his personal therapeutic regime—helping to organize the second North American Bioregional Congress, which was held in Leelanau County in 1986.

Meanwhile, I was still stuck in the orthopedics ward, feeling a lot of pain (when the drugs wore off), learning to use crutches, and having two more operations and an interminable course of intravenous antibiotics. About forty days after the accident, I was released, just in time to contend, on crutches, with my first full-fledged Michigan winter. I had another operation in the spring, was in a cast for a while, broke the steel plate that had been implanted to reinforce my thighbone, and had to have yet another operation, this one a heller that involved transplanting bone from my pelvis to help the healing of my femur.

A protracted misery, all in all. It kicked our marriage around badly. My being lame for a couple of years was indeed a handicap. But the saga is just about done. Phil has been hearty for the last couple of years, and I've been walking (if not running) and hauling capably for about a year. I am immensely grateful to have my love alive, and to possess two functioning legs. Without so much love and grace, things might not have turned out nearly so well.

Suffice it to say that the car crash wrecked and derailed our persons and our lives for a longer while than either of us would have liked. Some of those realities were conceptual news, some not. They all cast our characters, and my dream, into a new light.

It's not that I didn't think there would be trials, but that I thought that the trials would be of my choosing, and therefore to my liking. I imagined myself moving through them gracefully, in the fashion of movie heroines who defend their cabins from marauding outlaws and emerge glowing, victorious, with a smudge on the cheek and a wisp of hair come loose from the demure bun. That kind of struggle I was prepared for.

But the trying thing about trials is that I don't get to be the heroine. Often I become a pettish child or a lofty windbag, a self-righteous critic or a melancholy pessimist. The real trials are the hellish and mortifyingly imperfect mental states to which I regress in a clinch, and those know no loyalty to place, following me wherever I go.

With eyes softly unfocused by love, I misread my new context. The county is a beauty—Michigan's little finger (the back of your left hand's a map of Lower Michigan, see?), a lovely peninsula in Lake Michigan, rolling countryside accented with wooden barns, storybook orchards, chattering woods, and a few charming little villages. (The charming little villages, however, are swamped by summer, winter, and fall visitors, and second homes are mushrooming everywhere.) The county has long been dependent on the infusion of cash that arrives each year with the tourists and summer residents. The soul of Leelanau County is just about as prostituted by tourism as my old stomping grounds in San Francisco were. Likewise nearby Traverse City, capital of the region, a megalopolitan (eighteen thousand souls) Lake Wobegon east. On my first visit here, Phil took me to a dance. The teens were punked out, but they had rosy cheeks, and their sullenness was as much an affectation as the hairdos. Traverse City doesn't offer much to be bitter about. The central neighborhood harbors big clapboard houses on tree-lined streets. Downtown there are friendly salespeople, ample parking (save during tourist season), and a human scale. Front Street is a classic of the genre. The place boasts wholesome folks, year-round recreation, clean air, and a gracious bay front. All of which is why my California friend Sarah dubbed it AmericaLand. A theme park: step back with us in time to a simpler era of peace and prosperity.

Oh my, I thought on that first visit; here's a handsome little town that knows what it's got in the way of advantages and seems to have protected them. (Another infatuation-induced vision problem, it temporarily blinded me to the lengthening franchise strips lining the main routes into town. Want a burger? Need a T-shirt? Fudge? A motel room? We got 'em.) Before the scales fell from my eyes, though, Traverse City looked perfect. I liked the substantial quality of the local citizens (and still do). Most of the natives and new arrivals are here for the quality of life. Most of them are year after year braving the rigors of a northwoods winter, even having several kinds of fun with snow and ice. In the summer it's mom and dad and buddy and sis out on the waterskis or gone fishin'. To this jade, fresh off the boat from California, the American Way of Life didn't look half bad. And ecotopia should be pretty easy to start here, what with all the gardens and woodstoves already in place, and because of the discipline that winter demands.

I had idealized my new home. I got a kick out of moving to a place that almost nobody in San Francisco had ever heard of. I thought it might be good for me to learn about small-town life, life without *dim sum* and art films. I heavily overestimated the give of my personality. I had imagined that in no time I would fit right in, and, shoulder to shoulder, neighbor to neighbor, we would commence bioregional endeavor. Sigh. The impulse to change was neither strong enough to carry me into the mainstream, nor yet the mainstream into ecotopia. Instead I was welcomed into a close-knit, albeit geographically dispersed, counterculture of unreconstructed hippies, ecoactivists, and back-to-the-landers; doggedly determined volunteers; strong-hearted midwives; and accomplished artisans.

Everyone sort of knows everyone else, sometimes even in the biblical sense.

If in San Francisco I was becoming restive with my old friends for not being hippies, here I get restive with my grown-up hippie friends for not being more skeptical. But what our organic little community has that we lacked in San Francisco is a setting in which it is more possible to act on the conviction that our lives must be simplified in order to be sustained. And we have a community not just of interests, but of activities. Friends help friends with muscle and time, in the heat and in the snow.

Our "community," however, is scattered over two peninsulas (the Leelanau, and to the east the Old Mission peninsula, which cleaves grand Traverse Bay), and we are visibly distinct from the majority of the area's populace. On account of our reflexive opposition to development proposals, we are sometimes at odds with our neighbors over questions of land use and economic growth.

Born too late, it seems like I got here 'bout two days before ol' demon Progress grabbed the area by the throat (a misperception, no doubt, and typical of my unfortunate tendency to take things personally). Now the grass on this side of the fence appears to be the same shade of green as that on the side I recently departed. It took me a couple of years to notice that many of the locals were intent on selling their birthright for a mess of paté. Now Traverse City is sprawling towards us, and the farmlands are being split up into low-density suburbs. The local boosters are eager to promote the region. They perceive even industrial growth as necessary and desirable and are gleeful at being mentioned in national travel and business publications, rejoicing when national gatherings are held here. Traverse City's gnomes of Zurich are keen to invite absentee owners to develop further such presently polluting businesses as plastics and plastic coatings, oil drilling, printing, and photographic reproduction—for the "good" of the local economy. In short, this little paradise, like everywhere else, is fixing to go out with a tawdry bang. Phil and I, both being wordmongers, like to throw verbal caltrops in the path of such dubious progress. And, in addition to having words and thoughts, Phil is very good about picking up and running with an organizing challenge. As for me, here I sit, twelve miles outside of town, sniffing the flowers, trying to figure it all out, with my culture shock subsiding slowly.

The sad fact is that the eighties made it everywhere, even to lovely Leelanau County. Here also we confront the growth that is undermining the quality of life. "Be grateful for the snow," said my husband. "It's what keeps this place from being California." Despite the hard winters, we're poised on the brink. The agrarian economy is becoming less tenable; the tourism, which was attractive for being so clean, is starting to encroach on a wetland here, a boulevard there, and to skew grotesquely in the direction of the automobile the management plan for the nearby national lakeshore. Tourism is looking less like an easy answer to the problem of undergirding the local economy.

What I am learning from all of this is that there is no place to hide from the eighties, to say nothing of the nineties. The emblematic bad things in our culture—like Burger King and Big Mac—are here too; and among humans some of the simple differences and skillful means seem to be fading, although more slowly in the countryside than in town.

Deploring the frontier mentality that scarred the face of North America, I nevertheless sought an unspoilt frontier for myself where I could start fresh and this time live well and correctly. Deploring the rootlessness that has so many of us treating places as carelessly as Kleenex, I left a changing place I loved very much in hopes of finding a place where I wouldn't have to witness the late-twentieth-century despoliation, a place that would have the courtesy to stay the same. It seems foolish now that I thought that there could be a place anywhere overlooked by the opportunism of commercial civilization, but then I never have been much of a one to abandon the idea of an easy answer. The Brigadoon/Shangri-La fantasy falls into that category—the geographical-cure idea again.

What gives the disillusionment a keen edge is confronting how tough it is for ordinary folks to get on over, and recognizing how general and venal the mass culture has become. For instance, everybody's got to have a snowmobile, and the mental space occupied by such noisy, speedy forms of recreation is unlikely to be satisfied by a package of new-age notions and a sudden urge to take up nature study. These are the waters that must be navigated in order to arrive at a sustainable culture.

We talk about developing a culture of sustainability as though all that existed now were a vacuum. But part of what I had to come to understand in my new home was the existence of a different, and self-respecting, local culture. There is already a life in place here, complete with strengths to build on, and "weaknesses" to disturb the alien: differences. But my neighbors on Kasson Road know exactly where their water comes from, when the deer rut; and the women are canning fiends. They know how to grow food and put it by.

An object lesson in geography: We're way inland, a long way from the nearest port, so there's not a whole lot of cultural relativism here in the heartland of America. The Midwest is missing the Pacific advantage of exposure to people who have grown up in Buddhism, Confucianism, Taoism, or any other tradition differing from the Christo-Judaic worldview. While this insularity provides a certain coherence, it may slightly fetter the imagination. Small-town and rural midwesterners just want to think themselves good and righteous, decent and self-reliant (not such bad values to cultivate). They have little reason to compare and contrast their way of life with another. If they are discontent, it seems not to be from hankering after new worlds to explore.

The average Joe here is a good Joe, a GOP Joe, a guy who gets fed up after a 5-month battle with the snow. He likes his carbohydrates, and his physique betrays it. He hunts and fishes;

the family's into sports. He drives a late-model truck, or hunk of Detroit iron. Salt on the wintertime roads rots out the undercarriage, so he has to replace it frequently. The family (with, at minimum, a brace of kids) is churchgoing. Having lived through a serious recession a decade ago, they may be mindful of the possibility of another downturn and appreciative of the recovery that has made their ownership of a lot of things possible.

There are enough ways in which that description fits our household that our silhouettes, if not our souls, seem to be drifting mainstreamwards. I've lately discovered the comforts of Buick ownership; a couple of winters ago hubby bought a snowblower (but a small one, he is quick to point out), and we are both experiencing a marital thickening of our centers of gravity. For an avid couple of nonconformists, any drift towards normality is a little disappointing.

Back in California I reasoned that I would only be as strong as I was called upon to be, and that by thrusting myself into the simple life, I would grow new strengths and skills. In short, married life in the northwoods would be soul aerobics. I would come to Michigan and garden and eat tofu and heat with wood and be snowed upon and be miraculously relieved of my partiality to the free air of the city. I would get roses in my cheeks from the healthy diet and requisite exertion of country living. Yes, by the time I got around to writing this, I expected I'd be freckled and feeding on vegetables I had home-canned, or skiing out to the sugar bush to see how the sap was running. In short, I figured I'd be more of a plain citizen of the land community, including the community of humans.

Ah, nothing like an idea for a smooth surface unmarred by the hickies of reality. It's a good thing it's impossible to anticipate accurately the feel and texture of that wonderful new experience we crave. If it were, probably no one would ever try anything different, especially falling in love.

The real texture of this wonderful new experience unexpectedly included being sidelined by injury, and human inertia (mine). Consequently I've had a less spectacular and very different personal transformation. In addition to not being very good copy, this chafes my pride. As was the case in San Francisco, "community" does not necessarily equal "neighborhood." The most extensive contact I've had with my Kasson Road neighbors has been in putting out an APB on a lost kitten, and having the kitten retrieved by Maralene, the kind and friendly woman across the road. This generous soul has also lavished us with irises, asparagus, and a bushel of tomatoes. She says a garden won't grow unless you share from it.

A blessing of rural life is that you can't be too selective or exclusive about your dealings with people. There is no hiding out in a like-minded elite—specialty groups are too small to be viable. So us would-be intelligentsia are forced to acknowledge intelligence in its wide applications, an embodied and practical intelligence, concentrated most wonderfully on matters at hand. This motherwit is most becoming when, for instance, my simple-living midwife friend bolsters her daughter's feelings of self-worth, which are being trampled by the clotheshorsiness of her schoolmates.

Slowly, and meeting with resistance, the good real is edging out the one-dimensional ideal. Simple living is a great concept until you're called upon to show up again and again for physical demands that have lost their novelty. Community is a dandy thought until it's time to forfeit your time in solitude. You can't belong if you don't show up.

In these parts, to refer to somebody as "different" carries a considerable freight of unstated meaning. It's that "different is not a way I would be for anything, but it is tantalizing. I concede to the few the right to be 'different,' and if they come to ruin, it will be no surprise."

The tendency of everybody to mind everybody else's business makes for a safer, more closely knit, and, for the belonger, more congenial feeling to life. We leave our houses and cars unlocked around here. Add to this a pleasantly laid back, but not lazy, pace, and an absence of the hassles that inhere in communities of great size and complexity, and you get a way of living that is beguilingly *possible*.

The purveyors of local services and the functionaries of local government are fairly accessible and often responsive. Contentment just isn't the uphill proposition that it is in the cities. True, the fine line between contentment and self-congratulation gets crossed sometimes, but there is an equally fine line between a striving for self-knowledge and an anxious narcissism that gets crossed from time to time by members of the urban intelligentsia; we're talking cultural trade-offs here.

In saying goodby to all urban that, though, I took for granted, really underestimated, the courage, resourcefulness, and tolerance of the average city dweller. People here in Americaland have little occasion to tolerate diversity because that which there is is inward, secreted away. Population here is predominantly heterosexual white folks of northern European origins. Local folks just don't have to deal face-to-face with very many persons, cultures, or realities that challenge their worldview, only the local Indian bands, who bear the full brunt of our culture's ingrained racism. It all adds up to an insular kind of contentment and incuriosity that you would expect to lead straight to the kind of stability and rootedness that bioregional theory's so keen on.

Despite the occasional attacks of what Robert Theobald calls *"amondie"* (as opposed to anomie), when I redefine world as nature, excitement enough is mine. This Michigan weather changes so fast it seems like there are no transitions. Suddenly, one day in May, it was sultry enough for there to be distant thunder, harbinger of those bodacious storms that rumble throughout the late spring. The day before was suicide weather: hulking, indifferent gray skies; cold, blowing mist. Chilly enough to warrant firing up the heater. Had me wondering whether to break out the long johns for one last reprise of winter—or what I, with my simplified sunbelt-bred conception of seasons, would call winter. They say the Eskimos have a hundred words for snow. Sure enough, on live-in observation, snow defies generalization. Likewise, moments on the continuum of spring are many and various. Its scales overlap. The trilliums of early spring still glitter in the green-shadowed forest floor. But the sorrel and knapweed of summer are with us also, and it's breathtaking to witness how quickly it all flashes past. We're climbing to a peak experience of light and warmth and foliage and soon enough will begin our colorful descent to the subdued tones of winter. The symbol of the Tao leaps to mind; there is a little speck of winter awareness in this turning experience of summer. And I recall marveling at last winter's realization that the cold neutral landscape harbored a coming riot of life.

A seasonal climate is a good place for a smart but not wise novice to confront the doggedness of change in nature. One of the writ-large lessons of northern Michigan is the mutability of Earth, the dynamic of the year.

Westerners and Californians attest truly that their landscapes do pass through seasonal changes. But those changes are subtle moments: in Arizona it's the unfurling of a carpet of minute green seedlings, new life peeking up between the stones of the desert pavement, of ironwood brush bedecking itself with pale mauve flowers, paloverde keying up from olive to sulfur, and the saguaro's upraised arms being crowned with huge moony pearl blossoming tiaras.

In California the color of the grass is your clue—emerald in the winter rain, spangled with many-colored wildflowers by spring, sun-bleached and tousled surfer-blond by summer. Such are the seasons in the Sonoran and Shastan bioregions—not terribly inconvenient, excepting the rare extremes of drought and heat or drenching storms and syzygous tides. Nature's menace fades from awareness in a no-fault climate. To realize what's going on with the round of the year in those places takes some effort—a fine discernment. Otherwise these transitions melt into calendar time and are clumsily marked by holidays that promote mass-media versions of seasonal character.

At holiday time, when I was a schoolkid in Phoenix, we'd get aerosol cans of spray snow and flock the mullions; we'd write Merry Xmas on the picture window that looked out on faded green lawns and neighborhood palm trees. Getting into the reality that spray snow alluded to has been a fair challenge.

Carolyn Weed, an architect friend over in the next township, who, like me, is a product of both the Sonoran bioregion and the San Francisco Bay area, exclaimed at our first encounter, "What are you *doing here?* Do you know how *cold* it gets?"

When it's fall, the maple leaves flutter leisurely across my view as do the butterflies of summer, but the leaves evoke a different note. Winter's imminence is a little dreadful. On first seeing the perpetual rose in Phil's cheek, I assumed that coming north one was granted strength. I became as disdainful of sunbelt folks who avoided the snow for fear of getting their toys rusty as of the locals who stayed and constantly bitched about the winter. Now I are one.

When it's late December at the outset of a winter that's promised (by the *Old Farmer's Almanac*) to be a bonanza for the long-john industry, I find myself wondering whether the bare trees also experience it as cold. Here is a winter cold that penetrates all sensation, of shoveling snow and slipping on ice, of mining for wood and sliding on slushy roads. Winter is as stern as the sea. The penalty for failing to stand up to its discipline is guaranteed suffering.

Once, when a snowstorm dumped a foot of the pretty white stuff within twenty-four hours (which is nothing exceptional), it occurred to me that my continued existence hinged on an extended industrial metabolism of fuel and electricity. Drifts of snow on the windowsills, no longer symbolic, but actual water solidified by cold, ominously occluded the view. Its myriad forms and properties mostly involve more work. Any work that you do in and around the snow will be magnified, complicated, increased. Just dressing for it takes time—layers, heavy boots, the works. I had vowed not to become one of those who gripes about winter, but the whine doesn't seem to want to leave the equipment.

Here, where it snows, seasonal change can challenge your survival. It is possible to die of winter (although these days I imagine the presenting complaint is no longer exposure or starvation but adverse highway conditions and the Windigo, the northwoods version of the run amok). Midwesterners must engage in seasonal preparations throughout the year. Getting the wood up is a crucial endeavor that separates the ants from the grasshoppers. The former sweat their way through August, splitting and stacking; some time in late October, the latter try to get the best deal they can on pre-split and seasoned and hope that the spot where the pile's to go isn't already knee-deep in snow by the time the stove lengths arrive. Winter here puts hair on the chest and a plaint in the throat. The days become frighteningly short. Arising at a decent hour, hustling out through the chilled house to stoke up the woodstove, shivering as you put on the kettle, you get a little martyrish.

Winter lets us see things as they are, unbedazzled by the broadleaf festival of photosynthesis. The white curve of a hill is surgically precise. The capillary quality of the bare branches becomes undeniable; they are a root system for drinking the atmosphere. It is all stark, beautiful, unremitting.

Last January there still hadn't been much snow, to the great disappointment of the skiers. Such snow as there was arrived in November and was shopworn and corny by New Year's. The meadow's cheeks showed a stubble of dead weeds, and the dark bleak earth began to blemish the mantle of white. Nevertheless, it was a pretty sight, peaceful and all but mono-chromatic, relieved by the dense green of the pine and fir plantation on the west edge of the field. There's something reassuring about the sight of life in those green needles, the truth of its persistence despite the cold and gloom. It becomes easy to understand the ancient northern magic of the evergreen, and why we yet bring evergreens into our houses around the time of the winter solstice.

Winter is a dying and a turning inward, a skeleton time of slow cessation and deep stillness, a blunt annual lesson in mortality. It's a season that drags on long enough to tax everyone's ability to relate. The walls of the burrow shrink closer all the while and become sickeningly familiar. Earth earns a resurrection by moving through winter.

We all need to be taught about our powerlessness, our ephemerality. Some guys go to the wilderness to get their awe. I get mine by witnessing cold and snow. The struggle involved in business as usual in the face of such weather testifies to humanity's crazy will to order. We like a challenge. We put ourselves in places where just surviving is a triumph. Perhaps that is why Easter and its iconography make such intuitive sense. Things suffer, die, and are buried. The snow lingers endlessly in dirty, scrofulous patches before the miracles of green finally begin to blaze forth again.

For me, snow country is the end of the line. I can't kid myself that there's a better place than this to do what I can to save the Earth, or better people to do it with. In my life it's time to stop looking for an elsewhere. Time to adopt some land and nurse it, to reinhabit and name it Home.

• • •

Miraculous as the whole four-season show is, a lot of folks here, as they approach their middle years, head south during the months of late winter. Even the young bolt. Maybe the reason that so many people in the northeast and midwest are losing their tolerance for seasons such as winter is that most of their television images originate in southern California, eternally awash in sun. You don't see teevee stars suffering indignities like gooseflesh on the ass or the fundamental unchicness of long underwear. Let's face it: you have to be a bit of a stud to live in the frostbelt.

This move helped me realize that I've always wanted to be macho. I've always thought it would be cool to strut some stuff that was a little tougher than the next person's, to be noticeably rugged, or ruggedly noticeable. But I *hate* most endurance sports and competitive athletic endeavors. However, the last few years I lived in San Francisco, somehow it came easily to me to swim in the bay (from March until November, at least). That the bay waters are cold (60 degrees is high average) was impressive to people who couldn't take the chill. So in joining a funky, but alas upwardly mobile, old swimming club, I had lucked on to an activity that was doing for me what hard-core running was doing for the many.

In retrospect, I realize that in addition to obtaining a wild sense of vitality and a certain pride every single morning that I entered the water, I also had to deal with my fear of dying. Each day that I swam away from the beach, it was with a sense that I might not return. That possibility was vanishingly small, yet there were maritime adventures; there were return swims— during squalls, say—that were genuinely perilous. So it wasn't easy—it was difficult but possible. It wound up being a nice paradox. That image and a little self-image of fortitude were ransomed with the coin of fear. And there was the heartening splendor of seeing the sun rise over Aquatic Park from the water level, and a joyous brisk liberation from land and gravity.

The counterculture, and then the yuppie culture, has noticed that the mind-body schism made possible by affluence can be disastrous. We young moderns resort to elaborate means of getting physical experience. Yogic practice, fanatical running, bicycling, competitive sports, bodybuilding. All of these recreations are voluntary and may not cultivate the endurance necessary for the kind of labor required to dismantle industrial society and restore the Earth's productivity.

One summer afternoon a few days after a freak windstorm, I made a foray out to buy some toilet paper. (Every time I have to replenish the supply of this presumed necessity, I wonder what we're going to substitute for it when the trucks stop running.)

When I arrived in the village of Cedar, a few miles to the northeast, I discovered that both of the stores had had to close because the power lines were down. At the loading dock behind one store, a huge refrigerator truck was parked and panting while several hefty young men loaded it with carts full of the store's perishable inventory. The men were flushed, for it was clearly hard work, but they also appeared to rejoice in their ability to deal with the emergency. I imagine they would have come up with some solution even without the refrigerator truck. Seeing them rise to the occasion set me to thinking about what may be demanded of us in the coming hard times and what personal qualities it will be useful to have. If by chance the chips fall on the side of equity and against privilege, bodily toughness and skillful means will be essential.

Growing up in Michigan is like the Bay swimming, but more than a pastime. I was beglamoured by the green effulgence of a northern summer, and I envied Phil's strength and rosy cheeks. I wanted those appearances, not anticipating the aches and bruises that must precede the strength, nor the edgy fatigue that goes with outlasting the cold, awaiting the spring.

I certainly didn't plan on being an ignorant beginner most of the time, ignominiously doing half-assed jobs, or just plain quitting. My householding fantasy didn't factor in an endless sequence of compromises and delays and never getting exactly what I want. Although I understood that I would have to position myself for some new experience if I wanted to be forever young, I avoided recalling how trial and error feels.

A city trait upon which country life has yet to work its calming magic is urgency. It's the conceit that I can't plant or dig in the garden because I'm too busy trying the save the world with my typewriter. Even here in the sticks it feels like there's not quite enough time to get the learning experience. We, too, are stuck with having to be "efficient," as currently defined. We're trapped enough in a cash economy that it's difficult to come up with the initial capital requirement for gearing down—the land, the tools, the shelter, the seeds, the livestock, the waking hours. The start-up costs are many. Living simply in this climate requires a special wardrobe, some basic equipment, and, in fact, some connoisseurship in those acquisitions.

Hence, the inescapable conflict: the writer self wants to continue to take advantage of civilization and specialization. If somebody else will grow my food for me and tend to my energy needs and simplify the proposition of giving me shelter, I can continue to hole up in my studio, striking away at the flint of my being, hoping to give out with a spark that might ignite some other inflammable punk.

Gazing out that studio window at the progression of the seasons, I've begun to have a more palpable sense of the passage of time—that carpet being unfurled ahead, and rolling itself up behind me. I see that my lifetime is finite (obviousness, but never so gut-real as now) and that the clip at which I must explore and create within that finitude is picking up. At the end of any March, things start accelerating in realms cultural and biospheric.

The clouds pull back, the sun reemerges. Things are seething here, quickening: the ice has long since broken up, and the waters of life are rushing fast. The humans are in turmoil. The women are rising, questioning their lives, their charity, their ability to compromise just one more time. Possums, skunks, raccoons, and snakes are on the move, crossing roads, getting hit, rotting on the wayside. Birds are swooping low, darting past, mating, hemming together the skies and the Earth. There's a rush into the garden to see what's up. Here's the real excitement. The action is in the back eighty as April races past into May. It's that visceral sense of the ebb and flow of energy in nature, the brief seasons of opportunity and the slow ways of renewal, that the country knows and the city only thinks about.

We need to discover a means of making the information flow from city to country a circuit, rather than the one-way imperial propaganda it is now, with the allure and inappropriateness of city style and city timing undermining the differently earned contentment of rural life. What is it that the country has to teach the city? That the reserve is gone, for one thing. There's no unspoilt "out there" to repair to, once the affluence battle's won, or conceded. There is only everywhere Earth in peril, ground that wants defending, communities threatened, society in need of reconciliation with the land and of healing from within. As the endlessly quotable Peter Berg puts it, "Reinhabitation begins where you are." And, as we used to say in the sixties, the future is now.

SHAKING

◆

Bioregions are things like the Rocky Mountains, the Gulf of Maine, the Ozarks. All of us live in some bioregion or other. And once it's understood that we live in bioregions and that the idea of trying at least to live within the natural energy and life flows of these specific regions is possible, and that if we do that, perhaps we can save the biosphere—save the whole by saving the parts would be the idea—then a quickening spirit enters some of these fields that all of us have been aware of for the last decade at least but are largely unfulfilled.

I'm talking about renewable energy as being the primary source of our energy, of permaculture being the primary source of our food. Renewable energy in a bioregion has its own unique sources. Permanent agriculture has a home base. Decentralist politics has its constituency. "Act local" has its bioregion, and "think global" has its biosphere. It's a way to get a handle on realizing some of these sweeping changes that all of us would like to see take place.

Peter Berg
verbatim

GARRETT HARDIN ONCE POINTED OUT THAT NOAH WAS A GUY unusual in his readiness to heed a dire warning. "How can one believe in something—particularly an unpleasant something—that has *never* happened before?" Hardin asked. "This necessity must have been a terrible problem for Noah."

And, having heeded the dire warning, how to build an ark? Simple, but not easy. Reinhabitation using biological design is a constructive, positive, ecologically sensitive, decentralist response to the staggering problem of securing the human niche on Earth.

Wherever you happen, or choose, to do it, reinhabitation is the antithesis of the occupation we've got going now. It's humble, unprepossessing, baby steps, minute particulars. The following brief sketches of reinhabitory projects (each of which easily warrants its own book) compose an idiosyncratic, and by no means representative, sample of such works in progress.

My visits to the New Alchemy Institute took place some years ago, as did my visits to the Meadowcreek Project. It is in the nature of those places to develop and change quickly, thus these descriptions may be dated. Although I have had the pleasure of meetings with Wes and Dana Jackson of the Land Institute, I haven't had the experience of visiting their 188 acres of Kansas. What I know of their work is thanks to Dana's meticulous *Land Report,* published thrice annually, to admiring accounts of their work published elsewhere, and to Wes's stirring orations and majestic prose.

Led by the New Alchemy Institute in Cape Cod (which has, in fact, generated more than one book), the puttering towards a technics of reinhabitation has been under way for better than two decades. Founded in 1969 by John Todd, Nancy Jack Todd, and Bill McLarney, New Alchemy Institute set about devising integrated greenhouse, aquaculture, and waste-water purification systems that were synthetic ecologies. Owing to McLarney's strong piscatorial bent and training in aquatic biology, aquaculture (important because cheap protein is important) has long been a distinguishing feature of New Alchemy's advanced bioshelter designs. Upright cylindrical fish tanks do double duty as solar-heat storage; open fish tanks serve as rivers to circulate and cleanse gray water. Enveloping the production of a diverse array of foodstuffs, New Alchemy also has a long history of working with renewable energy sources, including wind generation and greenhouse design.

Because John Todd and Bill McLarney are both scientists, they established a rigorous standard for New Alchemy's research and publication. And for more than a decade Nancy Jack Todd's intellectual, poetic, and editorial gifts embellished much of the information produced by New Alchemy. In 1982 the Todds left New Alchemy to create a new organization— Ocean Arks International—whose purpose is to disseminate methods and practices of ecologically sustainable development throughout the world. Thus far they have accomplished the design of wind-powered workboats for Third World fisherfolks, and of sewage-treatment systems that use miniaturized aquatic ecosystems.

The original New Alchemy focus was on creating a science of biological design. It did and does demand strict attention to detail—the species of fish to be used in solar aquaculture; the relationships of plants, reptiles, and beneficial insects in the greenhouse ecosystems; the path of the sunlight and the gradation of moisture and temperature in the different bioshelters.

Specificity to place is not an overriding concern for New Alchemy in North America. (It is, however, paramount in McLarney's work in Costa Rica, where since 1973 he and his collegas have been building the Asocación de los Nuevos Alquimistas (ANAI), which engages in a wide range of place-specific, sustainable, development projects, including agroforestry, a reforestation cooperative, and refuge management.)

In 1975 New Alchemy received a big grant (probably about enough to buy one control knob on a Stealth bomber) from the Canadian government. It enabled them, in collaboration with Solsearch Architects, to build an "ark"—a self-contained bioshelter—in Nova Scotia. The ark, on Prince Edward Island, strove to be more organism than artifact. Its purpose was to provide a comfortable, deliciously provisioned home life despite the elements. It was a generic indoor tropics set in the Maritimes, a dwelling that would permit a kind of existence in that place that unaided nature wouldn't countenance.

In the years since the Todds' departure, New Alchemy has continued to earn respect and esteem and even some philanthropic support. Its members have been active participants in environmental issues arising on Cape Cod, as well as pursuing their particular researches. Under the directorship of John

Quinney, New Alchemy's maturation has progressed. A few years ago the institute embarked on a comprehensive planning process to "design" the New Alchemy Farm, which had hitherto grown on a project-by-project basis. The new thrust was to create a "model farm." With researcher Colleen Armstrong's guidance, New Alchemy's greenhouse work becomes ever more sophisticated and ingenious, with experiments in integrated pest management and the rediscovery of older methods, like the composting greenhouse.

As with virtually all the exploration along what energy maven Amory Lovins calls the Soft Path, it's research done on a shoestring. Building materials, machine parts, and equipment are often scavenged, painstakingly restored, and cobbled together. In most reinhabitory projects, resources are scant enough and work is plentiful enough that such hierarchy as exists exempts no one from labor. The leaders are workers. They may have to suit up for fundraising endeavors and information exchange, but their hands are beat up from digging in the dirt, from dipping around in ponds, from tool use.

The Land Institute in Salina, founded in 1976 by Kansans Wes and Dana Jackson, is a small but beautiful ag school whose research tends to emulate the wisdom of the prairie. Jackson, a plant geneticist, could not, even as an academic, quite bring himself to discount reality: conventional grain production is laying waste to the topsoil and costing inordinate amounts of petrochemical subsidy for traction, fertilization, and weed and pest control. The Jacksons' radical insight was to recognize the problematic nature of annualism in humanity's favored cultivars. Annual plants live a year and propagate themselves by producing a one-shot abundance of seeds. Because an abundance of seeds provides the surplus that leads to civilization, these are the plants that our ancestors so painstakingly domesticated back in the Neolithic, the grains on which the human diet is largely based. Their culture, however, takes an enormous toll on the soil. Annuals take rather than give because the plant's substance goes into seeds rather than roots, and roots are what hold and build and make humectant soil. By contrast, prairie plants are mostly perennials with deep, extensive root systems.

So the Land Institute has set about the painstaking process of trying to breed perennial plants that will bear a respectable amount of seed, and also to experiment with polyculture—planting together several different species whose particular needs for and contributions to soil nutrients may be complementary and mutually enhancing. The Land Institute's herbary—a living library of prairie plants—contributes to this work.

In contrast to high-tech genetic or chemical manipulation, this kind of agronomic research is slow and cautious, finicky. It can be traumatic, but only for the researcher; not, potentially, for the rest of the world's DNA. For instance, Thom Leonard, whose Grain Exchange, an organization dedicated to grassroots preservation of cereal diversity, has offices and plots located at the Land Institute. He must have been plenty dismayed when a windstorm blasted through and ripped the protective bags from the tassels of a hundred carefully cross-pollinated corn plants, literally blowing off a year's worth of experimentation.

All of this vital effort takes place on a small patch of land with a small group of associates and perhaps a dozen students. In addition to the plant research, the Land Institute also tinkers with windpower and solar architecture. Such modest diligence is dramatically different from NASA-style spectacles, and even from land-grant–multiversity–agbiz research complexes. It is so subtle that it takes some philosophy to understand that human survival and biospheric health could depend on these few earnest, ill-financed efforts carried on at homegrown institutes by handfuls of dedicated souls.

In 1979, following an essentially pedagogical impulse, two brothers, David and Will Orr, an academic and a businessman, respectively, founded the Meadowcreek Project. Situated in a beautiful Arkansas holler, long winding hours from any city, with hardwood forests on the uplands and a year-round stream running through the valley, the Meadowcreek Project is an educational institution with a curriculum in sustainability. Ozarkia is a tough place to make a living. The principal resource is scenery, and the danger is a colonial economy. So in addition to the basics—gardening and food production, renewable energy, passive solar, solar electricity biomass, and microhydro—Meadowcreek is also working on local economic development. The project has twelve hundred acres of forest, a wood-fired sawmill, solar kilns, and a wood-products shop employing local residents and students in a value-added strategy for utilizing their local raw materials at home. Meadowcreek stages conferences throughout the year and offers internships to college undergraduates. By the late eighties, nearly two thousand students and conferees were visiting each year, and further growth was planned. Meadowcreek's unique contribution is in making a practical synthesis—and application—of many technical methods, and in being both native to the Ozarks—rooted in place—and extensive—through its teaching and research.

New Alchemy, Meadowcreek, and the Land Institute are all rural projects, land based and essentially agrarian. Day by day they are figuring out ways to make it possible for people to stay down on the farm after they've seen Paree. But if re-inhabitation begins where you are, what about the millions of city dwellers? As Phil so pungently put it in our very first conversation, "Show me sustainability in Detroit." If in the sticks, reinhabitation is a peoples' science, systematic puttering, mimicking, a story of trial and error, in the city it's a nimble political skirmishing.

City people aiming at Earth stewardship and self-reliance face much greater practical challenges in getting at the soil and water. In cities it requires considerable time and effort to take responsibility for your own refuse, and there's not much you can do about your effluent. It's infinitely harder to demonetize and live simply. Cities have so effaced the contour and tissue of life, and are such imperial delusions of might and right, that the essential details of life support are unsustainably relegated to the hinterlands, out of sight and out of mind. Thus, people who devote themselves to figuring out how to make cities integral to local ecology, rather than tumors upon it, are the ultimate reinhabitory insurgents. I know of no reinhabitors in the Motor City, but the greenprints for urban sustainability are being roughed out elsewhere.

Planet Drum founders Peter Berg and Judy Goldhaft, and their shifting assortment of colleagues, have for many years worked out of their steep, Mission District, San Francisco Victorian, tending a ruffian vegetable garden out back. An urbane cabal, Planet Drum recently has been organizing the development of a sustainable city plan, a "Green City" vision. In keeping with the spirit of the thing, Berg decided it would be an apposite gesture to free the dirt under the sidewalk on the east side of the house. The point was to try planting northern Californian native species in the de-entombed soil, to see how a 5-foot-by-15-foot patch of restoration ecology might fare. Securing official permission to commit this Green City deed of sidewalk removal required some cajoling of officialdom. It was a civic chore. Prying up the concrete assumptions that crush biology out of urban planning altogether will be a heroic, lifesome endeavor.

Planet Drum Foundation has initiated the dreaming and discussing and, according to Peter Berg, "is currently preparing a Green City Program document developed from meetings with members of nearly one hundred Bay Area working groups, city departments, businesses, and advocacy organizations."

Describing some of the highlights of the proposals in an article in the *San Francisco Bay Guardian,* Berg listed:

> *Urban wild habitat:* Establish native vegetation corridors of wildness in the city, linking habitats so that wildlife can move unimpeded through urban areas. . . .

Urban planting: Reduce restrictions on locations for planting street trees and sidewalk strips. . . . Encourage donations of land for "vest-pocket" parks and neighborhood vegetable gardens.

Recycling and reuse: Institute curbside pickup of separated recyclables. Establish secondary-materials industries in neighborhoods—garbage should be seen as a resource. . . .

Renewable energy: Refit public buildings to demonstrate various uses of renewable energy sources and energy conservation. . . .

Smart transportation: . . . Adopt more mixed-use zoning policies to enable living, work and recreation sites in the same area. . . .

Neighborhood character and empowerment: Foster the formation of neighborhood design review boards to represent neighborhoods in the planning process. Create a municipal agency to advocate neighborhood and other nondeveloper views on transportation and land-use issues. Develop mechanisms to broaden neighborhood self-government.

Socially responsible small businesses and cooperatives: Create "small business incubators" featuring low-rent space and shared equipment during start-up. . . .

Sustainable planning: Solicit neighborhoods' visions of their futures and use them as standards for determining changes. Adopt "statutes of responsibility" that point out officials' responsibility to maintain the health of cities and their inhabitants. . . .

Celebrating life-place vitality: Assist small-scale localized media (murals, bulletin boards, neighborhood radio shows). Stage public celebrations of natural events (seasons, animal migrations, etc.). . . .

Deepened and informed by the sense of natural history, the primary technique of reinhabitation, wherever the home place, is community organizing: *we* empowering *us* to meet our basic needs sustainably, and in harmony with the greater life of our bioregions. In so doing, we will be indebted to the research and invention accomplished at little institutes like New Alchemy and the Land Institute. We can also study which means of local economic development might be appropriate and life enhancing where we are, after the fashion of the Meadowcreek Project. And we can bring creativity to the challenge of citizenship, exercising our rights and responsibilities in our neighborhoods and townships—intimate arenas where it's possible to know and see almost the whole being of any political actor.

Obviously, you can't get into the reinhabiting business without a place to do it. Consequently, place-defense is often step one in "saving the parts": securing the venue for changing lifeways and a sustainable culture.

Back when I was an urbanite living in a community where the ties to place were more sentimental than organic, my experience of community was far-flung, dynamic, and cerebral. From that limited basis of experience, I imagined that cultural and political interactions should be amenable to purposive reform programs, much in the same way that other people view ecosystems: that is, simplistically and fallaciously, as being amenable to greater "efficiency" and "productivity."

Of course, I had never really engaged in the political process until I moved to this rural-area-in-transition. Here, many people own land and have a vital economic interest in maintaining the freedom to dispose of that land at their pleasure. This tenure makes people rather less than malleable on the subject of ecological reform—the yeoman farmer/small landowner's cussed independence is no joke. It invites participation in local politics, the politics of land use.

A township is thirty-six square miles of Earth, a healthy chunk of stewardship. The township level of politics is where the land-use decisions in rural areas are made. And land-use decisions determine the livelihood of landowners and the life of life places, so all of us within these thirty-six square miles of Kasson Township have a vital stake in our township trustees' and zoning board's deliberations.

One hundred and fifty years ago, this society still condoned the owning of human beings as property, and supported the right of the slaveowner to do exactly what he pleased with his human chattel. As Aldo Leopold observed in *A Sand County Almanac,* those mores have changed, and so should our mores about land. A perfect analogy, but one likely to be regarded as romantic in Kasson Township, where getting a living entails a load of hard work, and where philosophies are forged in the struggle to make the land produce.

Every time I enter our township hall, I'm moved. It's an unexceptional building, isolated on a country road. In addition to housing our township meetings, it is also our polling place. On weekdays it's in use as a day-care center. Midnineteenth-century photographs of the Kassons, our founders, hang on the wall. Our founders had a geologically rocky row to hoe and wound up looking as stony as their furrows. It's a stirring thing to sit with one's neighbors and face conflicts (because that's usually what draws our attendance) over the right of the individual landowner to maximize his profits versus the desire of his neighbors to live the kind of life they either grew up with or moved here to enjoy.

The factions that show up for these meetings fraction out along various cleavages: old-timers versus newcomers, farmers versus suburbanites, entrepreneurs versus preservationists, with various individuals wearing various hats, depending on the particular issue. It's nonpartisan, case-by-case self-government.

Because a township is a specific place and quite knowable, one of the revelations at any township meeting is the personal knowledge of the local land-use history possessed by many residents. They know the territory better than they know the map, and sometimes to a depth of several generations' occupancy.

There's a lot of power vested in the township government, most of it negative, reactive. The board can impede change and regulate land use, but it can't directly do much about the economic situation that drives the desire to change zoning categories. The underlying attitude of several of the board members seems to be that it's not fair to prevent a landowner from disposing of his property as he wishes. The general attitude of the township residents who show up to speak, often against a proposed change, is *Not In My Backyard*. (And the NIMBY approach is fine with me if it works to put the brakes on land destruction, aka development.)

People speak their hearts at these meetings, and they often have to disagree, standing up, out loud, and in person, with people who are their friends, people who have befriended them, people who may be their in-laws, customers, or, more rarely, their employers. Face-to-faceness makes it hard on the trustees and zoning-board members who may have to declare themselves publicly as against an old friend's economic interest. Making these kinds of decisions makes them uncomfortable. Township government is politics at its nudest. All you have to do is show up and you're entitled to speak your piece. You get to act like a citizen. And you know, if you're planning to continue living in the township, that you're going to be dealing with these people again and again, so you'd better be decent, and you'd better know how to forgive.

A lot of what goes on in our township meetings is farmers seeking permission to put their land to some more-profitable use, in order to continue paying the taxes and to subsidize their property-owning and agricultural habits. A few extraordinarily enterprising souls have figured out how to survive by doing both. The local *patron*, through whose hands seems to have passed a good quarter of our township's acreage, is one of these. He sits on the zoning board and, like a good Old Testament patriarch, seeks to dispense justice and serve the commonweal. He does understand the implication of increasing environmental protection, *and* he hates to see land "lying idle."

He has a half dozen kids, all but one of whom live and work in the township, most of them in their father's enterprises — farming and gravel extraction. So he's well on the way to founding a dynasty. This man has made a good many friends along with a smattering of enemies. He's a courteous, knowledgeable, formidable adversary in a local dispute, and not a sore loser when issues don't go his way. Definitely a leading actor in the Kasson Township story—a powerful person, and decent, who has worked hard for what he's got, and he's got a lot.

The *patron* has been defeated by the organized township residents, so he doesn't have the process under control, nor, I think, would he want to. It was he who owned the landfill until recently, and he who wanted a rezoning to expand it. Another neighbor, however, an equally decent, hardworking man who both farms and teaches, and who lives even closer to the landfill than we do, mobilized the opposition to the change. Together we organized meetings with neighbors nearby, mailed campaign pieces, and promoted an intimidating turnout at the township and zoning meetings where the change was discussed and finally denied.

A good way to feel like a crackpot at a Kasson Township meeting is to try to draw the connection between what we do here and what happens to, say, the entire atmosphere. About once per meeting, I stand up and do crackpot duty, saying things like this: "'Everybody talks about the weather, but nobody can do anything about it' is no longer true. If our township decides to let the aspiring gravel-pit operator log off the two hundred acres that the guy in the buffalo-plaid shirt says he's hunted all his life, we will be doing something about the weather, something destructive, because deforestation is one of the causes of the greenhouse effect."

Hanging myself out there among people I'm bound to respect and taking the risk of earning their disapproval make my heart leap out of my chest. Yet I wish everyone could have the township experience. It's group process without benefit of pop psych, sociological homogeneity, or media. It's precious, effective, and crucial. Townships are small enough, and the gossip thorough enough, that you can't run on the Big Lie. Somebody knows somebody who knows you, who knows when you moved in, what you do for a living, and how you treat your piece of Earth. People can drive around, have a look, see what you're doing. Or they may be doing business with you. So they can know whether you're in the habit of telling the truth.

• • •

One morning friends of ours who are building themselves a new house (solar-photovoltaic, by the way; no connection to the grid planned) stopped by to chat about house building. The conversation, however, drifted to zoning issues in their rather swampy township, where Jane, the female half of the couple, is vice chairman of the township planning commission. She talked about the hazing that went on during her first year of membership, during which time, she said, most of her colleagues were flat-out rude and objectionable to her. By insisting on permitting procedures that would conform to the aims of the state's wetlands protection act, she became a burr. In order to do what she could to preserve the aesthetic qualities of her home place, which give her rapture, she mustered the guts and patience to endure the flak.

Soon enough, though, because she is the type who does her homework, and an able researcher, she earned the respect of her colleagues, including their township's largest landowner, who now lets her know, on the qt, that they "think alike." Her presence has emboldened another member of the board to become more overtly preservationist in his participation. So Jane is causing a ripple.

Such local activists-despite-themselves felt the civic impulse to deal with the central issue of land use. None of them started out with a burning desire to be a politician, or even has developed one in the course of service. But townships are the alpha, if not the omega, and township government is approachable enough that there's no excuse not to become involved. Would you call this green politics or plain citizenship of the land community?

I would like to imagine that our area is not exceptional in having people, even younger people, who are willing to dig in to these issues by functioning as citizens at the microlevel.

I like to imagine that in townships everywhere, especially where the priceless values of the rural landscape are on the block, individuals are dragging themselves off to board and commission meetings out of duty to the Earth rather than personal ambition, taking some knocks for trying to elevate the land ethic over the profit motive. By taking their stands and casting their votes, they are forced to suffer the discomforts of commitment. They're having to live in controversies and are learning how to work through the minutiae of compromise at the square-foot scale. That's got to be the hardest part of all—the inevitable "compromises." Losses for the land, in truth. Passing by those places for the rest of your days and bearing some responsibility for the condition they're in.

I surely don't mean to suggest that the process of township government is immune to venal manipulation or always responsive to Earth-minded citizenship like Jane's. Developers will try every trick in the book to convince township officials and citizens that what's good for General Motors is good for the U.S.A., trying to sell the ol' trickle-down theory with jobs, or an increased tax base as the enticement to local people in exchange for the sacrifice of their quality of life. There seems to be a whole industry of chart makers and map colorers whose products are rung in to dazzle the citizenry and to paint—or whitewash—a picture of the territory once we get the bucks extracted. It's media spending, a high-ticket embellishment that obscures the real stakes in these conflicts. A case like that is unfolding in a township to the west of us, in a resort area.

Here's the tale. In geological time a pretty little river was made not far from Lake Michigan's eastern shore. In recent historic time white settlers saw the river to be so clear and delightful that they named it the Crystal. Over the last hundred years people became quite fond of canoeing and fishing the river, or locating their cottages on its banks. Long before that, whole communities of plants, birds, insects, and animals had made their habitat along the Crystal. They throve on fairly well despite increasing human incursions. Most recently a very shrewd, very determined, and, some say, ruthless local resort developer decided that he must enhance his holdings and build a golf course along the Crystal River's meanderings. Despite his good intentions to mitigate the environmental damage that earth moving, turf sowing for construction, fertilization, and weed control (by herbicide application) entailed in building and maintaining a golf course, it was obvious to some of the locals that the Crystal River would certainly suffer, and for what they deemed a rather trivial purpose.

Yet half the township's residents supported his plans, either on account of being, or aspiring to be, in the same class as the developer, or on account of their immediate economic dependence on his enterprises; the other half, including wealthy retirees, summer visitors, and the natives, people who had grown up on the riverbank, wanted the river left alone. They thought that the developer should stick his golf course somewhere else. So these defiant citizens enlisted the help of some environmentalists and environmental attorneys from Traverse City. They began to try to mobilize effective community opposition to the proposed zoning change that would be required to locate a golf course on the river. Although jumping into such a fray was meat and drink to the paladin environmentalists from the city, taking a public stand and stepping out into controversy was not an easy thing for these citizens and, as it shaped up, the entire female membership of the township's zoning commission.

While the environmentalists were writing anguished, impassioned, and ultimately unpersuasive letters to the township's board, the developer was suavely circularizing all his local suppliers, suggesting that he could use their expression of support in the coming struggle for approval of the golf course. He commanded an army of experts to study the situation and analyze it and develop a plan for the most environmentally sound golf course ever built in a wetland. He also sponsored a series of what he called community workshops, which were ostensibly to inform the public about the development, and to solicit comments, but never to address his idée fixe about the site of the golf course. Why build it on the river rather than in any number of other possible sites nearby?

When the issue came up for a vote at the township's planning and zoning commission, I felt impelled to attend, just to be one warm body among many, to demonstrate that there was countywide attention being paid to this decision and that the commissioners had better think well about it.

When I arrived, I discovered that a few hundred other interested parties had had the same thought, and that the township hall was crowded to the bursting point. The developer's presentation was under way. I stood in the back and listened to the droning parade of experts, even a "turf pathologist," for pete's sake, display the proposal in the best possible light. I also began to pick out the familiar faces in the crowd: the lawyers, one tall, round-faced, and well built, a newcomer to these kinds of battles; literate, blaspheming, eloquent and scrappy. The other, a whittled kind of wispy-haired scholarly guy, renowned throughout Michigan for having—literally—written the book on environmental law, and known to wander into the terrain of myth and spirituality in his arguments before the public, if not the bench. There was the environmental dream couple, a soon-to-be-married pair of local activists, each, by dint of years of volunteer organizing, a keeper of the flame of environmental quality.

There was the hotheaded, impassioned journalist, a woman who had graduated from elementary school in this very town hall, and who can always be counted on for exhaustive, insightful gossip about everyone and everything, plus righteous, vociferous opinions on most of the affairs of the region. There were the good-hearted husband and wife, bedrock members of the alternative community, he a master painter, she an accomplished florist and apprentice midwife. They were there just because they care about the fate of the Earth where they live, and everywhere. There was the maddeningly neutral, but helpful, senator's aide. There was the covertly radical park ranger, a true naturalist, working at the nearby national lakeshore, barred by the politics of his job from publicly deploring Reagan-era parks management and tangential land-use issues. (This golf course issue was one because the river debouches into the lake through park lands.) There was even a born-again pagan, an Earth First!er.

Seven township planning and zoning commissioners sat sweating at the front of the hall. The hired experts swamped the listeners with a floodtide of numerical data, giving assurances in dubious terms: that environmental damage could be contained "to the extent possible" and promising only "measurable but slight" amounts of mitigation and pollution, respectively. One sanguine character allowed as how there'd be some use of "safe" herbicides. After their lengthy dog-and-pony show, lavishly illustrated with magic-lantern slides of bar graphs and pie charts, we had a little break. Then we settled in to hear the voices of opposition.

To hear first the voices of citizens opposed to the golf course construction was the decision of the board chairman, and some protest was raised by the golf course proponents, a boisterous lot, many of them sporting badges reading "FORE" ("That stands for 'F___ Our Resources and Environment,'" quipped the young lawyer). The chairman said that the rules of township-meeting conduct allowed for such a slight change in sequence of discussion and asked that people limit themselves to five minutes of comment. After admonishing that if their point was made by another speaker, folks should refrain from reiterating it, he began to work his way row by row, front to back, calling on the individuals who raised their hands.

The opponents of the golf course came in all stripes and sizes, and were speaking with a sincerity and moral authority that couldn't be hired. They spoke of their childhoods unfolding by the river, or of memorable summers spent in its vicinity. Representatives of state conservation clubs proclaimed the rarity of the river as a landscape and of its ecological value as a wetland. They pointed out that an alternative site was available for the golf course.

The defenders of the river had, on their own initiative and slender purse, gone out to find themselves their own volunteer experts. They located professors who could speak with scientific authority on the vulnerability of the river. The tenor of their comments was more emotional, but no less intelligent or informed, than that of the armies of the experts. The Earth First! guy capped it with a colloquial version of the tragedy of the commons (a theorem expounded by Garrett Hardin, holding that since it is in each individual's self-interest to exploit a resource held in common — like an attractive tributary — and since the harmful consequences of such exploitation are widely diffused, rather than directly affecting the exploiting individual, self-interest will counsel individuals to exploit, and the cumulative effect of their actions will be the destruction of the whole system). By the time all the opponents had had their say, they had reproduced the complete ecological argument, the natural philosophy.

As I sat there in that humming township hall, nodding my head in enthusiastic agreement with the conservation eloquence, I could feel the animosity of the golf course proponents growing. Finally, wielding the stick, the lawyers rose and told the commission why a decision to zone for the golf course could be challenged legally, and hinted at the possibility of a suit. The animosity erupted into catcalling when the senior environmental attorney approached the mike. Their hostility provoked his, and he lectured the board and citizens, threatening them with the law. It was an ugly moment. You couldn't say that it was *degenerating* into a conflict between stereotypes — it had been that from the start.

Hoping to serve as a peacemaker, I decided to speak. I expressed compassion for the board members, acknowledging the difficulty of their position, and respect to the developer for his persistence in his vision. Even if an environmental "victory" could be obtained by means of some legal technicality, I said, the larger question of providing a sustainable economy would still remain for the community to address, along with the need to learn, as a community, to live harmlessly on the land. My effort was diluted. The level of tension in the room stayed nerve-racking. I didn't see how any good thing could come of a situation that had been organized as a win-lose affair from the outset.

Same old pro-and-anti format, people forced to choose sides and seemingly no way to impress upon the culture that we must begin to think in terms of belonging to a system—that community has to be treated as a system belonging to, and dependent upon, the larger ecosystem. At that juncture in the struggle, the ecological rhetoric couldn't make a dent. The trustees voted to grant the variance to permit the golf course. The board split four/three, men voting for, women against. Seasoned observers of the local political scene figured that that vote had been a foregone conclusion. The developer, some said, had long before stacked the township's board with biddable members. Economic suasion certainly had to be a factor.

Although the township voted the zoning change, the friends of the river didn't give up. They got a referendum on the ballot to overturn the board's decision and lost. At that point they had exhausted local recourse and appeal to higher levels of government. They held on like bulldogs and waited for the state Department of Natural Resources to hold a hearing on the issue before granting permits for the construction to proceed. As was anticipated, a huge crowd showed up for that hearing. At the hearing the Friends of the Crystal River produced experts from all over the state who refuted different parts of the developer's argument, leaving it in shreds. The objective evidence was mounting. The DNR thanked everybody and went off to think about it. Most of the state's conservation organizations had joined the chorus against the development and were prepared to sue if the agency granted the go-ahead. It didn't, however, so now it was the developer's turn to threaten a suit. Meanwhile, the citizens of the township, enough of them, at least, were sufficiently fed up with the peremptory behavior of their elected representatives in this matter that they decided to try to get some new faces in the township government, but it didn't work. So the rifts in the community aren't changed or mended.

The situation posed a dreadful dilemma. On the one hand, the river must be saved at all costs—there's no latitude for sacrificing any natural systems, least of all wetlands; on the other hand, saving the river by any available means—lobbying the permit-granting agencies and, failing that, a lawsuit—would sow discord in the community, causing a fragmentation that might come back to haunt the wholistic types. If the final recourse were litigation, that might assure that the values questions underlying the case never got confronted but would be obfuscated by legal pragmatics. The whole unsatisfactory situation clearly points to the need for a new mode of community discourse and decision making, indeed, a whole new paradigm.

Yet the ecofascist in me finds it hard to trust even the outcome of a democratic process, let alone a paradigm shift, because the demos is, through no fault of its own, largely ignorant of biology. I fear that our culture is so confused and our information systems so polluted with irrealities that people will vote, time and time again, to let the golf course be built. And it already has been a dreadfully expensive learning process.

Turning a preservation battle into a win-win situation is a baffling proposition. If you want to save land that is privately held, you're going to have to deprive the owners of their development "rights." It's like freeing the slaves—the slaveowners take the hit, lose "property." And this "taking" is bound to go on, because there's far more land to preserve than there is government or philanthropic ability to purchase it and compensate the owners. So it is a win-lose situation as long as the dominant paradigm, which maintains that land can be owned, holds sway. Getting beyond that from here, and by here I mean

Leelanau County, if all of us are to come along, is hard to picture.

The other day's mail brought the latest newsletter from a think tank devoted to envisioning the paradigm shift. Reading it, I felt like a sturgeon cruising the black depths of a frozen lake, dimly aware of a group of brilliant figure skaters disporting themselves on the (temporarily) hard surface above, and of their practical irrelevance to my life. My reaction must signal a drift into a pose of anti-intellectual locale machismo and grassroots pragmatism, two attitudes I never much enjoyed contending with when I myself was in the abstraction-mongering racket.

Our area is peopled mainly by folks who wouldn't recognize a paradigm shift if it bit them in the ass. And I don't quite see how to apply the new paradigm in the—yes—*battles* involving the fine-grain complexity and diverse personalities in even so small a piece of turf as a county.

Positive and effective as direct participation in township government sometimes can be, as evidenced by our occasional success in organizing in our township, and Jane's individual impact on her township board, the rout and disarray in the township where lies the Crystal River point to the need for radical change in both the structure and process of local government. Because the nature of even local government bodies is representative, which, in practice, means hierarchical, those representatives who can take advantage of their hierarchical position will ensure that the structures are slow to change, especially because hierarchy erodes trust.

However, a change in the quality of the process is something that could emanate from many centers and begin to transform the nature of group interaction whatever the setting. I am talking about working from the soul outwards through an affinity group, or cell, a collective experience of wedding the personal and the political. One of the great blessings of our time is what we are learning about human communication; that its clarity or confusion is a reflection of the individual's inner life. So, it turns out, the ability to build trust in order to work in small groups with a harmony of wills towards any good end can be consciously developed using new, or reclaimed, knowledge and techniques. In other words, anarchism is becoming more of a practical possibility. (By anarchism I mean the assumption that we humans have within us the gift to organize for mutual aid, in nonhierarchical ways; we can, in fact, be good enough to associate freely, determine our own conduct, and work together to provide our basic needs.)

The clearest, most coherent, and persuasive writer and teacher of this knowledge in our moment is a witch named Starhawk. She is a brilliant contributor to the developing art of nonviolent social change. With her first two books, *The Spiral Dance* and *Dreaming the Dark,* Starhawk emerged as America's preeminent exponent of a contemporary paganism. Her work is a convincing argument against hierarchy of any sort, political, economic, or religious. It's also a straightforward introduction to the philosophy and practice of magic.

Starhawk's magic is a spiritual path, a tried and true method of nonegocentric self-realization and community building; a practice of directly awakening and acknowledging the spark of the divine immanent within each being. Starhawk's wide literacy—in psychology, sociology, history, and religion—produces an effective case for the personal being political.

During her decade in a coven, and through her work as a therapist, and from participating in affinity groups engaging in nonviolent direct resistance, Starhawk has learned some essences of group and individual psychodynamics.

In her third book, *Truth or Dare,* which could be her masterpiece, Starhawk stresses our mortal need for community and relates her understanding in good instruction for fostering the life and work of any group. She shares her experiences in therapy, in the craft, and in jail (for her antinuclear protest) with unstinting self-honesty. She offers use-tested anarchy theory, tangible work that can be done to create a culture of reverence for the Earth, resistance to structural authority, in short, a sustainable culture of freedom. Ever since encountering her courageous synthesis, I've been a Starhawk fan.

Once upon a time, I must confess, this book was going to have a whole chapter titled "The Trouble with Jesus." I was feeling a little menaced by the advent of eco-Christianity and wanted to take a poke at it. With that vague and petty intention contaminating a larger, worthier desire to call attention to the value of the alternative represented by paganism, I made a plan to interview Starhawk. In addition to a desire to have her speak directly to readers of these pages, I was cryptically hoping that she might assert the superiority of the Craft over the Gospel.

In May 1987 I returned briefly to San Francisco. My attempts, by mail and phone, to arrange a meeting with Starhawk were unsuccessful. Brazenly one morning I just showed up on her doorstep, seeking an audience. One of her housemates admitted and announced me. Starhawk, who was then in the homestretch on *Truth or Dare,* deliberated for a moment before allowing me to step into her workday for a little while. As I waited for her, I scanned the bookshelves in her study and saw evidenced a rigorous will to go to the primary sources of ideas in politics, religion, psychology, and feminism. When she entered, I was struck by the quality of her presence. She's a consolidated human: direct, intelligent, focused, disciplined, humorous, and principled; substantial, brave, and darkly handsome—not an overpowering person, but vital in a way that's all too rare (perhaps because it's a way that was arrived at through years of practice at developing and putting her inner strengths to the test, and people who do that are, as yet, rare).

We drank coffee out back in the garden, then walked the dogs in the neighborhood park before alighting a few more minutes in her study. As it developed, my "interviewing" was more talk than listen. What I really wanted, I guess, was to bounce some ideas off her, to touch base and make friends. Despite my journalistic fallibility, we had a beneficial visit. Happily, I learned from her a lesson in religious tolerance. Of the gospel, she said, "You can find anything in those texts. . . . So much depends on how they're interpreted." She said that the experience of traveling in Central America, of visiting Christian base communities and seeing liberation theology in action, had really changed her feeling about Christianity.

Knowing of my involvement with Earth First!, she offered this succinct critique of wilderness Malthusianism: "You can't build a liberating movement on writing off whole masses of people." Like Gloria Steinem, whose kind of niche Starhawk may be filling in the nineties, she insists that the concerns of Third World people are pivotal, and has not much respect for any purported Earth-saving movement that does not deal directly with racism and sexism.

Finally, she discussed the subject of *Truth or Dare:* "It has been a long and gradual historical process and had to do with the ways human society was reshaped to meet the demands of war as it was institutionalized; . . . war warps society around it in the pattern of hierarchy and domination, particularly the domination of women by men."

One of Starhawk's most attractive qualities is weighting the balance in favor of honest hope. Perversely, whenever I talk to a dedicated soul, I try to find out whether they mightn't, *entre nous,* be as pessimistic as I am. Ask a genuine witch her outlook, and you get an answer such as, "I do definitely believe in magic."

On account of that belief, and witnessing after long years of concerted and disparate efforts for arms control, the beginning of a lifesome paradigm shift in superpower conduct, some real evidence that activists' work can bear fruit, and their prayers be answered, Starhawk says, "We could do it . . . it's not all lost yet."

Moving the focus of responsibility from "I" or "they" to "we" also has to do with the sense of humility, an understanding distilled in savant Hazel Henderson's remark that "only a system can model a system." Power structures are centralized and exclusive, however benevolent the pose. No one among us, no clique, however well meaning, can be sufficiently diverse and comprehensive to project an adequate ethos for the good life for all of us everywhere. Bearing in mind that the nation-state is vicious when crossed, one must be more than a solitary dilettante in espousing anarchism and decentralism. Starhawk has given us a useful handbook for the endeavor. Meanwhile, trying to play both ends against the middle, I mutter "smash the state" and still feel obliged to write my congressional representatives and get out the vote.

Still, I dream of a society based on free organic association at a scale that permits consensus decision making with maximum local autonomy, a society whose strength is in egalitarian relationships, the beauty of smallness, and an informing ecological ethic. In the long run, and in the aggregate, the consequences of such small changes as forming affinity groups and engaging in tree planting, organic gardening and farming, energy conservation, economic cooperation, local entrepreneurship, voluntary simplicity, community-based education, grassroots political organizing, and widespread participation in meeting basic needs could add up to the hoped-for transformation.

HOUSEHOLDING

———————————◆———————————

Examine each question in terms of what is ethically and esthetically right, as well as what is economically expedient. A thing is right when it tends to preserve the integrity, stability, and beauty of the biotic community. It is wrong when it tends otherwise.

Aldo Leopold
A Sand County Almanac

EFFECTIVE POLITICAL WORK, IN THE CURRENT ERA, IS BASED IN self-knowledge, a commitment to work for peace among the factions within, as well as without. It requires the application of conscience in a lot of ordinary doings, and a long, compassionate struggle to reform one's conditioned reactions. The changes are hard won, always, and the degrees of change are as different as individuals.

So it seems with householding. There is a householding ideal to aspire to, one in which the household is, at the very least, harmless to its surroundings, approaching self-reliance in food and energy. Ideally, the service of those goals should produce aesthetic grace, a comely ark. Striving towards this ideal is powerful dharma yoga. The benefits spill over into the community and the polity.

The existence of largely self-reliant households physically refutes the necessity to pay the price for maintaining centralized sources and long lines of supply. Independence of household can contribute to independence of mind. People who are learning how to meet their own needs for food, shelter, energy, and information (because to do the former three involves research) can regard the political process with some clarity about where real power inheres (in the sun meeting the biosphere, in the awakened community), and not as victims or supplicants. Homesteading and householding, even just gardening, immediately let you know what forces you're genuinely subject to, and dependent on. The more independent of the money economy the household becomes, the less its members have to work for the government, by way of paying taxes, the majority of which have come to be spent on engines of war.

In our recent foray into householding, Phil and I wound up following a modified conventional path, and built a small and pleasant, rather dependent house. It is not so much an exemplar of sustainability as it is a triumph of community, for it was built quickly, and thanks to the same web of friendships that helped celebrate our wedding and heal our wounds.

One of the real-life events that made my story less than the sterling reinhabitory example I intended was the suddenness of the necessity for us to build ourselves living quarters. For the first three years of our partnership, Phil and I lived with Rob, our roommate, landlord, and best man. Having been a longtime studio apartment solitary, I awarded myself simple-living points for inhabiting this casually communal household. A worthwhile, impact-reducing trade-off, keeping the rent low and postponing the need for equipping another entire household. (And having an extra metabolism or two around the house kept things a little warmer and required less wood burning.) When Rob's wife-to-be and her daughters moved in, our ménage fissioned. Too many metabolisms. We were so thoroughly crowded that Phil and I decided it was high time to leave The Hovel and build a nest of our own. We'd bought five acres next door to Rob, so we already had a homesite, and likable next-door neighbors, with already-familiar tools. All we needed, we thought, was some lumber and a few permits. Piece o' cake.

Breaking ground was a point of no return, at which, even before the house was built, I began to feel some of the weight of home ownership and the sense that the place possesses you at least as much as you possess it. Home building is one of those life endeavors where the results are writ in stone— concrete block and mortar, anyway— and are rather more indelible and irrevocable than most of the projects your average urban Joe, Jane, or Stef get to do.

The realer it gets, the more protean the outlines, the more confounding the choices, the more distant the ideal. When you're sitting in your apartment or town-house, resting from your white-collar labors, abstractions like zoning and development and home building are easy to form opinions about.

God knows I certainly had a head full of judgments about all that stuff. Since environmentally sound theories existed about all those things, I figured it should be possible to chivvy human settlements into ecologically sound patterns. Alas, I had little concept of the kinds and number of decisions involved in life its ownself the American way. To build a home differently requires a commitment to buck the system and defy it every step of the way. To be outlaw owner-builders takes a little more mettle and preparedness than we were able to come up with on the spur of the moment.

The reasons we truckled under and played by rules we knew to be foolish in the long run were: haste, our visibility, and a grudging admission that if we wanted to work through various units of local government to demand environmentally sound land use, we couldn't be outlaws without being hypocrites, and hoist with our own petard (which parallels Friends of the Earth's reasoned stand on civil disobedience; can't have it both ways).

We feel that we should be free to do simple living, appropriate-technology innovations free from the constraints of outmoded building codes. However, we are grateful that there's at least some regulation around to constrain our less ecologically oriented neighbors who similarly think that they should be able to do whatever they damn well please with *their* pieces of Earth. Sigh.

By being in a hurry, we co-opted ourselves. Our capitulation began with the well permit. We, I especially, wanted running water. At our homesite, clean running water is two hundred feet down, so we didn't much fancy drilling the well by ourselves. Our neighborhood well driller wouldn't proceed without our having a proper permit from the health department. So in making application, we announced our intentions to officialdom, in the person of the tricounty sanitarian. If you fess up that the well is to supply water for even a semiconventional residence, even if you plan to minimize your water use by installing a composting rather than a flush toilet, you're required to install a septic tank and leach field to treat your gray water (which is dishwater and the stuff that rinsed probable pathogens off your body when you showered). Privies are illegal. Over time, however, septic tanks and leach fields also contaminate groundwater, and on our site, the excavation to install them had brutal effects.

In consequence of our dealing with the health department, our construction project got defined as a residence, which meant that sooner or later we were going to have to have a minimum of 720 square feet in our dwelling if we were to be able to obtain a building permit and all the other permits that secure our right, as law-abiding citizens, under the watchful eye of the zoning administrator, to bitch about other peoples' land abuse at township meetings along with our right to have our project inspected by the aforementioned watcher. Building at the township's minimum scale quantumed us into needing high finance and confronted us with the dismal chore of talking to bankers whose conventionality is bred in the bone. Banks are wont to insist on energy-gobbling features like electrical baseboard heaters to serve as backup to the rigors of wood heat. By virtue of neither of us ever having saved anything, or having been employed at a level that would admit of some credit credibility, our mortgage loan applications were indulgently chuckled at by the local financial community. Their rejections drove us into the arms of my father, who now kindly holds the mortgage to our little home. Thus, we purchased some privacy for our marriage by taking on a debt with intergenerational ramifications.

Being conscious of what doing business as usual means makes it all worse. "Growth R Us" has become my shorthand for the irony that avowed ecofreaks like Phil and myself built ourselves a modest dwelling that will be plugged into the local utility grid. That means we will be getting some percentage of our electricity from Big Rock, the decrepit nuclear power plant a few miles north on the shore of Lake Michigan. By tapping into the grid and being metered, we will constitute demand, and thus a rationalization for the construction of more power plants. Voting with our dollars. Industrial civilization is like a tarbaby. Touch it and you're entangled and besmirched. Building this house proved to be advanced curriculum in that.

For instance, there's the matter of the tree massacre. Our little chunk of land is a derelict tree farm, with jack, red, and scotch pines planted cheek by jowl. These poor trees have gone too long without thinning. What's more, the trees are suffering from an epidemic of ringrot, which undermines the trees just at grade, so they topple here and there after every storm. To clear a site for the house and driveway, we slaughtered a lot of those scroungy innocents. Worthless as they may be, those trees, as all trees, have character and are undeniably alive.

My role in the tree removal was to lop off the lower branches. Phil and his brother Jim chainsawed the trunks and felled them. They hauled out the stumps with a block-and-tackle, an elegant, ancient, hands-on device. It made the yanking a lot more intimate. Phil in his old beater of a Chevy truck would put tension on the line, and brother Jim would whack away at the roots until the tree's last clinging to the soil was sundered with a groan and a crack as the truck lurched forward. Bringing all those humid roots—private parts—to light was rapish. But we went on to another and another, until a score or more of the pines lay stacked to serve as poles for some future fence, and a devil's midden of stumps and roots was heaped to become a "wildlife lair."

It was killing, plain and simple. And that was just the hands-on slaughter. There is also the logging and milling by proxy that we commanded in order to provide the lumber for our little home. Everything is connected to everything else—all flesh is grass. There seems to be no living without taking life. (A modicum of existential guilt over that seems appropriate.)

If there was violence done in the site clearing, there was a gorgeous harmony of wills demonstrated in the wall raising, which was one of several climaxes to the project. Certain moments demonstrate beyond a shadow of a doubt the magic of willing, reciprocal giving. Amazing things can happen when we all pull together. This particular accomplishment was thanks to the strong backs and sheer guts of a small group of men friends.

Early in the day had come a thunderstorm, with occasional lashings of heavy rain. It looked like work on the house would not proceed. Phil repaired to the easy chair with the Detroit and Chicago Sunday papers; I seized the opportunity to catch up on my correspondence. Later in the day the rain let up. Phil and Rob and I headed over to the building site to raise the short north wall Phil and I had put together the day before. Phil had consulted The Hovel archive of *Fine Homebuilding* magazines and found a trick to raise big walls without cranes or multitudes. The technique was first to build a set of wall jacks—heavy-duty notched sticks, basically. You rest the wall on the first set of notches and then walk along back and forth, moving it up notch by notch. A clever idea, and it worked pretty well with the 8-foot-high wall, with Phil and Rob lifting, me pushing the jacks into place behind them as they advanced.

Then came the news that a couple of other friends we'd called for help would be able to come over. With just that sufficiency of help, the building of the 16-foot-by-30-foot south wall began. This took about an hour of learning more about how to use a hammer, how to do the tailoring that carpentry involves, persuading the wood to fit and fastening it, beginning to learn how to toenail, strengthening my grip on the hammer, and generally toughening up my right hand. During the flurry of making headers and nailing studs, I was reveling in the bright wit of our friends, their cooperativeness, humor, and awareness of the world around. The work went quickly, and the wall was completed, easily weighing in at a ton.

Wood is heavy, I learned as I worked with it a little bit. Dense and supple, it once was alive. It was strange to be thinking that these studs that we were cutting and nailing and hauling around once had been trees and that we had accepted their sacrifice, not quite taking it for granted. Driving nails into the studs, I thought how luxurious it is to have nails in such abundance that when one gets bent, we just throw it away. Before wire nails could be mass-produced, wood structures were, of necessity, pegged, dovetailed, mortised, and lashed together. There's a lot to reflect on in building a house.

The absence of a crane to raise the tall wall meant that it would have to be hove into place with human labor. That made it a very difficult and quite dangerous proposition, a feat that was exciting and appalling to watch. There were five good men and true available to the task. First they hiked the wall all the way up onto the four 8-foot-tall wall jacks. The wall was 16 feet high, a huge and twisty thing. It required mighty exertion just to lift it onto the first set of notches. And it got scarier from then on out. After they'd muckled it up to the topmost set of notches on the jacks, the men had to resort to pushing and shoving it up, then bracing it with 16-foot-long two-by-fours as their multipurpose tools. At that point the crew needed supreme confidence in the holding power of wood and nails. During this harrowing phase of the feat, one or more of the men was under the wall, which was supported only by the poles they were holding. One board would shudder, everyone would gasp, and the men held on.

If the wall were to slip, the obvious possibility was that several good men and true would be crushed and horribly mangled. Their lives literally did depend on being able to hold on and cooperate and agree, second by second, on their strategy. Like being at sea in a small boat in a storm, it was a situation that called for an essential concord, and an acute attention to the moment. Phil, who had led his friends out on this limb, allowed as how he'd never raised a 16-foot wall before. Therefore, he, and his cohorts, also all first-timers, were inventing a method, figuring it out as they went along, with 480 square feet of studs and sheathing torquing high and heavy over their heads.

It was a risky, foolhardy thing to do. Guts ball. It wasn't absolutely necessary to do it at that moment, nor to depend only on the available men, but once the dare was taken, the friends went through with it. While the actual deed was being done, I stood fixated on the sidelines, taking snapshots and praying madly. There was nothing I could have done to stop those brave fools, save pulling a gun on them had I had one. Peggy, Rob's bride-to-be, stood beside me for a while, watching and worrying audibly. The tension got to be more than she could bear, and so she went away. Then the tension of not knowing the outcome became more unbearable than that, so back she came. Meanwhile, her daughters, Erin and Annie, sat on piles of lumber at a distance, watching the spectacle with unemotional curiosity, mercifully innocent of the stakes of the game. I, too, thought of leaving the scene, of going away to find some relief from my fear, but I felt compelled to witness the exploit to the end, and it was a fascinating thing. The men knew their existential positions to a T: holding the boards, their faces reddening, scurrying to put in more braces, and, in a moment's breather, indulging in gallows humor, burlesquing their apprehension with comic faces.

Fate had assembled exactly the right organism of bodies and personalities for getting the job done. One man present, David, the computer genius and student of mysticism, dubbed himself Captain Safety and was metagutsy enough to insist on a gradual approach and the taking of such precautions as were possible. David was aggressively nervous about it, and a good complement to Phil and Russell, who between them have healthy enough egos to imagine doing such a chore single-handedly. The men in the middle were Rob, with whom Phil has worked on countless around-the-farm building projects, and Tim, a good-natured environmental chemist who acted as though he knew what he was doing, and was able to help helpfully.

It looked like the flag raising on Iwo Jima, a unit of humans entrained, required by the laws of mass and force to act in bodily concert. The farther the crew advanced, the greater grew the angle between the wall and the floor, the more the weight of the wall was transferred to floor and foundation, the lighter became the burden, until, at length, they eased it into the full upright position and capped that accomplishment with a lot of quick dashing, bracing, and nailing. Physics and geometry, all the inescapable miracles of gravitation—the daring of it was quite sensational. It was a victory of friendship, a triumph of helping, and at considerable risk of life and limb.

Russell asked me to phone Sally, his wife, to let her know he'd be a little late, as he headed down the driveway and off to meet her at the movies. No time to linger for some figurative champagne.

As I walked over to the farmhouse, I wept a little in relief, and at the beauty of the sacrifice and of everyday courage. I thought, too, of the sometimes extreme difference between men and women, of the way Peggy and I had felt and reacted— our doubt, caution, and, ultimately, horror, none of which was groundless. This in contrast with the go-ahead brashness of the men; the two attitudes necessary to each other, parts of a whole, as indivisible a dynamic as that of predator and prey. It beggars me to describe the holy truths and stark realities we all unselfconsciously beheld in that wall raising. There was a relief to have done with it, and it had been a privilege to witness. A lot more raw information latent in those minutes than in the protracted skein of conversations with the wisest of the wise, I'm telling you.

The moral of that story is that groups with a purpose can accomplish a lot and are not only uplifting but inspiring to witness. Our wall raising also laid a cornerstone of love.

When you hire things done, as we did the excavation, you allow yourself to be seduced by the ease and speed that skilled contractors with heavy equipment can offer. You purchase efficiency and forfeit learning. You begin to lose touch with the fine grain of things. Some very meticulous local guys had dug out our foundation, septic tank, and drain field. The boss wielded his front-end loader like a tweezers to pluck out the last few pine stumps. He segued neatly around a couple of young maples in the path to the drain field. Even so, about two tennis courts' worth of earth was laid bare, pine roots hacked and stripped, and, worst of all, a baby snake was killed. Its pale dismembered carcass lying in the wrack did not look to be a very good omen. Often, as I was sitting in my studio next door, a couple of hundred yards from our homesite, I'd hear my land calling. Crying, really.

It was recordbreakingly hot that house-building summer. By mid-June it was so dry that the bracken ferns in some spots were crumpled a dead and leathery brown, their heydey foreshortened by drought. On scorching days the scar from the septic-tank excavation throbbed.

"I must rescue it!" I'd think. The sweat and strain inevitable in any kind of restoration work are good penance. Heavy equipment is great for tearing things up in a hurry, but restoring even a crude semblance of natural order requires close-in research and stoop labor.

To call what's underfoot here soil is charitable. It's a beach, really. Glacial till. What with the glaciers, the loggers and their fires, and, most lately, the farmers, followed by us well-meaning householders, the land has had only a brief opportunity to clothe itself with humus, but hasn't been allowed to keep its clothes on.

After the initial shock of seeing what the excavation had wrought, I realized the urgency of seeding all that exposed dirt. Of course, the only seeds available locally on such short notice would be the exotics—lawn grasses, primarily—so that's what I went for, thinly consoling myself with the thought that at least I'd bought seeds that hadn't been treated with fungicides or pesticides. If birds or rodents chose to feast on them, at least we wouldn't be causing more incidental deaths. And even if that rye had grown (which, owing to the drought, it didn't), it would have stuck out like a sore thumb, a vulgar new patch of monoculture in our raggedy, weedy landscape.

After I bestirred myself to seed the slope, I sat back and awaited the rain that would surely fulfill my good intentions. When a rain came, I realized that while it was wetting down the seeds, it would be, if it kept up, capable of washing them, while cutting gullies, down the slope. Getting some organic matter on the bare place to protect the dirt and seeds became the next urgency. Phil and I took the beater Chevy to the farm of a neighbor—a man beset by too many griefs—who was clearing his barn of some old bales of hay. We took a few so I could begin, with the help of a southeast wind, to strew the hay across the slope in hopes of anchoring and nourishing the soil and offering some shade and protection to those pitiful grass seeds. After a sequence of dry days, to help some of those seeds to germinate, I tried hauling water. We dragged about forty gallons over to the slope in big buckets and spiked it with shovelsful of horse manure. Making many trips down the hillside with a watering can full of manure tea was very much like bailing with a thimble. I managed to wet maybe a tenth of the area before my leg gave out. I came away feeling defeated by the magnitude of even this minuscule restoration project.

Having a broken leg, and being less than completely ablebodied, which was the case that house-building summer, I could walk only so far and carry only so much before pain would tell me to back off for a while, restricting me to piddling efforts at strewing and raking nonnative grass seeds into that scalped slope. It seemed like I was able to seed only a small portion of it before my leg would give out, requiring me to abandon the soil-conservation efforts till the next day. Hauling water to coax that desperately needed ground cover was simply beyond my powers, and a damned frustration.

For the first few years I lived here, I cruised around Leelanau County, remarking the many scenes of soil destruction wrought by annual tilling and even just clearing, feeling holier than whomever because I was not party (except of course at the safe remove of being a consumer of certain agricultural products) to such exploitation and abuse. Pride goeth before a fall. Now our land use is making us a part of that soil changing.

As the dry building summer wore on, leaving the normal vegetation parched and suffering, and our denuded hillside bare and baking in the sun, I could hear the erosion. At night. In my sleep, even. Consequently, when the first gusty summer squall arrived to slake the land's thirst, I greeted it with mixed emotions, fearing that the naked slope might be gullying and washing downhill. Suddenly I could appreciate the vulnerability of the farmer, nervously eyeing the sky, knowing that everything depends on the weather, and there's not a damn thing he or she can do about it. The overwhelming responsibility of land stewardship hit me like a ton of bricks; it's like having a child.

Lately, whenever I'm feeling blue, I console myself by riping up knapweed plants. This lavender relative of the bachelor's button has an unbeatable takeover strategy. An average individual plant may produce a few score composite flowers. The seeds are pet-fur and pants-cuff hitchhikers; the dried stalks and stems tumble, scattering the seeds; the plants seem to germinate in almost any circumstances save burial under an iceberg. Like dandelions, they flower at any height, so mowing doesn't discourage them, and, I am told, their roots secrete a substance inhospitable to other plants. An ultimate weed, holding the potential to dominate just about any untended field in a short span of years.

During these droughty summers, while all the grasses and flowers were withering to tan, the knapweed maintained its dusty slate color and continued to flourish. Pursuing its multiple ways of propagation and dominion, it proves that laissez-faire land management just won't do. I regard the crude knapweed's expansionism in these times of trial as a cautionary metaphor. Weeds follow on disturbance and simplification. While I suppose we should be grateful for vegetation at all, it seems like a weed-ridden landscape is truly waste.

Thus, knapweeds have become for me a symbol of something bad, and I uproot them every chance I get. It's an absurd exercise—a half hour's determined yanking, with me thinking I am the destroyer of worlds, may clear a 10-foot-square area of mature plants only. Then I unhunch and see thousands and thousands more of them ready to burst into bloom and scatter their seeds a stone's throw from where I've been working. Or I look closer and see thousands of seedlings popping up right where I've been yanking. The process reminds me very much of my efforts at spiritual progress, trying to root out those character defects.

I regard my hostility to knapweed as an ecologically correct outlet for that basic life-destroying urge so popular among humans. It's okay to beat up on exotic species, I tell myself. So thorough is my prejudice that I was a little sorry to learn that knapweed has the redeeming virtue of being a good honey plant. "The only good knapweed is a dead knapweed," I want to be able to say. "Why don't you knapweeds go back where you came from?" Impurity is a hard thing to accept in either the composition of the field or the modesty of our lifestyles.

Barbara Ward, the late great world saver, once expressed the sentiment that the greatest unhappiness was not to be a saint. This despite the fact that by standards of more ordinary mortals, her efforts toward preservation of this lone Earth were prodigious. Still, she knew how much else must be done. Maybe she thought that by the standards of the necessary and ultimately possible she was falling short. How on Earth ever not to? Even ascetics who reduce their worldly possessions to a robe and begging bowl live off the charity of the householder, who, by extension, trafficks in worldly things—taking, getting, and spending—for the monk.

At times I wish that ignorance were still an available refuge. As long as there are undeniably real pioneers householding harmlessly, there's no satisfying excuse. Strictly speaking, living above subsistence level is doing avoidable harm to the planet and to traditional peoples. "Your wealth is our poverty," says Anishinabey leader Winona LaDuke.

Leaping from the specific to the general becomes increasingly defeating as my life becomes more enmeshed in specifics, starting with the specific of this particular body and the mind it accommodates, and rippling outward from there in widening circles of specifics. Perhaps it was the weight of my own complicity in such commonplace wrongdoing, and being appalled by the consequences of a thousand other such choices—all those tons of maturity being dumped on my feckless head—that had me more than once during construction utterly depressed and bleaked out, paralyzed at the typewriter keys and weeping, unable to make sense of it anymore.

Basically, the urgency we felt about getting ourselves into new quarters confounded our dream of doing it perfectly frugally, appropriate-techly, correctly. And this is a metaphor for our patchwork politics as well. A choice of immediate reaction sticks you with employing old-world expedients to gain new-age ground, trying, as our friend Gary says, to live in two worlds and not quite making it in either.

Consequently, Phil and I have backed into things, done them impurely, with encouragement from the system. We've killed trees and exposed soils and bumbled our way into township politics. We're landscaping with exotic plants and have a flush (albeit a pricey low-flush) toilet. What's more, I'm learning to write a book, to be married, to recover from an injury, to cook vegetarian, to enjoy the seasons, and to relate to a more tightly knit community than the one I departed. Quite a bit, actually.

It's even, superficially, pretty much what I'd intended, but the experience of it has a texture that I never could have anticipated. The big lesson is how little control I do have, and how many surrenders it has been necessary to make. The characteristic madness of our civilization is in trying to control rather than attend nature. My human failing has been in an obsession with directing rather than observing what in living makes sound process. It's the difference between ideas and wisdom, both needed in these parlous times, but in about a one-to-ten ratio. Wisdom is aware of infinite detail, and also chance. It's the result of paying attention long enough. It took a thousand or two nails to secure the subfloor to the floor joists. At the end of that chore, I knew how to hit the nail on the head (provided it was being driven through soft pine).

Digging up the garden space was very high, a mix of labors and discreet rituals. Our neighbor George invited me to clean out his deserted pigsty, offering, as my incentive, all the pig manure I could haul off. One drizzly October day I attacked that job and made off with a truckload of nonpareil soil amendment, leaving behind a clean concrete floor. Later that day in a downtown sidewalk encounter with our friend Julio, I proudly advertised my pigsty version of the Augean stables sweep (and, like an amateur thespian going out in stage makeup, I was still dressed in my filthy jeans and shit-caked boots). Julio wisecracked that I'd do just about anything to add to my résumé.

I rototilled the manure, along with some lime for sweetening, into the garden soil. Phil didn't want the garden to be an ordinary square, so I made it spiral. When that was done, I invited him to come and sow a handful of the winter rye that was to be the cover crop. I took off my shoes to put some barefoot body warmth into the earth as I broadcast the rest of the seeds and raked them into the spiral. Much better than straight lines when they sprouted all vivid later that fall and again in the spring. The spiral was a right touch.

The accomplishments of this householding will be ours to live with, as will the shortcomings. No contractors to blame. No hired help, just the strength of friendship providing the labor and, sometimes, just us, dragging ourselves over to do a few more things. It's all as basic as food and as rewarding as work can ever be. It's a great gift to be able to do it this way.

Ignorance of a better standard would be bliss, perhaps. However, not only do we know in broad terms how much closer it is possible to come to household self-reliance, we have a handful of friends whose households are living proof that where there's a will, there's a way. And even some of them have qualms about the toll their lifestyle is exacting from the Mother.

Although the funky home tour of a sustainable dwelling is by now a subgenre cliché, the fact that there are functional households predicated on maximum respect for the integrity of their local ecosystems and, by extension, the biosphere cancels a lot of excuses for not dwelling more sustainably. Contrary to aeronautical-engineering theory, bumblebees do fly. Our sustainably dwelling friends are even second generation, making colloquial application of the principles adduced by researchers such as the New Alchemists and the Land Institute. Our householder friends are making their own practical syntheses of the technics of sustainability, according to their slender means. What they are doing would be an uphill battle in a city, or in absense of a counterculture that respects and supports such attempts, often with the sweat of its brow.

Ecotopia must be crafted on the material plane. No amount of Aquarian Age wishing will make it so. Lifestyle and livelihood are pivotal moral issues.

Our civilization, call it Judeo-Christian or Indo-Aryan, is contemptuous of the organic world, an attitude that all but guarantees a short unhappy life for most of the creatures with

211

whom we share the planet. The short-timer syndrome, encouraged by looking to an unearthly hereafter as a way out, is buttressed by theologies that regard interaction among humans as the only moral arena worthy of address. This reduction of the living Earth and proclamation of a "Christian" value system, widely preached, if not practiced, while piously reaping the benefits of human and biological exploitation, is breeding ethical monstrosity. Tolstoy drew the picture: "I sit on a man's back, choking him and making him carry me, and yet assure myself and others that I am very sorry for him and wish to ease his lot by all possible means—except by getting off his back."

The "man" on whose back civilized peoples sit was identified by Gary Snyder in these lines from his poem "Revolution in the Revolution in the Revolution":

> "From the masses to the masses" the most
> Revolutionary consciousness is to be found
> Among the most ruthlessly exploited classes:
> Animals, trees, water, air, grasses.

What our ecotopian friends are doing is climbing down off the "man's" back. They don't see much point in tangling with issues outside of their watershed. They feel that their best hope of ameliorating planetary—and human—suffering is personally to quit oppressing the "masses." They're survivalists without the arsenals. But what they are doing is motivated by a larger, effective sense of generosity, of trying to behave considerately within the ecosystem and so to live in peace with all their fellow beings. It is about as pure as humans can get, along one axis of compassion, as Mother Teresa is pure along another.

Mark and Sue and their adopted son, 2-year-old Red Pine Charlie, live in northern Leelanau County, a half mile up a two-track from the county road. When snow and ice make the two-track impassable, they leave their truck at the road and ski or snowshoe in to their house. A lot of county homesteaders commute this way. On winter nights when Mark returns late from teaching classes at the college, or when they return as a family from one of their rare appearances at a neighborhood gathering, it is going that cold starlit distance that makes their most intense encounter with their home place. "Coming in during the winter can be real spooky," says Sue. "You can have a wilderness experience in your own backyard. It keeps you honest in some ways."

Together Mark and Sue hand-built the home they return to. Fifty years after the triumph of rural electrification, country futurists are unplugging from the grid. Mark and Sue's passive solar house has two wings whose south-facing panes angle out for maximum solar gain. The wings are linked by a hallway that houses a shower and a cement-block composting toilet. At the end of the east wing is a screened porch that serves as Sue's summer kitchen, a tolerably comfortable place for canning at the woodstove.

Modest garden beds terrace part of the south slope below the house, and below that, on level ground, a half-dozen small raised beds accommodate productive polycultures—"mini-forests." Using the square-foot gardening principle, Sue mixes root crops, shade-tolerant midstory crops, and taller leafy vegetables. "More than anything, creating a diverse community is important," she says. "We've got a complete ecology going." (Complete with toads and snakes, she says.) Sue's cash crop is edible flowers, a pretty sight around the old plantation.

The upper terraces are watered by a salvaged sprinkler system that the pair lucked into for a couple of bucks one day while they were jaunting around the county. A photovoltaic panel down by the well gobbles up the sun's energy, stores it in a couple of golf-cart batteries ("I got 'em off a guy who decided solar wouldn't work," Mark crows. "They're just wanting to pump water."), and power a 12-volt pump purchased from a local hardware store. "This rainbird thing blows me away," says Sue.

It took me a little while to understand why they thought

this dinky solar-powered sprinkler system was such a big deal. Then I thought about what hard work hauling water is, for one thing, and, for another, how uncommon it is to be generating your own electrical power—electricity that doesn't come off a grid, that doesn't originate at a dam, coal-fired plant, or nuclear facility. No wonder their glee.

"If there's a problem, it's your problem," says Mark. He devised his energy system, and when it's on the fritz, he fixes it. There's no Big Brother to call. And in the dead of winter, this Gyro Gearloose's job is made all the more challenging by bitter winds and snow.

Our official interview took place on a splendid summer day, and we sat on the deck. The background music to our conversation was the little tikka-tikka-tikka sewing machine noise of their wind generator twirling merrily in the sunny breezes. Thus the energy that eases their simple living comes: in waves and pulses. "We live our lives so differently . . . whenever it's windy and sunny and I have dirty clothes to wash, we *have* to dump the electricity." There's an ebb and flow to living in a place of climatic extremes.

"This hillside has always been so brutal . . . it was so goddamn hot you just couldn't stand it," says Sue, recalling the conditions when they began camping at their site seven years ago. Now those extremes are beginning to be tempered by the foliage of the young maple trees that have grown big enough to shade the front deck, and by the presence of their gardens.

Funky though it may be, their sustainable dwelling is a showplace of appropriate technologies, definite gee-whiz material. I asked them why, what provoked them to what are, relative to the status quo, such extremes of simplicity and self-reliance? As with Dave Foreman's inability to trace his ecological radicalism to any single cause, so with Mark and Sue. There was no sudden awakening. Although it diverges dramatically from the mainstream, Mark and Sue see their way of living-in-place, their decision to be land based, not as a departure but as a homecoming and a continuity. For some reason, they just kept tending in the direction of household sustainability. Above all, their choice of this way of living was not an intellectual thing.

"It's really about place centeredness," said Mark. "We kept coming here since we were kids."

Mark and Sue are both from southern Michigan. Like a lot of others in the industrial flats downstate, their families came north for the summer, and every other possible speck of time, to make contact with nature. "The whole bottom half of the state goes north," said Sue. Children in exodus, they developed their ties to northern Michigan and to each other early on.

Sue had grandparents who lived with woodstoves, who bathed and washed in hand-filled tubs, who grew what they ate—survivors from a time when such practices were not an ethical dare but simply functions of necessity and experience. (And that time was not so long ago. Rural electrification didn't reach Kasson Township until the year I was born.)

Mark and Sue are, by long habit, fearless doers: midwestern ingenuity. (Lots of Michiganders are conversant with machines—the state is half full of people who know how to build cars, after all, so rigging up a wind generator is not such an inconceivable feat.) They met in high school. They did their growing up together, and they love each other and their adopted son.

"You are wild! And people can't handle you!" Mark cries to his mate. "He's wild, too," he says, indicating Piney, bestowing the ultimate praise.

When Mark went to Ohio for college and graduate school, Sue went along. He got a doctorate in communications, she a master's in natural resources. For a time, while Mark was teaching, they were protoyuppies, Sue riding a commuter train from the Planned Unit Development in Cleveland to an architectural firm downtown.

In all they spent ten years away, first in Ohio, then Indiana, where they both taught at Purdue. Sue refers to that decade as "that journey of ugliness."

"We never felt at home anywhere we lived. We both suffered desperately for water," said Sue. "I also remember really missing the winters."

By the time they were approaching the nadir of their tolerance for academe (and its for them), Sue was developing a kind of persona that didn't exactly jibe with the commercial spirit at Purdue's ag college, where Earl Butz was "a god."

While the horticulture department had Ph.D.'s on grants from NASA and Dow engaging in what Sue derided as "gene-splicing botany strangeness," she, by then an assistant professor in landscape architecture, had found her bibles: *The Whole Earth Catalog,* Planet Drum's *Raise the Stakes,* and Richard Britz's *The Edible City Resource Manual.* She was organizing symposia and bringing Berg and Britz to the campus. With Mark, she was organizing an early bioregional group in Lafayette, the Wabash Landschäft.

As part of her job, Sue had to take over the administration of a Department of Energy grant: "Documentation of passive energy-conserving features of historic structures and districts of the eighteenth to twentieth centuries." She and Mark had bought a farmhouse outside of Lafayette and were, in effect, making a demonstration site of it, implementing techniques described in the research the Department of Energy grant was producing. The house had a wood-burning furnace and a convection-loop cooling system. It had a solar greenhouse and a flat-plate collector. Sue grew all her vegetable starts. Mark was continuing the work with "solar gizmos" he'd begun in Columbus.

When Sue submitted the grant report, the Department of Energy, by then under the Reagan administration, shredded it. "That crushed my whole sense of reality," she said. And in addition to that shocking waste, the diametric opposition between Sue and her department was aggravating.

"My chances for tenure weren't real terrific," she said. In a confrontation with her department head, she lost, trailing

Mark by a couple of years in getting fired. "Getting fired," he said, "helped a lot." It cast them out into the garden.

Their natural inability to assimilate into any megainstitution blossomed into an outlaw mentality, with an accompanying sense of persecution (understandable enough nowadays in any land-based people). Sue admits to a degree of misanthropy. "I felt most at home and at peace when I was with the Mother. Our ten years of chasing around hardened that attitude. I don't like humans, in a lot of ways," she confessed. "I pay too much attention to what people do. I feel like I'm living in a kangaroo court," she says, mentioning yesterday's radio irony of "sitting in my solar house, using my solar calculator, listening to Paul Harvey saying that solar power doesn't work."

The cobbled-together style that began to affront their genteel neighbors on Purdue's faculty row back in their Lafayette days has blossomed into full-blown ramshackle makeshift scrounger functionality. "In Lafayette," says Mark, "it was sort of like Beverly Hillbillies, I guess. We were trash there, and we're trash now—look at all this shit around," he says, waving at the semiordered piles of reusable stuff that he's bound to transform into something someday. The difference, he says, is that "we don't feel weird here." And, indeed, in Leelanau County, there's nothing unusual about back-to-the-land hippies living amid heaps of possibly usable rubble.

For all the dearth of hard-edged slick, Sue and Mark hold themselves to a strict standard of practice in their household economy. Their craft, consciences, and consciousness are highly developed, as witnessed by the fact that Sue, despite being thrilled by the sprinkler system, was worried that their groundwater use (which is necessitated by what is perhaps a chronic, man-made, and certainly epochal drought) might be "usury." "We use 180 gallons in the garden and 50 in the house" [per day; standard garden pumps run through 20 gallons per minute]. "How many other people do you know who could even answer that question?" Mark asked.

Really, their household economy is no stricter than nature's, upon which it is modeled, using renewable energy flows and nutrient cycling. "It takes me five years to get soil to where it will grow anything," says Sue, explaining that the garden beds have already absorbed three layers of manure and top-soil, scores of truckloads hauled in from the horse barn down the road.

Their acquaintance with Mother Nature is unsentimentally direct. Their land is typical of northern Michigan: "so sandy and dry; the weather changes are so severe . . . the winters here scare me . . . the winds . . . it has its own horrible harshness, but none of it scares me as much as the human strangeness that I went through," says Sue. When Mother Nature cuts up rough, she says, "I can take that criticism from her."

"You don't get paranoid when she whaps you up side the head," is how Mark puts it.

Are these extraordinary people? Certainly their way of life has uncommon integrity, and that way of life is working on them, heightening their personal integrity and vision. A few years ago they were still frustrated intellectuals, still living in daily conflict with the ways of the Earth. Purchasing their land was the beginning of a peace. Creation of their home and gardens was the formation of an organism, its membranes permeable to all forms of energy. Just to the extent of their physical and cultural isolation, they are discovering themselves to be enveloped in what Mark describes as "fields of energy that are just f___ing *potent*."

"There's a lot of something still out there," says Sue. "I think we're very fortunate that the Indians are here, that other species and planes of consciousness are here."

Such a spiritual experience is indigenous. It's a function of awed nature study, of learning the plants ("I can't explain finding morels [a local wild mushroom, very tasty] in any other way than metaphysical," says Sue, wondering at the strange in-stantaneity of their emergence and the fleetingness of the flow-ering of irises and lobelia, offering to the apt their beauty and medicinal powers.) It comes of the wizardry of invention: learning to transform the sun's rays and the wind's stirrings into electrical current—enough to pump water, light the house, play the stereo. In a world of wounds, these endeavors are spiritual disciplines. Because Mark and Sue wanted out of urban hypocrisy and waste, they became adepts. They're tough; they labor; they study; they're not fearless, but they are courageous. And for all that, the Mother zaps crackling energy into Mark's brain and laves solace on Sue's solitary soul. These are the winnings of raising the stakes.

Because they are wedded to a particular place and are living in community with their land, something ultrareal—the dimension of the cosmos in nature—reveals itself to Mark and Sue. Staying put, becoming attuned to the energy flows around and within their land, they receive visions and associate with the subtle beings that also occupy their place. Such magic doesn't follow on mysticism or religiosity. It is, like their ecological integrity, an outgrowth of living in a certain place in a certain way. These less visible realities await discovery by anyone willing, even professors. Mark and Sue honor their gods of place by tinkering with photovoltaic panels and finicky transplanting of pubic-hair-size garden starts. This is a muscular form of devotion. In Mark and Sue we see not piety, but a virtue that consists in minute particulars, in a rapt attention to the great life around them and a conscientious choice of the proper sphere of endeavor.

FATE AND FAITH

The Tyger

Tyger! Tyger! burning bright!
In the forests of the night,
What immortal hand or eye
Could frame thy fearful symmetry?

In what distant deeps or skies
Burnt the fire of thine eyes?
On what wings dare he aspire?
What the hand dare seize the fire?

And what shoulder & what art,
Could twist the sinews of thy heart?
And when thy heart began to beat,
What dread hand? & what dread feet?

What the hammer? what the chain?
In what furnace was thy brain?
What the anvil? what dread grasp
Dare its deadly terrors clasp?

When the stars threw down their spears,
And water'd heaven with their tears,
Did he smile his work to see?
Did he who made the Lamb make thee?

Tyger! Tyger! burning bright
In the forests of the night,
What Immortal hand or eye,
Dare frame thy fearful symmetry?

William Blake

The woods are not exactly full of morels, but diligent searching is sometimes rewarded. Mushroom hunting, for the semirationalist, involves wandering short-sightedly in the woods, scanning the ground at your feet, hoping to discern the matte ebon fungus among its cognate shapes on the forest floor—the tiny lean-tos of leaves pushed up by fiddleheads in their striving to the light, the absorbent dark butts of toppled saplings, the shadows inside fallen beechnuts—all of these living and dying elements of the surface can hook the eye into a moment's attention. Seeing the evident relations and identities of things—their proportion, their color, their contours—discloses harmony, mutual aid, survival of the subtlest.

Being in the woods is being in church. On my knees, digging down through the pale layers of fallen leaves for leeks, I can see how life works to bring itself into existence and to proliferate in its forms. A vast community of microorganisms, numberless companions to the trees in their centuries-long endeavor of niche building and niche filling, is making leaves into soil, black, rich, clean, and alive. The vitality of this climax community is insistent. Three weeks after the snowmelt, there are thousands of maple seedlings bursting towards a spot of sun; citron-colored leaves unfold from bronze sheaths at the tips of frail-seeming beech whips.

A host of other aspirants pokes up through the duff: some of the yellow trout lilies screw themselves through insect-chewed holes in fallen maple leaves then try to burst the cincture. Legions of others grow free beside them, demurely keeping their faces to the ground. This becoming modesty doesn't dissuade the occasional bee from venturing within to sup. Scattered wild violets sweetly bloom in white and yellow as well as the traditional purple. Trilliums are strong and lusty, abundant in many places. Their three-petaled flowers gleam white mostly, sometimes pink, and, very rarely, carmine.

It is impossible not to imbibe the peace of the forest, even as the moods continue to change and flow. Leaving the woods, I try to step between the lilies, but there seems to be no way not to crush some of their handsome dappled leaves with these brute lug soles. I tread on a young beech and bow it. Playing god. If it's strong, it will recover from the blow. And I may never know whether it did or not, because it looks so much like every other treelet in the woods.

There's nothing to fear—it's just life: the keening of two trees whose topmost branches are caught and scraping together in the wind. This growing awareness of these huge dances and pulses, and of the waves of liberation and repression sweeping through humanity, leaving turbulence and change in their wake, is a highly mixed blessing. The age-old imponderables assert themselves. Among them the question: To what good end am I spending my years enriching, yeah, cramming my mind with observations, perceptions, reflections, sagas, and ideas when one of these days those three coddled pounds of nervous tissue will be nothing but lunch for the conqueror worm? (Now that's the kind of thought that can send you skittering after a god concept.)

Imagining that Gaia needs a unified field of human consciousness for her self-awareness is becoming a widespread humanist myth. Sounds like a make-work project to me, a rationalization. Humans want purpose, and our species a meaning, but becoming the biosphere's ego, if that's what we're doing, is costing an inordinate amount of life in tuition. It's not a satisfying answer to the question: What are we here for? I can't explain it, but my gut tells me that reducing the biosphere for trivial purposes, even maturing a metaconsciousness, is evil. Faustian. Consciousness at times seems, both individually and collectively, to be more a curse than a blessing. (*Vide* Hamlet, the ingrate.) Consciousness of a human sort was not required for Gaia to create an atmosphere conducive to life, or for the design and maintenance of a climax forest. Because we are blinded by our own species' self-interest, humanity alone, even as a particularly gifted species, is insufficient to the task of teaching or apprehending ultimate values. Only a system can model a system. Beyond consciousness, it is also important to regard wild nature, to strive for atonement with it, and to understand its supramoral quality. Of course, there has to be some of it left if we're going to grasp the lesson, but the gurus are vanishing fast.

The trees try to keep on growing. Even saints become cantankerous, but the steadfastness and generosity of trees is enduring. Take the maple tree, for instance: sweet and entertaining, boundlessly useful. Teacher of death and rebirth. Deciduous trees, maples most brilliantly, are in constant, obvious transformation, year after year. Tendering their leaves up to the sun, gathering and storing that energy, changing from a welcoming green to a blazon of red, then surrendering their substance to the soil, dropping their foliage to the forest floor, creating yet another haven for life below, just as, in season, the leafy branches above have been a haven. In addition to these blessings, maples raise and sweeten the Earth's waters in the spring; a glass of maple sap is a tonic like no other. A maple will give its life and keep you warm, with flames dancing bright as its leaves did earlier. It will even be your table or your floor. If that isn't a boundless, holy giving, what is?

A year or so ago a freak storm from Wisconsin blasted east across Lake Michigan and savaged our peninsulas. It was astounding to watch the inky front race in at eighty miles an hour, tossing piles of scrap lumber about and hurling raindrops parallel to the ground. I wouldn't dare drive my car as fast as those winds flew. Awesome was the word for it. I sat cowering in my studio, wondering if it would withstand the blow, abashed by my powerlessness. That gale looked as if it could have blown this little establishment, including me and the cat, clean away, just like Dorothy and Toto.

The storm let us see what the natural death of a tree looks like, as opposed to the far more common images of stumps, logging trucks, and piles of wood chips glittering like coins. There was enough force in those masses of air to split and snap a bunch of good-size trees in the woods all over the peninsula. It flung big branches like lances. Since I have done a little wood splitting, I have some appreciation, right in my muscles, of the kind of energy it takes to shatter a tree trunk. And I, with my still-broken leg and a husband who, in our auto accident, had so very nearly escaped being broken off in his prime, was aghast at the violence of it, the unsettling sight of heartwood laid bare by the abrupt rending of a great limb, or the scything of an entire trunk. Images as harsh and sickening as a compound fracture. Violent death but not unnatural. Sudden, nevertheless, a type of dying that I personally would rather not submit to.

A few days after the storm, I was traveling the backroads and pondering why only some trees and only some branches were ripped away by that howling westerly. The unknowable numbering of days is such a vast mystery. The little oak seedlings we had planted a couple of years earlier were indeed as sturdy as oaks, and small enough to be unscathed. Despite the dry spells, they've kept making comebacks, refledging themselves at least three times one summer. If they survive into ripe old age, their boles will embody the story of this year. This drought year might scribe into them some fallibility that will be their undoing when the next crazy storm strikes, perhaps when they're just at their prime. So it seemed that there was a hint of destiny in those deaths and maimings, that it is, finally, up to the tree to withstand the wind or capitulate and that the qualities that decide which it is to be are laid down in the tree's tissues long before the final tempest arrives. So it is with human individuals, with the species, and with different cultures. Early on we incorporate the natural causes, or imbibe the slow-acting poison, whether they be physical or spiritual, that will account for our deaths at the appointed hour.

Had that storm been in any wise an impartial force or random event? As an act of "god," it lay beyond human reasoning, but was neither patternless nor purposeless. However, neither the pattern nor purpose could be framed by mortal consciousness. So the storm was just a storm, and also a handy metaphor for a big discontinuity, some civilizational shock devastating enough to arrest the ravages of greed and growth and wipe the assumptions clean. The savage part of me has longed for that for years.

The approaching millennium is a picnic for eschatologists. The harmonic convergence idea, with its neomythic roots and plausible schema of periods of disintegration, upheaval, and renewal, its call for the self-election of 144,000 boddhisattva types, is certainly symbolically relevant to our historic moment.

We were promised a purification time by the prophets of harmonic convergence, kind of an ecohippie rendition of the fundamentalist Rapture. To superimpose a mystical pattern on the ruck of events—seismic activity, aviation disasters, stock market plunges—is a way of acknowledging that the shit is hitting the fan, while imagining that in the long run it's going to be okay, maybe even better. The trouble is it's not quite explicit whether the long run is scheduled for planet Earth or out in the interstellar plasma. Hence, my secularist qualms about the opiate quality of harmonic convergence (or harmonica convention, as Daryl, the local wit, had it). For me, it's a neighborhood issue, and I have long cherished Gregory Bateson's lucid clarification of it:

> By survival, I mean the maintenance of a steady state through successive generations. Or, in negative terms, I mean the avoidance of the *death of the largest system about which we can care.* Extinction of the dinosaurs was trivial in galactic terms, but this is no comfort to them. We cannot care much about the inevitable survival of systems larger than our own ecology.
>
> in "Time Is Out of Joint"
> from *Mind in Nature: A Necessary Unity*

The panoplied procession of the seasons bears in the understanding that time never stops. If we allow ourselves the long luxury of the geologist's perspective, there's no question of the possibility of renewal. Which, along with the humans-as-Gaia's-psyche idea, is another dangerous heresy, the notion that our generation may *not* be solely responsible for the fate of life on Earth. After Joan McIntyre visited a Hawaiian volcano and observed the upwelling magma, she concluded that for humans to think of "saving" the planet might be yet another form of hubris. To hear her talk about what she had learned from looking into the crater—a sense of the immensity of creation through time—confounded, a little, my sense of righteous urgency. I fear that it's dangerous for life on Earth when humans absolve themselves by time's infinitude. Yet I think McIntyre's truth, and Bateson's, are complementary and counsel calm perseverence and a sense of what is a meaningful sphere for our care.

Thanks to their hardihood and ability to function in a collective, there are more than a few people hereabouts who aren't quite as nervous as the nonsavage, timid part of me is about what may lie on the other side of the harmonic convergence. There's a certain nerve present: the old hold-your-nose-and-go-racing-off-the-high-board spirit, and a widespread, sometimes awkward, sometimes simply powerful free-form neopaganism that makes a decent augury for some kind of transformation, nuclei for new communities and new patterns of relationship to the Earth.

Our countercultural enclave is earnestly reaching towards a spirituality in which the awe and divinity are immanent in Earth and human spirit. Some effective, nonhierarchical community building goes on in our circles. Many of the seekers speak in terms of a psychospiritual transformation, an evolutionary leap in consciousness to a humanity free of greed and egocentrism. It might not be so impossible.

Manured by the madness of the postwar era, and the intensification of that madness in the eighties, remarkably positive countertendencies have blossomed—the civil rights movement, the human rights movement, the peace movement, feminism, environmentalism, Green politics, and bioregionalism. A great many fine, everyday people have invested their faith and their lives in these ideals.

Although I have my reservations, I can't help but remember the scene in Peter Pan where, as Tinkerbell's light is flickering out, Mary Martin turns to the television audience and begs us all to repeat, "I do believe in Fairies, I do believe in Fairies, I do believe in Fairies." Tink's life depended on it, and while my belief in fairies may have been less than complete, chant I did out there in television land. Harmonica virgins, permaculture, paradigm shift, transformation, greening of America, class struggle, civil disobedience, peacemaking, biocentrism, ecotage—all are necessary fairies. Sufficient belief in any or all of them might help to turn the tide. Believing in them fosters certain qualities of heart and mind, demands a certain innocence. It means abandoning despair. Strangely, I find that a choice between believing in fairies and believing that this planet's number is up ain't pleasant. Couldn't there be existentialist ecologists who persist in trying to do right by the planet without benefit of metaphysics?

Hope wears strange guises. Ectoplasm. Chlorophyll. And there aren't too many existentialists in foxholes. As the human species begins to conjure with what it has done and what it must face, no doubt more and more of us will become interested in finding some shared sense of higher power to help us in our self-, but not, I hope, Earth-transcendence.

Humans will make their god—and gods—in their own images. Usually it's enough for me to understand that I'm embedded in god, which to me is the forward intelligence of the biosphere. But humans need symbols to contain spiritual expression, and those images may be as personal as local, and even family, dialects. So there's talk of subtle bodies and esoteric studies, kabbalism, astrology; all matter of schematics for the unknowable engross the mind and inform the soul. At times it all seems like an artistic endeavor.

"What is the point of all this specificity?" I asked our learned friend Phil Holliday after his spellbinding erudite theological discussion on the differences between Greek and Latin Christianity, on the esoteric understanding of the nature of different orders of spirits—devas, kachinas, ancestors—and beings on the order of Gaia herself, all of which hinted at a less than magisterial role for Christ in the cosmos.

We were driving Phil home after an evening with friends. One of the other guests was an avid eco-Christian who at one point remarked that he owed "everything" to Jesus. Knowing how difficult evangelists are to satisfy, I'm always a little uncomfortable around them. On the ride home I suspicioned darkly and out loud that the current effort on the part of a number of ecologically minded Christians to reconstrue the gospel as an injunction to Earth stewardship was just the latest tactic in a 2-millennia-long campaign by the church universal to digest any viable belief system outside its sway or beyond its power to dominate.

I said I could not see much hope for the necessary restructuring of our relationship to the life of the planet as long as the operative myth is that creation was made by God for man to tend rather than the image that nature brought forth humanity, which developed goddesses, gods, and God as a vocabulary. That remark uncorked Phil Holliday's pedagogy, an argument beyond me to reproduce, but which culminated in a sociology of divine beings. Underlying my question was the attitude that belief in such orders and arrays of beings must be essentially a matter of taste, and therefore elective. My sense is that god concepts are a form of projection, that they are realest in the minds of the believers. Intellectual and creative folks will labor harder to construct satisfying theologies, but there's nothing objective to believe in except the fruits of the condition of believing. Weigh me some god.

There are two paths by which to approach this conundrum: Why believe? and Why not believe? In answer to my first question about all the details of the deities and the devas, which question betrayed my feeling that such elaborated god imagery was primarily aesthetic, Phil Holliday said, "The reason is that it's true."

Now it's one thing when a well-meaning backwoods eco-freak tells you he's given his hort to jeezus, and quite another when one of the smartest, most illuminating friends you've ever had tells you that the devas' family tree is observable fact. It sets you to thinking, Why not believe?

Like Bioregional Sue, I feel fortunate to live near woods and fields and swamps. All I have to do is look out the window to find endless evidence of something divine—the infinity of relationships among all living things; the staggering fact that every insect, every stem of grass, every flower is an individual; that the plants know how to do what they do and the animals as well. In grasshopper time, a kitten, with no instruction, knows how to chase those insects, while they, endowed with abilities to crawl, leap, and fly, know how to escape, for the most part. I am glad that we live in a time where these phenomena have become fit objects of study, with scientists beginning to make these creations and interdependencies explicit and accessible to civilized minds. I sometimes wonder what hunger our souls could possibly have that cannot be met by a contemplation of the patterns of life on Earth. In biology there's even the promise of eternal life provided you don't mind interpreting that life as becoming food for another's life and enjoying simple molecular persistence.

I find my mantra and prayer often to be just "Thank you god, thank you god, thank you god." Capital G god being to me not the principal of that karmic high school in the sky, but Mom, the bringer-forth of all life, the largest system that I can possibly care about, the system which, demonstrably, cares for me. I try to keep my own spirituality simple, and to be respectfully curious about the rest.

Whether or not God is true, our lives individually, and now the life of the planet, are determined by the nature of the gods we serve, even if one's god is not-god. Joseph Campbell wrote of this in the third volume of his monumental tetralogy, *The Masks of God:*

... the findings both of anthropology and of archae-
ology now attest not only to a contrast between the mythic and
social systems of the goddess and the later gods, but also to
the fact that in our own European culture that of the gods
overlies and occludes that of the goddess—which is nevertheless
effective as a counterplayer, so to say, in the unconscious of
the civilization as a whole.

Psychologically and sociologically, the problem is of enormous interest; for, as all schools of psychology agree, the image of the mother and the female affects the psyche differently
from that of the father and the male. Sentiments of identity
are associated most immediately with the mother; those of
dissociation, with the father. Hence, where the mother image
preponderates, even the dualism of life and death dissolves in
the rapture of her solace; the worlds of nature and the spirit
are not separated; the plastic arts flourish eloquently of themselves, without need of discursive elucidation, allegory, or
moral tag; and there prevails an implicit confidence in the spon-
taneity of nature, both in its negative, killing, sacrificial aspect ... and in its productive and reproductive.

Is it any wonder that "shadowing" the much trumpeted fundamentalist Christian revival there is a resurgence of goddess
worship, neopaganism, and polytheism? That the cost of
monotheism, or simple materialism, has been a disastrous
disharmony with the spirits of the Earth seems inarguable.

If in industrial civilization nothing (except perhaps the
almighty dollar, pound, mark, or yen) is sacred, to most traditional, land-based people, nothing in their world is not
sacred—and vital. Everything in and around ordinary life has
mana. These are the people to whom the gods appear as
kachinas, devas, and totems. In such sacred societies, everyone
had a place in the larger scheme of things, and the quality of
one's inner life—thinking good thoughts, making ritual
observance—was of real consequence. When the sense of in-
terplay among the natural, the human, and the subtle world
is vivid, the human impact on the environment is slight.

Several years ago, at the beginning of my stint at *CoEvolution*, we published an article on Sherpa culture that clarified those ideas unforgettably. The article, titled "Mountains as Gods, Mountains as Goals," by Thomas Laird, described what has happened to the Sherpa people since the advent of mountaineers and the monetization of their culture. Traditional Sherpas regarded the Himalayas as divine, a belief that kept their world in balance. Laird quoted one old Sherpa, Renzen:

> This year the Swiss come to climb one goddess of ours. You call her Numbur. They give the government in Katmandu lots of money [the climbing-permit fee] so it is good for them there. Here it will give some people work and money for a while.
>
> But how would you feel if someone came and climbed up on your head? She will be angry but they live so far from her that they do not care what humor she is in. We will lose animals, the young ones at birth. We will have too much water or not enough. Our harvests will be poor. Or the young men will be killed with the Sahibs on the mountain.

Following the mountaineers have come tourist hordes. Laird described the "ill effects of such mass tourism—large-scale deforestation, the resulting erosion of the delicate high-altitude environment, and societal disruption among the Sherpas."

> The origins of environmental disruption are easy to trace. The tourists demand big bonfires at night. But the trees that grow in the areas where most of the tourists are concentrated take one hundred and fifty years to reach maturity. Fifty percent of these forests have disappeared in the last ten years. Topsoil erosion is increasing because of the deforestation. Field productivity is declining because of the loss of topsoil. Flash floods also occur because without the trees, the rainfall runs off the land at a faster rate. It was not tourism alone that set off this deforestation, but also the earlier destabilization of the population balance through the introduction of the potato. The two have had a cumulative effect.

In an odd way many of the things that the older Sherpas said would happen if they "offended the goddess" have in fact happened, even including those that seemed, originally, the hardest for the Western mind to accept, such as changes concerning the fertility of the land and the availability and flow of water. Perhaps the concept of a "mountain goddess" is more complex than it first appeared to be.

I wish that I could believe, or know, as certainly as my friend Phil Holliday, or any old lama. I *am* convinced that mere ego is not sufficient to the task of directing a life in harmony with the Earth. Whether or not some larger consciousness exists, it is good to act as if there were, to show a little gratitude for and awe before the mystery. To say grace while partaking of the feast of life, to feel kinship with and respect for all other life-forms.

As a home-grown devotional exercise one recent April morning, the hippie in me wanted to free my soles from their winter prison. I wanted to get out and touch the Earth, to get some skin information. Off I went and discovered, through the nerve endings of heel, arch, ball, and toes, such qualities as: the ubiquitous industry of the mole tribe—nearly everywhere I walked my heels sank into their tunnels; the overall yieldingness of this sandy soil—it seems to rebound a little as you walk upon it; the irregular field for vegetation—the crisp coarse tickle of moss and lichens, the unctuous depth of the grassy swale, the tetanus stab of forgotten barbed wire, and the nasty stiff pokes of knapweed stems. Stimulus. This carpet rises up to the tread, varied, lush, cool—alive underfoot.

How wise the animals are to have come by the rugged foot-pads that allow them to brave, unshod, places I'd never dare visit. My cat prowls the old wooden barn, a structure pathetically near collapse, artifact of sweat and ingenuity, with hand-hewn beams from the woods out back and a manger made from saplings struck down in their youth eighty years ago. The earthen floor of the rickety barn's basement is layered with manure from cows that are not even memory, but supposition. Upstairs are the leavings of a busted generation of poor white trash, and the never-to-be-reclaimed garage sale offal of a succession of transient hippies. Broken glass, boards with rusty nails positioned like bunjee stakes—a real no-human's land. However, my cat, by virtue of her appropriate size, design, and agility, finds there a rich inviting realm of pigeons and mice and crannies to snare her curiosity. Her way of being is simply awareness of all possibilities, from finding a snack to being snatched by a hawk passing overhead.

We humans seem to have been fated by anatomy and then consciousness to imagine ourselves as being uniquely independent from the ecological ground of being. Knowing what we know now, we are essentially incapable of going back to that undifferentiated awareness. Besides, in nature there's no "back" to go to. All but the tiniest fraction of the wilderness that birthed us is gone. So we must conceive a way to go forward. I think that this will consist in, among other things, discovering the grace of death, in making peace with it. Heading into the cycle and accepting our destiny also to be prey, and to give life again to other organisms.

My recent brushes with Phil's near-mortal trauma and my own dread of dying under the knife have taught me that I'm not there yet, not at that point of philosophical acceptance. I don't mean to be casual about the anguish and suffering caused by dying. Death is a brute fact and can be cruel, but it's insanity to rebel against it, finally.

In Bihar, India, the disease of smallpox was venerated as a manifestation of the goddess Kali. Probably by no coincidence, Bihar was the last redoubt of the smallpox virus, and during the World Health Organization's successful campaign to eliminate smallpox infection, medical teams had to forcibly treat or inoculate the last few villagers clinging to their belief and harboring the disease.

One could deplore such belief as a "primitive" rationalization of a reality that could only lately be changed; or one could ponder the ecological wisdom of a religious philosophy that intuited the biological function of fatal infectious disease, even in the human population.

When I lived in San Francisco, I belonged to an Episcopal church, Trinity, whose rector, Robert Cromey, is a clergyman of true courage and encompassing vision. Thanks to San Francisco's numerous and valiant gay population, and to Bob Cromey's openness and passion for justice, much of Trinity's congregation and clergy was gay.

As AIDS began to strike more and more people, ministering to their needs became an increasingly important activity of Trinity's congregation and of innovative, compassionate groups throughout the city. Passively from my pew, I witnessed the proliferation of works of mercy. In San Francisco and other cities, AIDS spurred the flowering of efforts to help people learn to care for the sick and dying and to learn well how to die, as well as medical intervention and personal self-care to arrest the disease. Surely the learning going on between those sufferers and succorers is of a sort that is at once both mortal and transcendent. The courage of the humans involved, and the enlightenment they win from confronting directly their human finitude and death's immensity, is a gift of redemption to the whole culture.

The appreciation of death, as embodied in the Bihari cult, and as it may be developing in the minds and hearts of those who are dying and those who are sitting lovingly with the dying; the opportunity finally to embrace death's implacable truth, could be one of the hardest, clearest diamonds kicked up in our ecological scuffling on planet Earth. We can't not die. The sages have held that a mindful death is preferable to a death that's sudden or violent. It may be about arriving at repose. Dying well, and living with dying, wearing the garment lightly, may be the last best human achievement.

Meaningful as it is, ecological concern requires an ongoing confrontation with death and dying as well as life and living. It is mourning leavened by wonder, awe checked by grief.

I live in what's arguably a very beautiful place. I work with a seemingly unspoiled scenic view unfurled at my feet. But wait. There are those corrugations running straight up the hill to the south, lingering reminders of the time when this field was in corn. There's the gaping maw of a junk automobile. There's the piebald cover of lichens on the near hill, indicative of just about no soil fertility. There's trash vegetation over-taking the field, the wretched knapweed and an expanding patch of fruitless blackberry canes. The beauty of the view is a matter of vacancy and shape, of neglect, not of the land's fundamental health. Better it should be neglected than ex-ploited, I suppose, but better still would be to restore it, which would mean going over those forty or so acres on one's knees with tweezers.

So a beautiful view is also a depressing view, depending on who's looking. It takes a peculiar personality to keep on looking at things from an ecological perspective for years on end. It's wearing, living alone in a world of wounds. Yet at the same time it is inspiring simply to behold the infinite miracles and evanescent beauties alive in the remnants.

The last outburst of unalloyed hope in my bosom came when I was newly returned from the first North American Bioregional Congress, and wholly in love with Phil Thiel, my husband-to-be. It wasn't merely infatuation-intoxication-inflation: it was the effect of finding a partner, experiencing, in that moment, a reconciliation of opposites, a balanced enough being to con-tain a positive vision. In that blissful, energized state, happy endings seemed assured all 'round. But the new wore off of it; and the new place, and the adjustment to the new life, so worthwhile, proved to be much grittier than I could have guessed. (The way my mind tricks me into growing is to forget that good and easy are two different things.) It has all recolored the feeling-tone of these reminiscences and my conclusions, but not in rose. However inevitable that toning-down, I learned that a loving heart is what sustains the carrying-on through all the personal reactions to our planetary condition. To be right does not gladden the heart of an ecological gloomsayer. We suffer this together.

Sometimes despair at the unchecked destruction of this beautiful planet, mocking decades of countercultural, "special interest" striving, pushes me beyond wanting to line the bunker with freeze-dried goods and a bag of gold into fantasies of mindless abandon. From survivalism to nihilistic hedonism. What's the use? Let's party!

At other times, this despair has alienated me from my own species. Some part of me, I confess, does not rejoice to see new couples start new families and join life's procession by that path. In wondrous birth and perfect little babies I also see future trouble for planet Earth. Down in the depths, there is a part of me that regards humans as Gaia's worst affliction. It is a horrifying soul content, but I must own it. It's the kind of attitude that, writ large, becomes a Nazi. My higher self, the self that for ethical, if not rational, reasons chooses hope, knows better. The principle that life is sacred must include us. Whenever humans, for any reason, even righteous self-abnegation or plain guilt, abstract themselves from the total fabric, things worsen.

The signing of the INF treaty occasioned another little surge of what Anne Herbert calls "honest hope." I doubted that such a thing could be possible, but it was surely a case of answered prayers, the accomplishment of millions of humans yearning and working for peace over the years. Maybe it would work for the global ecosystem. A turnaround from our present path would be of amazing magnitude. But then so was our transition from the Paleolithic. The human species knows epochal transition in its bones, and has a faint but tastable memory of a world and life in balance.

If we were to take up the challenge, what would be the particulars? Other than learning well how to die, which we all must do regardless, what do we need to do in order to "live by life," as Jim Dodge felicitously puts it?

Saving species, which means saving their places, is at the heart of it. It could entail a logging-road blockade, a product boycott, a sidewalk-removal project, or the urgent preservation of endangered plants and animals. Our generation has produced some heroes and heroines in this line. Working in the badly used environs of my hometown, Phoenix, is Gary Nabhan, an ethnobiologist, plant ecologist, and naturalist. He is presently the assistant director for research and collections at the Desert Botanical Garden. In addition to his scientific attainments, Nabhan is a fine author. His books *The Desert Smells Like Rain* and *Gathering the Desert* (which won the Burroughs prize for writing in natural history) are graceful, sensitively observed descriptions of the indigenous culture and agriculture of the Sonoran Desert.

Before coming to work at the Desert Botanical Garden, Nabhan lived in Tucson, where, with a number of colleagues, he helped organize Native Seeds/SEARCH, a program dedicated to retrieving, propagating, and disseminating seeds from increasingly rare crop plants grown by native people in those arid regions.

A profile of Nabhan in the *Denver Post's Empire* magazine described this work:

> The method is simple but arduous. Traveling by truck over back roads, and, at times, into roadless canyons on burros, Nabhan and other scientists track down rare seeds— usually preserved by elderly Indians who still practice the old ways of farming—and beg or buy a handful. They plant the seeds, carefully saving seed produced from new plants until they have a few pounds, which they then distribute to the Indians, scientists, and a network of serious hobbyists.

Nabhan gathered more than hardy, well-adapted seeds in his travels among the Indians. He also got wisdom, which he shared in "Kokopelli, the Hump-Backed Flute Player," an article in *CoEvolution Quarterly*.

I sense that much of the ecological destruction wrought by people participating in certain religious traditions is not considered by them to be spiritually impoverishing in any way.

In contrast to this view, there still exist traditional (though not *unchanging*) communities in which the way that one farms and concerns himself with wild resources has everything to do with the spiritual life of the community. Some of these are Native American communities, which have associated with them agricultural fields that have been tended for centuries.

When, after having admired Nabhan from afar for several years, I had the opportunity to meet with him at the Desert Botanical Garden, he told me that he had shifted his attention from agricultural matters to rescuing DNA.

"The boddhisattva vow seems to be my agenda right now," he said. "The most important thing that I can do is save species. . . . I really don't care to see any more desert land put into agriculture . . . future generations will benefit from their [the species'] presences . . . biological diversity is really what counts in the long run . . . my ideas can come and go, but they're not [worth] as much as other species."

"It's the deep ecology / Saint Francis argument," this humble, dedicated, and quite beautiful young scientist continued. "Accept the right to life of the poorest thing around you and accept that you're no mightier than that . . . deflating yourself of all artificial reasons for living . . . live for the essence of life in you."

· · ·

One July day in 1988, as this work was approaching completion, a dessicating wind blew fiercely for hours, parching the pitiful remnants of green in the field. The grassy swale was drying up like the last watering hole in the veldt. Even the blades at the heart of it were crackling. The hardy mullein was curled crisp; its flowering this year seemed against all odds. Beyond the reach of the garden sprinkler, the saffron and sulfur hawkweed hurried up their blossoming and cast their seeds to the wind. Only the infernal knapweed seemed to be prospering in the drought, and bare sand was beginning to emerge between them. The illusion of fat was burnt out of the landscape. No more slack.

The drought makes graphic the truth that water is the essence of all living bodies on Earth. Hydraulic necessity for flowers to turn their pretty faces towards the sun. Helps leaves to stretch their surfaces taut for maximum solar gain. You can't really grasp the importance of rain until you've seen a maple-beech woods looking limp and disconsolate.

There hasn't been enough moisture for the wild strawberries to eke out any of their succulent morsels. (The first year I came here there were wild strawberries in such abundance that Rob could gather a quart in a single morning. That's a lot, considering that a wild strawberry is no bigger than a damsel's nipple. We brushed our teeth with wild strawberries that year.)

This year and last, though, we've received very little rain. Perhaps we don't deserve any. The crops are stunted and withering in the fields. As in the Greek myth, the Earth Mother, Demeter, is withholding her abundance as lament—and punishment—for the rape of her daughter Kore in the underworld. That myth resounds today in the crunching of dried lichens underfoot, in the languid pattering of famished grasshoppers scattering with every footfall.

This dry desolation is acute for its moral dimension. Some scientists say that this may be the first result of the greenhouse effect. All the combustion and deforestation industrial man has been doing has created a denser envelope of carbon dioxide, methane, and chlorofluorocarbons around the planet, which is retaining more of the sun's heat. With help from agribusiness, this climatic change could desertify the farmbelt. That searing windy afternoon, I halfway expected Wisconsin to blow by. Exceeding Earth's carrying capacity, we humans have pushed the ecosystem beyond the margin of forgiveness and are due to reap the whirlwind.

Because this bad weather may well be the result of every-day actions, like driving and consuming mass-produced goods (especially forest products), I find myself, finally, feeling responsible, accusatory, guilty, and self-righteous all at once. M. Esther Harding, a Jungian psychologist, suggests that such a global sense of guilt is a function not of personal humility but of inflation—the arrogance of taking responsibility for a whole civilization's practices. I can relate to that. Most days I have as little compassion and understanding for the other poor saps participating in this geophysical debacle as I do for myself. So I oscillate continually between blaming self and blaming others. The self-righteousness that stems from knowing, if not doing better, however, is no substitute for an attitude of compassion and detachment.

We do not make ourselves, Harding said, and it is hubris to think as though we did. Thinking we should be able to tailor our own makeup to suit our own tastes is like thinking that nature may be improved upon. No one of us—individual, generation, people, or nation—made this ruinous civilization. We humans are impelled to expansionism by our very DNA. So it bespeaks a lot of nerve to take on one's shoulders the weight and to imagine that one could have even a minuscule role in, or responsibility for, transforming it, rendering it harmless. Yet, paradoxically, we all do . . . everyone enjoying the fruits of consciousness anyway.

Things being how they are, why bother? Children, for one thing. Justice for the next generation There's Sara Neri Carhart, whose sublimely peaceful tawny face, adorning her arrival announcement, confronts me from my windowsill portrait gallery. I think it only fair that she; and my godchild, Stephanie Wingfield Reinhardt; and Stef's brother, Max; and young Scott Marsden Hanna; indeed all their siblings everywhere, be able to enjoy the experience of wandering in a meadow, philosophizing at forty, provoked to thought by the variety of wildflowers and the presence of great rodent and insect realms underfoot.

No children should be cheated of the truth in sweet water or the shock of a grouse exploding from its covert.

Of course, there is other innocent life that suffers from our tragic failure and inability to save it all today. There's the phenomenon of the thousands of tribes of birds that have come to be, the metamorphoses of caterpillars and tadpoles, the twinkling of fireflies, the delicate valor of the wild geranium's petals, the emergence of nymphs to the flashing pied beauty of trout. How wrong it seems that any of these wonders should be destroyed, for any reason! Which leads directly to the boddhisattva vow. How to find a psychic balance in relationship to this task of stewardship and protection, the torments of being part of the problem, and the grief at watching the planet suffer?

If I knew it were all going to end tomorrow, I guess I'd finish the paragraph, water the apple trees, and go for a swim. But could I find it in my heart to forgive myself and my species? What choice have I?

Making common cause with all the spirits of place is called for, listening to their prompting. If enough of us assumed the spiritual discipline of tending nature's sacred precincts—sought to abandon our little selves to the wisdom of the greater Self—then perhaps there could be wildflowers, and long, drenching midsummer rains to instruct those little girls and their brothers when it comes their time to venture into reflective woman- and manhood.

Regardless of the urgency and of the time available to us, the work remains the same; to take ecological responsibility for our lives, restore the Earth, and build effective community, reclaim our true sources of knowledge.

When my mining-engineer granddad was a young husband and father in Michigan's upper peninsula, he made a food garden every year and recorded the plans in his diaries. Fifty years later, in his garden in Montecito, California, he kept a compost heap and almost instinctively husbanded his household's organic matter. Somehow this old engineer was not completely taken in by the postwar miracles of synthetic fertilizers and pesticides. He was a lot of things, but one thing he wasn't was a waster. His insistence on repairing tools and coffeepots, clothing, and any useful object, fixing them and utilizing them till they disintegrated into their original atoms, was a source of amusement, chagrin, and maybe secret pride to his children. In his frugality my granddad was on to something—the principle that in a hungry world, waste is immoral. I claim that as part of my ancestral heritage.

I claim as my blessing Jim Dodge's wisdom that our job is just to get it started right. Thanks to a quite wonderful community of friends—local folks who are knowing but not cynical—I've got a house in which to consider Thoreau's question, "What is the use of a house if you haven't got a tolerable planet to put it on?"

The house has a garden whose outcomes I'm extremely curious about. When I look out my studio window at the old cornfield, I dream about turning it into a prairie. I look at the slopes, thinking they might be hospitable to nut trees. When I am not smarting from the world of wounds, my imagination is restoring and transforming a few acres of land, furnishing the means of rural self-reliance, fantasizing doing some local organizing. I don't know if that's what you'd call hope. It's more like irreducible desire.

Life will out. There may be less diversity of life by the time we're done with Earth, but on any spring morning there can be no doubt that no matter what havoc humans wreak, there will be some green things peeping up through the sandy poor soil, and six- and eight-legged, may be even four- and two-legged, creatures stirring through that growth. To me, hope is a thing with chlorophyll.

We may be going forth into the apocalypse, maybe towards utopia. Whichever, the path seems to lead through the garden.

Samhain 1988

BOOK LIST

———————◆———————

BECAUSE THIS IS NOT A SCHOLARLY WORK, WHAT FOLLOWS IS NOT so much a bibliography as a book list. It includes Books That Changed My Life and books that I consulted in writing *Whatever Happened to Ecology?* Virtually all of them contain information towards ensuring that what happens to ecology is a lively continuation.

Abbey, Edward. *The Monkey Wrench Gang.* Salt Lake City: Dream Garden, 1985.

Adler, Margot. *Drawing Down the Moon: Witches, Druids, Goddess-Worshippers, and Other Pagans in America Today.* Boston: Beacon Press, 1986.

de Angulo, Jaime. *Indian Tales.* New York: Hill & Wang, 1962.

Atwood, Margaret. *The Handmaid's Tale.* Boston: Houghton Mifflin, 1986.

Baldwin, J., ed. *The Essential Whole Earth Catalog.* New York: Doubleday, 1986.

Bateson, Gregory. *Mind and Nature: A Necessary Unity.* New York: Bantam Books, 1980.

————. *Steps to an Ecology of Mind.* New York: Ballantine Books, 1972.

Berg, Peter, ed. *Reinhabiting a Separate Country: A Bioregional Anthology of Northern California.* San Francisco: Planet Drum Foundation, 1978.

Blake, William. *The Portable Blake.* Edited by Alfred Kazin. New York: Viking Press, 1946, 1968.

Bleibtreu, John. *The Parable of the Beast,* New York: The Macmillan Co., 1968.

Bly, Robert, ed. *News of the Universe: Poems of Twofold Consciousness.* San Francisco: Sierra Club Books, 1980.

Bodner, Joan, ed. *Taking Charge of Our Lives: Living Responsibly in a Troubled World.* San Francisco: Harper & Row, 1984.

Bowden, Charles. *Blue Desert.* Tucson: The University of Arizona Press, 1986.

_____. *Killing the Hidden Waters: The Slow Destruction of Water Resources in the American Southwest.* Austin: University of Texas Press, 1977.

Brand, Stewart, ed. *The Last Whole Earth Catalog.* Menlo Park: Portola Institute, 1971.

_____. *The Next Whole Earth Catalog.* New York: Random House, 1981. Original edition, 1980.

_____. *The Whole Earth Epilog.* San Francisco: POINT Foundation, 1974.

Britz, Richard. *The Edible City Resource Manual.* Los Altos: William Kaufmann, 1981.

Brower, David R., ed. *Only a Little Planet.* New York: McGraw-Hill, 1972.

Callenbach, Ernest. *Ecotopia: The Notebooks and Reports of William Weston.* Berkeley: Banyan Tree Books, 1975.

_____. *Ecotopia Emerging.* Berkeley: Banyan Tree Books, 1981.

Campbell, Joseph. *The Masks of God: Occidental Mythology.* New York: Viking Press, 1964.

Capra, Fritjof, and Charlene Spretnak. *Green Politics: The Global Promise.* New York: E. P. Dutton, 1984.

Carson, Rachel. *Silent Spring.* Boston: Houghton Mifflin, 1962.

Dasmann, Raymond. *The Destruction of California.* New York: The Macmillan Co., 1965.

Devall, Bill, and George Sessions. *Deep Ecology: Living as if Nature Mattered.* Salt Lake City: Peregrine Smith Books, 1985.

Ehrlich, Anne H., and Paul R. Ehrlich. *Earth.* New York: Franklin Watts, 1987.

Ehrlich, Dr. Paul R. *The Population Bomb.* New York: Ballantine Books, 1971.

Eisler, Riane. *The Chalice and the Blade: Our History, Our Future.* San Francisco: Harper & Row, 1987.

Foreman, Dave, ed. *Ecodefense: A Field Guide to Monkeywrenching.* Tucson: Earth First! Books, 1985.

Gitlin, Todd. *The Sixties: Years of Hope, Days of Rage.* New York: Bantam Books, 1987.

Goldsmith, Edward, and Nicholas Hildyard, eds. *The Earth Report: The Essential Guide to Global Ecological Issues.* Los Angeles: Price Stern Sloan, 1988.

Griffin, Susan. *Woman and Nature: The Roaring Inside Her.* New York: Harper & Row, 1978.

Grossman, Richard and Richard Kazis. *Fear at Work: Job Blackmail, Labor and the Environment.* New York: Pilgrim Press, The United Church Press, 1982.

Gustaitis, Rasa. *Wholly Round.* San Francisco: Holt, Rinehart and Winston, 1973.

Hardin, Garrett, ed. *Population, Evolution, and Birth Control: A Collage of Controversial Ideas.* San Francisco: W. H. Freeman, 1969.

Harding, M. Esther. *Psychic Energy: Its Source and Its Transformation.* Princeton: Bollingen Series X, Princeton University Press, 1963.

Hart, Alexandra, ed. *North American Bioregional Congress II Proceedings*. Forestville: Hart Publishing, 1987.

Henderson, Hazel. *Creating Alternative Futures: The End of Economics*. New York: Berkley Windhover Books, 1978.

_____. *The Politics of the Solar Age: Alternatives to Economics*. New York: Anchor/Doubleday, 1981.

Herbert, Frank. *Dune*. New York: Berkley Publishing Corp., 1975.

Herold, J. Christopher. *Mistress to an Age: A Life of Madame de Staël*. New York: Harmony Books, 1958.

Hinckle, Warren. *If You Have a Lemon, Make Lemonade: An Essential Memoir of a Lunatic Decade*. New York: G. P. Putnam's Sons, 1973.

Hopkins, Gerard Manley, *The Poems of Gerard Manley Hopkins*. 4th ed. Edited by W. H. Gardner and N. H. MacKenzie. Oxford: Oxford University Press, 1970.

Jackson, Wes. *Altars of Unhewn Stone: Science & the Earth*. San Francisco: North Point Press, 1987.

Jung, Carl Gustav. *Memories, Dreams, Reflections*. Edited by Jaffe, Winston, and Winston. New York: Pantheon, 1963.

Keen, Sam. *Faces of the Enemy: Reflections of the Hostile Imagination*. San Francisco: Harper & Row, 1986.

Kleiner, Art, and Stewart Brand, eds. *News That Stayed News: Ten Years of CoEvolution Quarterly*. San Francisco: North Point Press, 1986.

Kohr, Leopold. *The Breakdown of Nations*. New York: Routledge, Chapman & Hall, 1986.

_____. *Development Without Aid: The Translucent Society*. New York: Schocken Books, 1979.

_____. *The Overdeveloped Nations: The Diseconomies of Scale*. New York: Schocken Books, 1978.

Kropotkin, Peter. *Mutual Aid: A Factor of Evolution.* Toronto: Black Rose Books, 1988.

Lappé, Frances Moore, and Joseph Collins, with Cary Fowler. *Food First!: Beyond the Myth of Scarcity.* New York: Ballantine Books, 1979.

Leopold, Aldo. *A Sand County Almanac.* New York: Ballantine Books, 1970.

Lillard, Richard. *The Great Forest.* Jersey City: Da Capo Press, 1973.

Lipset, David. *Gregory Bateson: The Legacy of a Scientist.* Boston: Beacon Press, 1980.

McClure, Michael. *Scratching the Beat Surface.* San Francisco: North Point Press, 1982.

McIntyre, Joan. *The Delicate Art of Whale Watching.* San Francisco: Sierra Club Books, 1982.

_____. *Mind in the Waters: A Book to Celebrate the Consciousness of Whales and Dolphins.* San Francisco: Sierra Club Books, 1974.

McNeill, W. H. *Plagues and Peoples.* New York: Anchor/Doubleday, 1977.

McPhee, John. *Encounters with the Archdruid.* New York: Farrar, Straus and Giroux, 1971.

Mander, Jerry. *Four Arguments for the Elimination of Television.* New York: Morrow, 1978.

Merchant, Carolyn. *The Death of Nature: Women, Ecology, and the Scientific Revolution.* New York: Harper & Row, 1980.

Milne, Lorus J., and Margery Milne. *Ecology Out of Joint: New Environments and Why They Happen.* New York: Charles Scribner's Sons, 1977.

Mitchell, John G., and Constance Stallings, eds. *Ecotactics: The Sierra Club Handbook for Environment Activists.* New York: Pocket Books, 1970.

Myers, Dr. Norman, ed. *Gaia: An Atlas of Planet Management.* New York: Anchor/Doubleday, 1984.

Nabhan, Gary Paul. *The Desert Smells Like Rain: A Naturalist in Papago Indian Country.* San Francisco: North Point Press, 1982.

_____. *Gathering the Desert.* Tucson: The University of Arizona Press, 1985.

Nash, Hugh, ed. *Progress as if Survival Mattered: A Handbook for a Conserver Society.* San Francisco: Friends of the Earth, 1981.

Orwell, George. *1984.* San Diego: Harbrace, 1983.

Peattie, Donald Culross. *A Natural History of Trees of Eastern and Central North America.* 2d. ed. New York: Bonanza Books, 1964.

Platt, Rutherford. *The Great American Forest.* Inglewood Cliffs: Prentice-Hall, 1971.

Porter, Eliot. *The Place No One Knew: Glen Canyon on the Colorado.* San Francisco: Sierra Club Books, 1966.

Reisner, Marc. *Cadillac Desert.* New York: Viking Penguin, 1986.

Richter, Conrad. *The Fields.* New York: Alfred A. Knopf, 1946.

_____. *The Town.* New York: Alfred A. Knopf, 1950.

_____. *The Trees.* New York: Alfred A. Knopf, 1940.

Roszak, Theodore. *Person/Planet: The Creative Disintegration of Industrial Society.* Garden City: Anchor/Doubleday, 1978.

Rothenberg, Jerome, ed. *Technicians of the Sacred: A Range of Poetries from Africa, America, Asia, and Oceania.* New York: Doubleday, 1968.

Shepard, Paul, and Daniel McKinley, eds. *The Subversive Science: Essays Toward an Ecology of Man.* Boston: Houghton Mifflin, 1969.

Shepard, Paul. *The Tender Carnivore and the Sacred Game.* New York: Charles Scribner's Sons, 1973.

Shi, David E. *The Simple Life*. Fairlawn: Oxford University Press, 1985.

Singer, Peter. *Animal Liberation: A New Ethics for Our Treatment of Animals*. New York: Avon Books, 1975.

Starhawk. *Dreaming the Dark: Magic, Sex & Politics*. Boston: Beacon Press, 1982.

_____. *The Spiral Dance: A Rebirth of the Ancient Religion of the Great Goddess*. San Francisco: Harper & Row, 1979.

_____. *Truth or Dare: Encounters with Power, Authority, and Mystery*. San Francisco: Harper & Row, 1987.

Stone, Christopher D. *Should Trees Have Standing? Toward Legal Rights for Natural Objects*. Los Altos: William Kaufmann, 1974.

Theobald, Robert. *The Rapids of Change: Social Entrepreneurship in Turbulent Times*. Indianapolis: Knowledge Systems, 1987.

Todd, Nancy Jack, and John Todd. *Bioshelters, Ocean Arks, City Farming: Ecology as the Basis of Design*. San Francisco: Sierra Club Books, 1984.

Todd, John, and Nancy Jack Todd. *Tomorrow Is Our Permanent Address: The Search for an Ecological Science of Design as Embodied in the Bioshelter*. New York: A Lindisfarne Book/Harper & Row, 1980.

Turner, Tom. *Friends of the Earth: The First Sixteen Years*. San Francisco: Earth Island Institute, 1986.

Udall, Stewart L. *The Quiet Crisis*. New York: Holt, Rinehart and Winston, 1963.

ORGANIZATIONS
AND PUBLICATIONS

◆

THE FOLLOWING ORGANIZATIONS AND/OR PERIODICALS ARE personal favorites. I rely on the publications and regard the organizations' work as essential to keeping a diversity of life on the planet. My short list is just a fraction of the thousands of citizen groups and nongovernmental organizations doing needful work. Please, when you write to inquire about memberships or subscriptions, enclose a buck. None of these do-gooders is suffering from excessive funding.

Akwesasne Notes: A Journal for Natural and Native People
Mohawk Nation
P.O. Box 196
Rooseveltown, NY 13683-0796

Amnesty International U.S.A.
(organization)
322 Eighth Avenue
New York, NY 10117-0389

Asociación de los Nuevos Alquimistas (ANAI)
(organization)
1176 Bryson City Road
Franklin, NC 28734

Buddhists Concerned for Animals
(organization)
300 Page Street
San Francisco, CA 94102

Citizen's Clearinghouse for Hazardous Wastes
(information clearinghouse)
P.O. Box 926
Arlington, VA 22216

Cultural Survival
Cultural Survival Quarterly
(organization and periodical)
11 Divinity Avenue
Cambridge, MA 02138

Daybreak: American Indian World Views
(periodical)
P.O. Box 98
Highland, MD 20777-9989

DECENTRALIZE! Nonviolent Radical Decentralist Strategy
(newsletter)
P.O. Box 3531
Washington, DC 20007

Deep Bioregional Action Examiner and Green Hippie Intelligencer
(newsletter)
P.O. Box 748
El Prado, NM 87529

EARTH FIRST! The Radical Environmental Journal
P.O. Box 2358
Lewiston, ME 04241

Earth Island Institute
Earth Island Journal
(organization and periodical)
300 Broadway, No. 28
San Francisco, CA 94133-9905

The Elmwood Institute
The Elmwood Institute Newsletter
(organization and periodical)
P.O. Box 5805
Berkeley, CA 94705

The Grain Exchange
(organization)
The Land Institute
2440 East Water Well Road
Salina, KS 67401

Green Synthesis: a Newsletter and Journal for Social Ecology, Deep Ecology, Bioregionalism, Ecofeminism, and the Green Movement
P.O. Box 1858
San Pedro, CA 90733-1858

In These Times
(weekly newspaper)
1912 Debs Avenue
Mt. Morris, IL 61054

The Land Institute
(organization)
2440 East Water Well Road
Salina, KS 67401

Manas
(weekly newsletter)
P.O. Box 32113
Los Angeles, CA 90032

The Meadowcreek Project
(organization)
Fox, AR 72051

National Abortion Rights Action League
(organization)
1101 14th Street, NW
Washington, DC 20005

New Alchemy Institute
(organization)
235 Hatchville Road
East Falmouth, MA 02536

Ocean Arks International
Annals of Earth
(organization and periodical)
10 Shanks Pond Road
Falmouth, MA 02540

Planet Drum Foundation
Raise the Stakes
(organization and periodical)
Box 31251
San Francisco, CA 94131

**Planned Parenthood
Federation of America**
(organization)
810 Seventh Avenue
New York, NY 10019

Rainforest Action Network
(organization)
300 Broadway
San Francisco, CA 94133

TRANET
(newsletter/directory)
P.O. Box 567
Rangely, ME 04970-0567

Whole Earth Review
(quarterly magazine)
27 Gate Five Road
Sausalito, CA 94965-9925

World College West
101 S. San Antonio Road
Petaluma, CA 94952

The Wrenching Debate Gazette
(newsletter)
1801 Connecticut Avenue, NW
2d Floor
Washington, DC 20009

Zero Population Growth
ZPG Reporter
(organization and periodical)
1400 Sixteenth Street, NW
Washington, DC 20036

TREE DUES

Biologist Peter Warshall estimates that sixty-four 20 to 25 year-old softwoods (loblolly pines, say), each yielding about 125 pounds of paper, were cut and pulped to produce the first printing of *Whatever Happened to Ecology?* What a green world it would be if for every book purchased, one planted a tree!